EDL WORD CLUES ™·
L

Senior Author

Helen Frackenpohl Morris
Educational Developmental Laboratories

Consultant

Arthur S. McDonald
Nova Scotia Department of Education

Lesson Authors

Nancy Joline
Alan Petraske

Test Authors

Paul A. Fuchs
and
Mary Ellen Grassin
Rumson-Fair Haven (N.J.) Regional High School

INTRODUCTION

What do you do when you encounter a word that is not familiar? Do you stop to look it up, do you try to analyze its parts, or do you look for clues in the way the word is used in its setting or surroundings?

There are several methods that may be used in unlocking the meaning of unfamiliar words. But the quickest and most practical approach is knowing how to use the context, or the words around the unknown word, to unlock its meaning. This method is called using context clues or "word clues."

You may say, "Why not look up all unknown words in a dictionary?" The dictionary is, of course, one of our most valuable tools in meeting and dealing with new words. You can't get by without it. But there are many times a dictionary will not be available. Even if you're reading with a dictionary near at hand, you don't want to stop every few minutes to look up a word. The chain of thought would be interrupted so often that you would lose much of the pleasure and profit in your reading.

Let's look at some of the ways we can get the meaning of a word from context without looking it up in the dictionary.

1. One way to use context clues is to look for a *synonym*, or a word that has the same meaning. Sometimes a writer or a speaker will give a synonym for an unfamiliar word just to make sure that we understand it. For example, look at this sentence:

    "When an atom undergoes fission, or splitting, a tremendous amount of energy is released."

    In this case, the author thought that you might not know the meaning of *fission*, so he or she provided a synonym—*splitting*.

2. Another context clue is a definition or explanation that precedes or follows a difficult word. For example, you might not know what the word *quandary* means, but by studying its use in the context of this sentence, you could find its meaning:

    "When a person cannot choose between two solutions to a difficult problem, this is called being in a quandary."

    This sentence makes it very clear that *quandary* means a state of perplexity or uncertainty.

3. At other times, the context may give us a fairly good meaning of a word by telling what it is like or even what it is not like. We might call these clues of similarities or differences. Do you know what *opacity* means? See if you can figure out its meaning from these two sentences:

    "The opacity of various materials differs greatly. We know, for example, that transparent substances, such as air, glass, and water, have almost no opacity. Light passes directly through them."

    Now you know that *opacity* means something that is different from air, glass, and water, or something that is not clear or transparent. When materials are clear or transparent and light passes through them easily, they are said to have no *opacity*. Therefore, you can reason that *opacity* must mean "a blocking of light."

4. Another way to use context clues is to notice the circumstances in which the word appears. When you are aware of information given in connection with a word, you can "put two and two together" and guess its meaning. Read this sentence in which the word *feasible* is used:

    "The mountain climbers searched desperately for a feasible means of rescuing the injured man. They finally decided that the only way they could reach him was by lowering another man on a rope."

    It is not difficult to see that *feasible* has to do with being able to effect, or accomplish, something. *Feasible*, therefore, means "capable of being done."

There will be times when none of these four approaches will work. When you cannot use context clues, you must use the dictionary. But even then, you will need to use context clues in order to select the appropriate dictionary definition. The dictionary might give you the generally accepted meaning or perhaps a number of different meanings. It is up to you to choose the correct meaning and adapt it to the context with which you are working.

The WORD CLUES series will help you use context clues to discover the meanings of unfamiliar words. This series consists of seven books on a variety of reading levels. One way to find your starting level is to use the *EDL Word Clues Self-Placement Guide*.* It will help you find the WORD CLUES book with which you should start.

*EDL Word Clues Self-Placement Guide. Copyright© 1975 Educational Developmental Laboratories, Inc.

Dictionary entries for Books J, K, and L are taken from SCOTT, FORESMAN ADVANCED DICTIONARY by E. L. Thorndike and Clarence L. Barnhart. Copyright© 1979, 1974 by Scott, Foresman and Company. Reprinted by permission.

HOW TO USE THIS BOOK

WORD CLUES is a programmed book. It teaches you in a step-by-step fashion and tells you immediately whether you are right or wrong.

You don't read the pages in this book in the usual way. You have probably noticed that the pages are divided into bands of white and gray. Each of these bands is called a frame, and all of the frames are numbered. You work through the book "by the numbers," turning the page for each new frame, and **working only on the right-hand pages.** After starting with frame 1, you go on to 1a, 1b, 1c, 2a, 2b, 2c, etc.

Each of the 30 lessons in the book starts with the beginning of a story. You then complete 30 frames to help you master ten words. The three frames for each word are labeled *a*, *b*, and *c*.

The *a* frame Here the word is introduced. It is divided into syllables and its pronunciation is given. Say the word to yourself. This may help you think of its meaning. If you are not sure of the pronunciation, refer to the pronunciation key on the inside back cover. Then read the sentence or sentences in which the word is used. Looking at the way the word is used, write a definition or synonym in the space provided. If you are not sure, guess. This is not a test but rather a way to help you find out how well you know the word's meaning.

The *b* frame The word is used again. This time, the setting contains more clues to the meaning of the word. Find these clues and use them to complete the meaning, or synonym, exercise in this frame. Then check to see if you were correct by turning the page and looking at the extreme left of the *c* frame. If you were wrong, circle the correct meaning, and then read the sentences again with this meaning in mind.

The *c* frame The dictionary entry* appears at the left. When a word has multiple meanings, study all of them. Also notice if the word can be used as several parts of speech. If other forms of the word are given, study these too. Notice any pronunciation changes.

The right side of the *c* frame gives you a chance to see if you understand how the word can be used. You will find two kinds of exercises: usage exercises and analogies. For some of the usage exercises you will need to refer to the dictionary entry. Other times, you will have to rely on your experience.

The analogy exercises deal with relationships between pairs of words. A definition of analogy is "likeness in some ways between things that are otherwise different."

To complete an analogy exercise, you need to figure out how two words are related, and then apply this knowledge to another pair of words.

Here is one type of analogy:

Winter is to **summer** as **day** is to

    a. light
    b. night
    c. cold
    d. warm

Winter and summer are opposites. To complete the analogy, you select the word that is the opposite of day. The answer is, of course, choice c—night.

Sometimes analogies deal with synonyms, as in this example:

Rough is to **crude** as
    a. coarse is to smooth
    b. bark is to tree
    c. tender is to gentle
    d. cruel is to kind

Here you look for a choice in which the words are synonyms. The answer is choice c, because tender and gentle are synonyms.

Notice the difference between the two examples given so far. In the first, you looked for *one word* to complete the analogy. In the second, you looked for a *pair of words* that are related in the same way as the words in the first pair.

Here are some additional kinds of analogies:
PART-WHOLE: **Leaf** is to **plant** as **page** is to **book.**
FUNCTION: **Write** is to **pencil** as **paint** is to **brush.**
QUALITY: **Smooth** is to **satin** as **coarse** is to **burlap.**
You will encounter other kinds of analogies as you work through the lessons in this book.

A special kind of punctuation is used to express analogies. It looks like this:
Smile : cheer :: frown : worry
This would be read as:
Smile *is to* cheer *as* frown *is to* worry. This special punctuation is used in all of the analogy exercises in this book.

When you have finished the *c* exercise, check your answers by turning the page and looking to the left of the next frame. If you were wrong, circle the correct meaning and then reread the exercise to see why you were wrong. You are then ready to proceed to the next *a* frame.

Whenever you use WORD CLUES, be ready to give it your complete attention. Never leave a word until you are sure you understand its meaning or meanings.

Now you are ready to start on frame 1.

*Dictionary entries are taken from SCOTT, FORESMAN ADVANCED DICTIONARY by E. L. Thorndike and Clarence L. Barnhart. Copyright© 1979, 1974 by Scott, Foresman and Company.

BOOK L
ANSWER KEY FOR MASTERY TESTS

Lesson 1	Lesson 6	Lesson 11	Lesson 16	Lesson 21	Lesson 26
1. e	51. b	101. c	151. b	201. d	251. e
2. e	52. c	102. d	152. e	202. a	252. d
3. b	53. d	103. e	153. d	203. b	253. e
4. b	54. d	104. b	154. a	204. c	254. b
5. c	55. b	105. d	155. c	205. e	255. c
6. c	56. c	106. c	156. e	206. c	256. d
7. a	57. e	107. e	157. d	207. b	257. e
8. e	58. a	108. c	158. b	208. d	258. d
9. b	59. e	109. d	159. b	209. c	259. a
10. c	60. d	110. c	160. d	210. e	260. b

Lesson 2	Lesson 7	Lesson 12	Lesson 17	Lesson 22	Lesson 27
11. b	61. e	111. b	161. a	211. b	261. b
12. b	62. c	112. c	162. e	212. e	262. c
13. a	63. b	113. a	163. d	213. a	263. c
14. c	64. d	114. b	164. a	214. b	264. d
15. e	65. e	115. a	165. e	215. d	265. a
16. e	66. d	116. c	166. c	216. e	266. e
17. c	67. b	117. e	167. e	217. d	267. c
18. d	68. b	118. b	168. c	218. b	268. b
19. e	69. c	119. d	169. e	219. a	269. d
20. a	70. d	120. e	170. b	220. b	270. a

Lesson 3	Lesson 8	Lesson 13	Lesson 18	Lesson 23	Lesson 28
21. a	71. a	121. e	171. a	221. d	271. c
22. b	72. e	122. d	172. c	222. a	272. e
23. b	73. c	123. e	173. c	223. c	273. c
24. e	74. b	124. d	174. d	224. d	274. e
25. d	75. d	125. e	175. d	225. a	275. a
26. d	76. a	126. b	176. b	226. e	276. c
27. b	77. b	127. d	177. a	227. b	277. a
28. e	78. e	128. d	178. b	228. a	278. b
29. d	79. d	129. d	179. e	229. d	279. e
30. b	80. a	130. a	180. c	230. c	280. d

Lesson 4	Lesson 9	Lesson 14	Lesson 19	Lesson 24	Lesson 29
31. a	81. b	131. a	181. e	231. e	281. d
32. d	82. e	132. b	182. a	232. b	282. c
33. a	83. a	133. c	183. b	233. d	283. a
34. e	84. b	134. c	184. c	234. b	284. e
35. d	85. a	135. d	185. e	235. e	285. e
36. a	86. c	136. a	186. a	236. c	286. a
37. d	87. b	137. c	187. e	237. b	287. b
38. d	88. e	138. d	188. d	238. d	288. c
39. d	89. e	139. a	189. d	239. e	289. a
40. b	90. c	140. e	190. e	240. b	290. e

Lesson 5	Lesson 10	Lesson 15	Lesson 20	Lesson 25	Lesson 30
41. e	91. c	141. a	191. c	241. a	291. e
42. c	92. a	142. b	192. d	242. b	292. c
43. c	93. d	143. e	193. c	243. d	293. c
44. d	94. a	144. d	194. d	244. a	294. a
45. e	95. b	145. d	195. a	245. c	295. d
46. d	96. d	146. e	196. e	246. d	296. c
47. b	97. b	147. b	197. e	247. e	297. e
48. b	98. e	148. c	198. d	248. a	298. b
49. b	99. a	149. b	199. a	249. d	299. d
50. c	100. e	150. c	200. b	250. a	300. b

ANSWER KEY FOR BOOK L POSTTEST

1. c 2. b 3. c 4. d 5. a 6. b 7. b 8. a 9. c 10. c 11. b 12. a 13. a 14. b 15. d 16. a
17. a 18. c 19. b 20. d 21. b 22. d 23. d 24. b 25. d

LESSON 1

Northern Neighbors

Joe Andrade, the social sciences instructor at Central High, was the man responsible for the Northern Neighbors tour through Canada. The trip was open only to graduating seniors. Expenses were kept to a minimum. The journey would be made by train, with frequent stops for side trips, camping, and backpacking.

26a

a droit (ə droit′)

Sally, who was an **adroit** young woman, immediately began to question all the workers who kept plants in their offices.

Write a definition or synonym:

51a

ad a mant (ad′ ə mənt, ad′ ə mant)

The Crusades began when men grew **adamant** in their desire to regain the Holy Land from the Moslems who occupied it.

Write a definition or synonym:

76b

Her **gossamer** gowns danced and drifted in the slightest breeze. They enhanced her fragile beauty.

Gossamer means:
—**a.** light and filmy
—**b.** expensive; lavish
—**c.** rare and exotic
—**d.** tasteful; elegant

101b

Mr. Stanton, the director, said that the academy was fully accountable for the education and welfare of its students. He hoped that Linda and the other new students would accept this **tutelage.**

Tutelage means:
—**a.** franchise
—**b.** privilege
—**c.** guardianship
—**d.** surveillance

126c

ho mo ge ne ous (hō′mə jē′nē əs, hō′mə-jē′nyəs; hom′ə jē′nē əs, hom′ə jē′nyəs), *adj.* 1 of the same kind, nature, or character; similar. 2 made up of similar elements or parts; of uniform nature or character throughout: *The population of the island was homogeneous because there were no foreigners there.* 3 (in mathematics) of the same degree or dimensions. [< Medieval Latin *homogeneus* < Greek *homogenēs* < *homos* same + *genos* kind] —**ho′mo ge′ne ous ly,** *adv.* —**ho′mo ge′ne ous ness,** *n.*

ANALOGY homogeneous : heterogeneous ::
—**a.** segment : component
—**b.** bulwark : mainstay
—**c.** simultaneous : series
—**d.** robust : hardy
—**e.** concave : convex

1

176b

By not casting their votes, citizens may **invalidate** the right to have a voice in their government. There is no value in possessing a right if it is not exercised.

Invalidate means:
__a. ignore
__b. nullify
__c. avoid
__d. neglect

Go back to page 154 and continue on frame 176c.

201a

pseu do nym (süd′ n im)

Early in his career, Tim Farrell decided not to use a **pseudonym.**

Write a definition or synonym:

Go back to page 154 and continue on frame 201b.

226a

b

junc ture (jungk′ chər)

At this **juncture,** the chief chimp decided that Paul and Paula must have flown the spaceship themselves, incredible as it seemed. She sent for the two humans immediately.

Write a definition or synonym:

Go back to page 154 and continue on frame 226b.

b, c

LESSON 26

Vincent Van Gogh: Tormented Genius

In his dress, his behavior, and his artistic goals, Vincent Van Gogh (van gō′), the great nineteenth-century Dutch painter, remained a tormented outsider. The intensity of his search for creativity and self-discovery alienated him from his middle-class family, from the workers and laborers he painted, and from his fellow artists. When he began painting, his work was rough and unpromising. When his life's work was completed, he had created some 600 paintings, which have established him as one of the world's great artists.

Go back to page 154 and continue on frame 251a.

275c

a

cen sure (sen′shər), *n., v.,* **-sured, -sur ing.**
—*n.* 1 expression of disapproval; un- favorable opinion; criticism. 2 penalty, as a public rebuke or suspension from office. —*v.t.* express disapproval of; find fault with; criticize. See **blame** for synonym study. [< Latin *censura* < *censere* appraise] —**cen′sur er,** *n.*

1. If you are **censured** you are:
   __a. "casting the first stone"
   __b. "rapped on the knuckles"
   __c. "given a going-over"
   __d. "dressed down"
   __e. "dressed up"
2. Which of the following is *least* like **censure** in meaning?
   __a. taunt __b. chide __c. scold

Go back to page 154 and continue on frame 276a.

300c

b

quin tes sence (kwin tes′ns), *n.* 1 the pur- est form of some quality; pure essence. 2 the most perfect example of something: *Her dress was the quintessence of good taste and style.* [< Medieval Latin *quinta essentia* fifth essence; with reference to a fifth element supposed by medieval philosophers to be more pervasive than the four elements (earth, water, fire, and air)]

Which of the following characteristics does the **quintessence** of a thing possess?
__a. mediocrity __d. triviality
__b. perfection __e. incompleteness
__c. purity

The End

2

1a

vac il late (vas′ ə lāt)

Connie's parents **vacillated** before permitting her to join the tour.

Write a definition or synonym:

26b

Sally's clever, quick-witted questions kept the workers off guard. She was **adroit** enough to collect information without letting anyone realize how much she was learning.

Adroit means:
___a. relentless
___b. rapid
___c. skillful
___d. honest

51b

The Crusaders pledged their lives to regain the Holy Land. The Moslems, however, were just as **adamant** in their determination to remain in the Holy Land. Wars over the Holy Land lasted for almost two generations.

A synonym for **adamant** is:
___a. unyielding
___b. remitting
___c. dauntless
___d. devious

76c

a

gos sa mer (gos′ə mər), *n.* 1 film or thread of cobweb spun by small spiders, which is seen floating in the air in calm weather. 2 a very thin, light cloth or coat. 3 anything very light and thin. —*adj.* like gossamer; very light and thin; filmy. [Middle English *gossomer* goose summer, name for "Indian summer," as the season for goose and cobwebs]

Gossamer *cannot* be described as:
___a. delicate ___e. durable
___b. coarse ___f. tough
___c. rugged ___g. airy
___d. fine ___h. wispy

101c

c

tu te lage (tü′tl ij, tyü′tl ij), *n.* 1 office or function of a guardian; guardianship; protection. 2 instruction. 3 a being in the charge of a guardian or tutor. [< Latin *tutela* protection]

Check the sentence(s) in which **tutelage** is used correctly.
___a. The child was placed in the tutelage of a responsible young man.
___b. After college he went on to graduate school to continue his tutelage.
___c. They wanted a reliable watchdog for tutelage.
___d. Her tutelage ended when she left school.

127a

e

im pe tus (im′ pə təs)

Write a definition or synonym:

The success of Jamestown provided the **impetus** for other Europeans to start settlements in the New World.

300b

In their painting and their poetry, Japanese artists ruthlessly remove all superfluous elements, leaving only the **quintessence** of their subject.

4.

Quintessence means:
- __a. faint resemblance
- __b. purest form
- __c. original source
- __d. last vestige

275b

Several writers harshly criticized the leaders of industry for the sweatshops they ran. In addition, the writers **censured** the government for not taking action against such working conditions.

Censure means:
- __a. reprove
- __b. censor
- __c. abuse
- __d. interrogate

250c

a

rel e gate (rel/ə gāt), *v.t.* **-gat ed, -gat ing.** 1 put away, usually to a lower position or condition. 2 send into exile; banish. 3 hand over (a matter, task, etc.). [< Latin *relegatum* sent back < *re-* back + *legare* send with a commission] **—rel/e ga/tion,** *n.*

Check the sentence(s) in which a form of **relegate** is used correctly.
- __a. He was relegated to the presidency.
- __b. I relegated the work to my assistant.
- __c. Criminals are sometimes relegated to isolated places.
- __d. I was relegated to top position in the class.

225c

c

pon der ous (pon/dər əs), *adj.* 1 very heavy. 2 heavy and clumsy: *A hippopotamus is ponderous.* 3 dull; tiresome: *The speaker talked in a ponderous way.* **—pon/der ous- ly,** *adv.* **—pon/der ous ness,** *n.*

ANALOGY ponderous : lithe ::
- __a. pinnacle : apex
- __b. diligent : slothful
- __c. tolerable : formidable
- __d. copy : replica
- __e. ordain : glorify

LESSON 21   Cartoon King

b, d

I have to admit I enjoy telling people that I know Tim Farrell. Not everybody has a world-famous cartoonist as a friend. Of course, I haven't seen Tim since his comic strip caught on. He's been too busy writing and drawing the adventures of Penny Dreadful, the strongest little girl in the world. But I've known Tim since we were kids. When I read about Penny and her friends in the Sunday papers, the stories take me back to my own childhood.

176a

c

in val i date (in val' ə dāt)

Write a definition or synonym:

Citizens should not allow their right to speak their minds to be **invalidated.**

1b

Connie's parents usually came to decisions quickly and stood by them. This time, however, they **vacillated** until they met the leader of the tour.

Vacillate means:
- __a. brood
- __b. postpone
- __c. meditate
- __d. waver

---

c

26c

a droit (ə droit′), *adj.* 1 resourceful in reaching one's objective; ingenious; clever. 2 skillful in the use of the hands or body; dexterous. See **deft** for synonym study. [< French < *à droit* rightly] **—a droit′ly,** *adv.* **—a droit′ness,** *n.*

Which of the following mean the *opposite* of **adroit**?
- __a. inept
- __b. awkward
- __c. silly
- __d. convenient
- __e. appropriate
- __f. coordinated

---

a

51c

ad a mant (ad′ə mənt, ad′ə mant), *adj.* 1 not giving in readily; firm and unyielding; immovable. 2 too hard to be cut or broken. [< Latin *adamantem* < Greek *adamantos* the hardest metal < *a-* not + *damnanai* to tame, conquer. Doublet of DIAMOND.] **—ad′a mant ly,** *adv.*

Check the sentence(s) in which **adamant** is used correctly.
- __a. Adamant substances like diamonds can be used for cutting glass.
- __b. He picked up an adamant and hurled it through the window.
- __c. He jokingly called the stale biscuits adamant.
- __d. She was adamant in her refusal to go.

---

b, c,
e, f

77a

u surp (yü zėrp′, yü sėrp′)

Sir Mordred attempted to **usurp** King Arthur's position.

Write a definition or synonym:

---

a, d

102a

sec u lar (sek′ yə lər)

In his first lecture, Mr. Stanton made it clear that the academy was a **secular** institution.

Write a definition or synonym:

127b

After the founding of Jamestown, Plymouth and Massachusetts Bay were settled. Certain religious groups, such as the Pilgrims, had always dreamed of settling in a land where they could worship as they chose, but it was the success of the Jamestown colony that gave them the **impetus** to act.

Impetus means:
- __a. courage
- __b. good example
- __c. acumen
- __d. incentive

d

175c

e lec tor ate (i lek′tər it), *n.* 1 the persons having the right to vote in an election. 2 territory under the rule of an elector of the Holy Roman Empire. 3 rank of an elector of the Holy Roman Empire.

Check the sentence(s) in which **electorate** is used correctly.

__a. When the electorate was over, everyone agreed that the best candidate had won.
__b. Are you old enough to electorate?
__c. The electorate should be well informed.

---

b

200c

aus ter i ty (ô ster′ə tē), *n., pl.* -ties. 1 sternness in manner or appearance; harshness; severity. 2 severe simplicity. 3 a strict limiting or rationing of food, clothing, etc., in order to conserve national resources. 4 **austerities**, *pl.* severe practices, such as going without food or praying all night.

Check the sentence(s) in which **austerity** can be correctly substituted for the italicized word.

__a. The *harshness* of the abrasive had worn away the enamel.
__b. The *severity* of their regimen soon hardened the recruits.
__c. The *severity* of the weather was unusual for that time of year.
__d. *Self-denial* was the monk's way of life.

225b

The poor, bewildered humans seemed defenseless. The chimps were far too quick and agile to be struck by the slow, clumsy hands of the **ponderous** humans, even though the humans weighed twice as much as the chimps.

Ponderous means:
__a. vagrant
__b. astounding
__c. heavy
__d. heedless

250b

Many Western women seek the opportunity to have careers in addition to caring for their homes and families. However, most women in Ibn Saud's sheikdom do not protest when they are **relegated** to a sheltered life at home.

Relegate means:
__a. banish
__b. retire
__c. admit
__d. entice

---

b, e

275a

cen sure (sen′ shər)

As working conditions grew worse, public **censure** of big business increased.

Write a definition or synonym:

---

d

300a

quin tes sence (kwin tes′ ns)

Mr. Nakamura claimed that the **quintessence** of delicate beauty is found in Japanese art.

Write a definition or synonym:

6

1c

d

vac il late (vas′ə lāt), v.i., -lat ed, -lat ing.
1 waver in mind or opinion: *A vacillating person can't make up his mind.* 2 move first one way and then another; waver. [< Latin *vacillatum* wavered] —vac′il lat′ing ly, adv. —vac′il la′tion, n.

ANALOGY vacillate : decide :: forget :
__a. thirsty
__b. angry
__c. remember
__d. remark
__e. lose

27a

a, b

big ot (big′ ət)

Sally was almost sure that those plants held the key to the mystery. She confided in the chief of security at Tektron and discovered that he was a confirmed **bigot**.

Write a definition or synonym:

52a

c, d

ac ri mo ni ous (ak′ rə mō′ nē əs)

The Crusades gave the Europeans a chance to acquaint themselves with the spices, ornaments, and rugs of the Moslems. A great demand arose in Europe for these items. Eventually the cities of Italy became engaged in **acrimonious** competition for this trade.

Write a definition or synonym:

77b

Arthur's right to the throne was established when he pulled the sword Excalibur from the stone. Mordred's efforts to **usurp** King Arthur's throne threatened not only Arthur's supremacy but also the stability of the entire kingdom.

Usurp means:
__a. to use illegally
__b. to confiscate
__c. to seize without right
__d. to conquer

102b

Because the academy was **secular,** it had no connection with a church and gave no instruction in sacred matters. However, Mr. Stanton stressed the importance of a personal sense of morality.

Secular means:
__a. neutral
__b. atheistic
__c. not religious
__d. specialized

127c

d

im pe tus (im′pə təs), n. 1 the force with which a moving body tends to maintain its velocity and overcome resistance: *the impetus of a moving automobile.* 2 a driving force; cause of action or effort; incentive: *Ambition is an impetus to work for success.* [< Latin, an attack < *impetere* to attack < *in-* + *petere* aim for]

Check the sentence(s) in which **impetus** is used correctly.
__a. Coffee is an impetus.
__b. The ball's impetus knocked the racket from the player's hand.
__c. She had a sudden impetus to sneeze.

175b

Although the preliminary choices and decisions are made by political leaders, the ultimate choice and victory of one candidate depends on the entire **electorate**.

Electorate means:
— **a.** those who support a candidate
— **b.** those who donate money
— **c.** those with high rank
— **d.** those who have the right to vote

~~200b~~

A period of **austerity** was necessary because the nation's treasury had been severely depleted. Most people were willing to do without normal conveniences and services until prosperity was restored.

Another word for **austerity** is:
— **a.** propriety
— **b.** strictness
— **c.** conservation
— **d.** surveillance

225a

b, e

pon der ous (pon′ dər əs)

At this point in the movie there is a long close-up of the horrified faces of the Stargazers. Then the camera shows a group of **ponderous** humans being attacked by a crowd of chimps. The humans look as savage and as uncomprehending as wild beasts!

Write a definition or synonym:

250a

b, c, e

rel e gate (rel′ ə gāt)

Although a woman's role is changing fast in Ibn Saud's sheikdom, most females continue to be **relegated** to a subservient role.

Write a definition or synonym:

274c

c

sub sid i ar y (səb sid′ē er′ē), *adj., n., pl.* **-ar ies.** —*adj.* 1 useful to assist or supplement; auxiliary; supplementary. 2 subordinate; secondary. 3 maintained by a subsidy. —*n.* 1 person or thing that assists or supplements. 2 company having over half of its stock owned or controlled by another company: *The bus line was a subsidiary of the railroad.* [< Latin *subsidiarius* < *subsidium* reserve troops]

Which of the following can be correctly described as **subsidiary**?
— **a.** the main theme of a symphony
— **b.** an outlying division of a business
— **c.** a government agency
— **d.** a parent company
— **e.** a subservient position
— **f.** a junior high school

299c

c

ab ject (ab′jekt, ab jekt′), *adj.* 1 so low or degraded as to be hopeless; wretched; miserable: *to live in abject poverty.* 2 deserving contempt; despicable: *the most abject flattery.* 3 slavish: *abject submission.* [< Latin *abjectum* cast down < *ab-* down + *jacere* to throw] —**ab ject′ly,** *adv.* —**ab ject′ness,** *n.*

ANALOGY abject : glorious ::
— **a.** deficient : vigilant
— **b.** sterile : exploited
— **c.** pleased : satisfied
— **d.** foolish : astute
— **e.** impetuous : magnanimous

2a

c

de mean or (di mē′ nər)

Almost everyone was impressed by the forceful **demeanor** of the tour leader.

Write a definition or synonym:

27b

The chief of security was unwilling to admit that a mere woman such as Sally would have any worthwhile suggestions. His prejudice against women who work for a living made him a **bigot** in Sally's eyes.

A **bigot** is a person who is:
___a. thoughtless
___b. unpleasant
___c. intolerant
___d. intelligent

52b

As time passed, greed fostered hostility, and the rivalry among the cities became more **acrimonious**. With increasing competition, any friendliness that might have existed disappeared without a trace.

A synonym for **acrimonious** is:
___a. bitter
___b. emotional
___c. unceasing
___d. accelerated

77c

c

u surp (yü zėrp′, yü sėrp′), *v.t.* seize and hold (power, position, authority, etc.) by force or without right: *The king's brother tried to usurp the throne.* —*v.i.* commit usurpation. [< Latin *usurpare* < *usu* through use + *rapere* seize] —**u surp′er,** *n.*

Check the sentence(s) in which **usurp** can be correctly substituted for the italicized word.
___a. He *seized* her hand and declared his love for her.
___b. She fired her assistant for trying to *take* her job.
___c. She *seized* the thief and put handcuffs on him.

102c

c

sec u lar (sek′yə lər), *adj.* 1 not religious or sacred; worldly: *secular music, a secular education.* 2 living in the world; not belonging to a religious order: *the secular clergy, a secular priest.* 3 occurring once in an age or century. 4 lasting through long ages; going on from age to age. —*n.* 1 a secular priest. 2 layman. [< Latin *saecularis* < *saeculum* age, world] —**sec′u lar ly,** *adv.*

Which of the following can be described as **secular**?
___a. a sequoia tree
___b. a supreme court
___c. a monk in a monastery
___d. a hymn
___e. a priest who does not belong to a religious order
___f. a trip around the world
___g. a diplomat
___h. a parochial school

128a

b

neb u lous (neb′ yə ləs)

Write a definition or synonym:

The Pilgrims could never be accused of being **nebulous** in their aims.

175a

e

e lec tor ate (i lek′ tər it)

The final decision is made by the **electorate**.

Write a definition or synonym:

200a

, e, f

aus ter i ty (ô ster′ ə tē)

A period of **austerity** followed the establishment of the new government.

Write a definition or synonym:

224c

d

pan de mo ni um (pan′də mō′nē əm), *n.*
1 place of wild disorder or lawless confusion.
2 wild uproar or lawlessness. **3 Pandemonium, a** abode of all the demons; hell.

Which of the following expressions describe **pandemonium**?
___**a.** "hullabaloo"
___**b.** "tumult and confusion"
___**c.** "bolt out of the blue"
___**d.** "trick of fate"
___**e.** "fire and brimstone"
___**f.** "quick as a flash"

249c

c

pes ti lence (pes′tl əns), *n.* 1 any infectious or contagious epidemic disease that spreads rapidly, often causing many deaths. 2 the bubonic plague.

Which of the following can be helpful in controlling **pestilence**?
___**a.** doctors   ___**d.** insect control
___**b.** good sanitation ___**e.** drugs
___**c.** hospitals   ___**f.** germs

274b

Industrial monopolies were created when one company acquired over half the stock of its rivals, thus transforming them from independent operations to **subsidiaries** of the parent company.

A **subsidiary** is:
___**a.** a competitor
___**b.** an independent company
___**c.** a company owned by another
___**d.** a successor

299b

Although Lucy expected to find starvation and the misery of **abject** poverty in Asia, she learned that the Japanese, who enjoy the highest standard of living in Asia, were generally prosperous.

Abject means:
___**a.** opulent
___**b.** ostentatious
___**c.** wretched
___**d.** despotic

2b

Mr. Andrade's character was evident in his general **demeanor.** The way he spoke, the manner in which he held his head and body, and the way he walked all suggested his quiet strength.

Another word for **demeanor** is:
___**a.** composure
___**b.** manner
___**c.** composition
___**d.** expression

---

c

27c

big ot (big′ət), *n.* person who is bigoted; intolerant person. [< Middle French]

A **bigot** is most likely to be:
___**a.** liberal   ___**d.** modern
___**b.** high-principled ___**e.** magnanimous
___**c.** narrow-minded

---

a

52c

ac ri mo ni ous (ak′rə mō′nē əs), *adj.* bitter and irritating in disposition or manner; caustic.   **—ac′ri mo′ni ous ly,** *adv.* **—ac′ri mo′ni ous ness,** *n.*

1. Which of the following words is *least* similar to **acrimonious**?
___**a.** acrid   ___**d.** hostile
___**b.** indifferent ___**e.** affable
___**c.** harsh
2. **Acrimonious** can be used to describe:
___**a.** a piece of glass
___**b.** an angry debate
___**c.** a savory stew

---

b

78a

e dict (ē′ dikt)

King Arthur might have issued an **edict** regarding Mordred's fate. Instead he chose to meet him on the field of battle. The outcome of the battle was that Mordred was killed and Arthur was wounded.

Write a definition or synonym:

---

b, e, g

103a

gauche (gōsh)

Many of the new students seemed to feel **gauche** at the dinner party where they met the instructors at the academy.

Write a definition or synonym:

128b

Certainly, the Mayflower Compact which the Pilgrims drafted was not **nebulous** concerning the rules of government under which their colony was to operate. These simple, understandable rules served to guide their colony well.

Nebulous means:
___**a.** ambiguous
___**b.** contradictory
___**c.** ingenuous
___**d.** vague

174c

cau cus (kô′kəs), *n.* 1 u.s. a meeting of members or leaders of a political party to make plans, choose candidates, or decide how to vote. 2 any similar meeting for the private discussion of policy. —*v.i.* hold a caucus. [probably < Algonquian *caucauasu* elder]

ANALOGY caucus : election :: plan :
___a. sear
___b. tabulate
___c. ire
___d. dupe
___e. test

d

199c

mer ce nar y (mèr′sə ner′ē), *adj., n., pl.* -nar ies. —*adj.* 1 working for money only; acting with money as the motive; hireling. 2 done for money or gain. —*n.* 1 soldier serving for pay in a foreign army. 2 person who works merely for pay. [< Latin *mercenarius* < *merces* wages < *merx, mercis* wares] —mer′ce nar′i ly, *adv.* —mer′ce nar′i ness, *n.*

Which of the following can be described as **mercenary**?
___a. brigadier general in the U.S. Army
___b. philanthropist
___c. Foreign Legionnaire
___d. non-profit organization
___e. soldier of fortune
___f. "gold digger"
___g. "forty-niner"

c

224b

When Paul heard the loud sounds of scuffling and shouting, he was so startled that he dropped his pineapple. He ran to the front of the cage to see what could be causing such **pandemonium.**

Pandemonium means:
___a. celebration
___b. consternation
___c. complications
___d. uproar

249b

Common forms of **pestilence** include smallpox and yellow fever. The sheik told the Cassidys that these diseases will be eliminated as soon as his people could be persuaded to take the necessary shots or vaccinations.

Pestilence means:
___a. bacteria
___b. illness
___c. epidemic
___d. crime

274a

sub sid i ar y (səb sid′ ē er′ ē)

A person could gain control of an entire industry by starting with one company and then acquiring **subsidiaries.**

Write a definition or synonym:

a, b

299a

ab ject (ab′ jekt, ab jekt′)

As a child in the United States, Lucy had never seen **abject** poverty.

Write a definition or synonym:

a, c

12

b

2c   **de mean or** (di mē′nər), *n.* way a person looks and acts; behavior; manner.

Check the sentence(s) in which **demeanor** is used correctly.
__**a.** Her demeanor was characteristic of her station in life.
__**b.** Her report card indicated poor demeanor.
__**c.** The queen's demeanor is stately.

28a

c

con nois seur (kon′ ə sėr′)

Sally's idea seemed quite plausible to the director. He was a true **connoisseur** of exotic plants.

Write a definition or synonym:

53a

1. e
2. b

ar du ous (är′ jü əs)

It became **arduous** for the other European countries to compete with the Italians in trade with the Middle East and China.

Write a definition or synonym:

78b

Arthur was a sovereign with limitless authority. The **edicts** he proclaimed were posted throughout the kingdom and were to be obeyed unquestioningly.

An **edict** is:
__**a.** a citation
__**b.** a request
__**c.** a decree
__**d.** an aide

103b

One of the new girls told Linda that she felt so clumsy, she was "all thumbs" when she met the instructors. Linda told her that she had no reason to feel so **gauche**. After all, each of the students would someday be world-famous!

Gauche means:
__**a.** cumbersome
__**b.** awkward
__**c.** ponderous
__**d.** inane

---

d

128c   **neb u lous** (neb′yə ləs), *adj.* 1 hazy; vague; confused. 2 cloudlike. 3 of or like a nebula or nebulae. —**neb′u lous ly,** *adv.* —**neb′u lous ness,** *n.*

Check the sentence(s) in which **nebulous** can be correctly substituted for the italicized word.
__**a.** The line between talent and genius is *hazy*.
__**b.** They became *confused* at the intersection.
__**c.** There is a *cloudlike* spot in the sky.

13

174b

A major responsibility of party leaders is the planning of campaigns and overall strategy. A caucus is held to accomplish this end.

A **caucus** is:
__a. a prenomination vote by party members
__b. a preelection rally
__c. a canvassing of party members
__d. a planning meeting of party members

199b

After the fighting was over, these **mercenaries** were glad to be allowed to leave the country. They would search for other governments which might pay them for their military skills.

A **mercenary** is:
__a. a career officer
__b. an idealist
__c. a hired soldier
__d. a war correspondent

224a

pan de mo ni um (pan' də mō' nē əm)

Suddenly there was **pandemonium** outside the cage where Paul and Paula were being held.

Write a definition or synonym:

249a

pes ti lence (pes' tl əns)

Pestilence is another problem which Ibn Saud intends to obviate.

Write a definition or synonym:

273c

can dor (kan'dər), n. 1 a saying openly what one really thinks; honesty in giving one's view or opinion; frankness and sincerity. 2 fairness; impartiality. [< Latin, whiteness < *candere* to shine]

Check the sentence(s) in which **candor** is used correctly.
__a. The judge decided the case with candor.
__b. A little white lie is sometimes kinder than candor.
__c. His candor made him a valuable spy.
__d. She sunburned easily because of the candor of her complexion.

298c

in un date (in'un dāt), v.t., -dat ed, -dat ing. 1 overspread with a flow of water; flood. 2 overspread as if with a flood: *Requests for free tickets inundated the studio.* [< Latin *inundatum* flooded < in- onto + *undare* to flow < *unda* wave]
—in'un da'tor, n.

Check the sentence(s) in which a form of **inundate** is used correctly.
__a. The company was inundated with Christmas orders.
__b. She was inundated with surprise.
__c. The basement was inundated by the storm.

d

d

, e, f

, d, e

3a

a, c

par a pher nal ia (par′ ə fər nā′ lyə)

Surrounded by her **paraphernalia,** Connie waited for the group at the train station.

Write a definition or synonym:

28b

The director was an authority on the type of plants the missing worker had been growing in his office. He was often called on to evaluate similar plants in local flower shows. This was a task that only a **connoisseur** could perform.

A **connoisseur** is:
__**a.** a capitalist
__**b.** an expert
__**c.** an influential man
__**d.** a dealer

53b

Portugal recognized how **arduous** it would be to compete with the Italians, who were closer to the established trade routes. However, if the Portuguese could find a new route, competition might become easier.

A synonym for **arduous** is:
__**a.** difficult
__**b.** impossible
__**c.** inappropriate
__**d.** unprofitable

78c

c

e dict (ē′dikt), *n.* 1 decree or law proclaimed by a king or other ruler on his sole authority. See **proclamation** for synonym study. 2 any similar order or command. [< Latin *edictum* < *edicere* proclaim < *ex-* out + *dicere* say]

Edict can be used to describe which of the following?
__**a.** an announcement by a store that it will be closed on a holiday
__**b.** an announcement by a dictator that traitors will be shot
__**c.** a verdict of "not guilty" given by a jury
__**d.** a ruling by the United States Supreme Court

103c

b

gauche (gōsh), *adj.* lacking grace or tact; awkward. [< French, literally, left] —**gauche′ly,** *adv.* —**gauche′ness,** *n.*

1. Check the expressions that mean the same as **gauche.**
   __**a.** having a "green thumb"
   __**b.** "putting one's foot in it"
   __**c.** having "two left feet"
   __**d.** "slippery as an eel"
   __**e.** "barking up the wrong tree"
2. Which word means the *opposite* of **gauche**?
   __**a.** elegant   __**b.** astute   __**c.** suave

129a

a, c

con ver sant (kən vér′ sənt, kon′ vər sənt)

It was not long before the settlers became **conversant** with the plants and herbs that could be used as medicine or as food.

Write a definition or synonym:

298b

b

Lucy knew that the rice paddies are **inundated** during the rainy season. The rice requires this soaking. Farmers sometimes must wade knee-deep in water and mud to care for their crops.

Inundate means:
- __a. plant
- __b. cultivate
- __c. irrigate
- __d. flood

273b

c

Although some industrial magnates would speak with **candor** about the size of their fortunes, they would undoubtedly be less open about the means by which they acquired their wealth.

Candor is:
- __a. ingenuousness
- __b. exultation
- __c. deference
- __d. frankness

248c

c

ob vi ate (ob′vē āt), *v.t.,* **-at ed, -at ing.** meet and dispose of; clear out of the way; remove: *obviate a difficulty, obviate danger, obviate objections.* [< Late Latin *obviatum* met in the way < Latin *obvius.* See OBVIOUS.] —**ob′vi a′tion,** *n.* —**ob′vi a′tor,** *n.*

Which of the following would you be most likely to **obviate?**
- __a. an obstacle
- __b. an insurmountable problem
- __c. a roadblock
- __d. an ally
- __e. risk in carrying money
- __f. a problem

223c

d

suc cu lent (suk′yə lənt), *adj.* 1 full of juice; juicy: *a succulent peach.* 2 interesting; not dull. 3 (of plants, etc.) having thick or fleshy and juicy leaves or stems. —*n.* a succulent plant. [< Latin *succulentus* < *sucus* juice] —**suc′cu lent ly,** *adv.*

Which of the following could be described as **succulent?**
- __a. cold cereal   __d. an intriguing plot
- __b. a dull person   __e. cactus
- __c. a ripe tomato   __f. a stalk of wheat

199a

b

mer ce nar y (mûr′ sə ner′ ē)

Write a definition or synonym:

The defeated government had many **mercenaries** in its army.

174a

1. c
2. b

cau cus (kô′ kəs)

Write a definition or synonym:

District and county leaders are asked to attend **caucuses.**

3b

In addition to her luggage, Connie had brought a camera, a radio, a pair of field glasses, and two notebooks. Keeping track of her **paraphernalia** would be a full-time job!

Paraphernalia means:
__a. luggage
__b. sporting goods
__c. equipment
__d. excess baggage

---

b

28c

con nois seur (kon′ə sèr′), *n.* a critical judge of art or of matters of taste; expert: *a connoisseur of antique furniture.* [< Old French < *connoistre* know < Latin *cognoscere.* See COGNITION.]

Which of the following would *least* likely be **connoisseurs?**
__a. a student   __d. a beginner
__b. a dealer   __e. a critic
__c. a professional __f. an amateur

---

a

53c

ar du ous (är′jü əs), *adj.* 1 hard to do; requiring much effort; difficult: *an arduous lesson.* 2 using up much energy; strenuous: *an arduous climb.* [< Latin *arduus* steep] —ar′du ous ly, *adv.* —ar′du ous ness, *n.*

1. Which of the following would be most **arduous?**
  __a. getting dressed for a party
  __b. pushing a car
  __c. walking home from the local theater
  __d. spending money
2. Studying can be very **arduous** for some students.
  Yes__   No__

---

b, d

79a

al le go ry (al′ ə gôr′ ē, al′ ə gōr′ ē)

Some people interpret the legends about King Arthur as **allegories.**

Write a definition or synonym:

---

b, c
, c

104a

pseu do (sü′ dō)

Linda paid little attention to the **pseudo-**sophistication of some of the other students.

Write a definition or synonym:

129b

If they had not quickly become **conversant** with the new and different diet, they would not have survived that first hard winter. Among other things, the Pilgrims learned to plant corn, to harvest cranberries, and to prepare wild turkey.

A synonym for **conversant** is:
__a. congenial
__b. familiar
__c. agreeable
__d. learned

173c

c

col lo qui al (kə lō′kwē əl), *adj.* used in everyday, informal talk, but not in formal speech or writing; conversational. Such expressions as *clip* for *punch* and *close call* for *a narrow escape* are colloquial. —col lo′qui al ly, *adv.*

1. Which of the following correctly describe(s) **colloquial** speech?
   __a. dignified   __c. casual
   __b. sedate   __d. ignorant
2. Who is most likely to use **colloquial** language?
   __a. a judge   __b. a sportscaster

198c

d

bour geois (bur zhwä′, bur′zhwä), *n., pl.* -geois, *adj.* —*n.* 1 person of the middle class, as distinguished from an aristocrat or a worker or peasant. 2 person who owns property or who is engaged in business or commerce, as an owner, partner, etc. —*adj.* 1 of or characteristic of the middle class. 2 like the middle class in appearance, way of thinking, etc.; ordinary; common: *bourgeois attitudes.* [< French < Medieval Latin *burgensis* town dweller, citizen < Late Latin *burgus* town. Doublet of BURGESS.]

Check the sentence(s) in which **bourgeois** is used correctly.
   __a. He was not seriously ill; he merely had a bourgeois head cold.
   __b. He was of the nobility, but his wife was bourgeois.
   __c. Newspaper headlines are usually set in bourgeois type.

223b

The fruit appeared to be rather dry on the outside, but when Paul sliced it open, he found that it was dripping with juice. The next five minutes of the movie show the Stargazers eagerly devouring the **succulent** fruit.

Succulent means:
   __a. savory
   __b. rare
   __c. palatable
   __d. juicy

248b

Disease and illiteracy are two of the problems Ibn Saud would like to **obviate**. To remove them, he has sponsored widespread health and education programs.

The meaning of **obviate** is:
   __a. recognize
   __b. conceal
   __c. dispose of
   __d. make manifest

273a

b, c

b

can dor (kan′ dər)

In those days a man would boast of his millions with a **candor** which we would find surprising today.

Write a definition or synonym:

298a

a, c

in un date (in′ un dāt, in un′ dāt)

On the train ride from Nagoya to Tokyo, where Mr. Nakamura had a business meeting, Lucy noticed the terraced tea plantations and the **inundated** rice paddies.

Write a definition or synonym:

18

3c

c

par a pher nal ia (par′ə fər nā′lyə), *n., pl.*
or sing. 1 personal belongings. 2 equipment;
outfit. [< Medieval Latin < Greek *para-*
*pherna.*a woman's personal property besides
her dowry < *para-*[1] + *phernē* dowry]

Check the item(s) that would be considered
paraphernalia.
__**a.** conduct   __**d.** tennis racket
__**b.** speech   __**e.** appearance
__**c.** transistor radio

29a

d, f

la tent (lāt′ nt)

Sally learned that the man who had stolen the plans
also took his plants to and from the office. Sally knew
she had the answer! Like many reporters, Sally had
a **latent** talent for police work.

Write a definition or synonym:

54a

b
Yes

co erce (kō érs′)

Portugal made no attempt to **coerce** the Italian
traders into surrendering their monopoly of the
trade routes.

Write a definition or synonym:

79b

The various characters could easily personify
different human attributes. For example, King
Arthur might represent Honor, Sir Mordred could
depict Evil, and their conflict the age-old fight
between good and evil. The meaning of an **allegory**,
however, is always subject to personal
interpretation.

An **allegory** is:
__**a.** an ambiguous story
__**b.** a symbolic narrative
__**c.** a fairy tale
__**d.** a descriptive tale

104b

A few of the students tried to simulate a worldliness
and experience which they did not actually possess.
Linda found this **pseudo**-sophistication as
unconvincing as it was unattractive.

Pseudo means:
__**a.** feigned
__**b.** inept
__**c.** ingenuous
__**d.** naïve

129c

b

con ver sant (kən vèr′sənt, kon′vər sənt),
adj. familiar by use or study; acquainted:
conversant with many fields of study.

Check the sentence(s) in which **conversant** can be
correctly substituted for the italicized word.
__**a.** She saw a *familiar* face in the crowd.
__**b.** "Let's get *acquainted*," said the stranger.
__**c.** She was *acquainted* with French customs.

173b

While Hoover generally gave formal political speeches, Smith's talks were **colloquial.** His style of delivery was the same for large gatherings as for small groups.

A synonym for **colloquial** is:

__a. hackneyed
__b. unchanging
__c. conversational
__d. vehement

198b

The **bourgeois** element is often divided. Members of this group may sympathize with the businessmen because of their commercial interests, or with the proletariat, because they, too, would like to advance.

The meaning of **bourgeois** is:

__a. government
__b. commercial
__c. neutral group
__d. middle class

223a

c, d

suc cu lent (suk′ yə lənt)

The chimps assumed that the true owners of the spaceship had perished. Paula and Paul were herded into a truck and carted off to the zoo, where they were offered two **succulent** pineapples.

Write a definition or synonym:

248a

c, e

ob vi ate (ob′ vē āt)

Ibn Saud and many of the other sheiks are attempting to **obviate** social unrest.

Write a definition or synonym:

272c

a

av id (av′id), *adj.* extremely eager; greatly desirous: *an avid desire for power. The miser was avid for gold.* [< Latin *avidus* < *avere* desire eagerly] —**av′id ly,** *adv.*

1. Check the phrase(s) in which **avid** is used correctly.
   __a. avid satisfaction __d. avid solitude
   __b. avid collector __e. avid affinity
   __c. avid reader
2. Check the word most like **avid** in meaning.
   __a. fervent
   __b. covetous
   __c. agitated

297c

a

com prise (kəm priz′), *v.t.,* **-prised, -pris ing.** 1 consist of; include: *The United States comprises 50 states.* See **include** for synonym study. 2 make up; compose; constitute: *Fifty states comprise the United States. The committee is comprised of five members.* [< Old French *compris,* past participle of *comprendre* < Latin *comprehendere.* See COMPREHEND.]
➤ **Comprise** has recently developed a meaning that is the reverse of its original one, perhaps by being confused with *compose.* Although some people insist that it can mean only "include," more people now use it to mean "be included in."

Check the sentence(s) in which a form of **comprise** can be substituted for the italicized word.

__a. Her church *embraces* all races.
__b. He *embraced* his sister tenderly.
__c. A heterogeneous society *includes* all sorts of people.

20

4a

c, d

plain tive (plān′ tiv)

The train whistle made a **plaintive** sound as it pulled out of the station.

Write a definition or synonym:

29b

Sally had never dreamed she could solve a crime, but her interviews at Tektron made her think she had a **latent** ability which was now becoming apparent. She was sure the secret plans had been hidden in the pots that held the plants.

Latent means:
__a. new
__b. refreshing
__c. burning
__d. hidden

54b

Portugal did not use military force or other means to **coerce** the Italians into sharing their trade routes. Instead, the Portuguese sought their own.

A synonym for **coerce** is:
__a. weaken
__b. convert
__c. compel
__d. convince

79c

b

al le go ry (al′ə gôr′ē, al′ə gōr′ē), *n., pl.* **-ries.** a long and complicated story with an underlying meaning different from the surface meaning of the story itself, told to explain or teach something: *Bunyan's "The Pilgrim's Progress" is an allegory.* [< Latin *allegoria* < Greek < *allēgorein* speak figuratively < *allos* other + *agoreuein* speak publicly < *agora* public place or assembly]

An **allegory** is never:
__a. obscure   __d. complex
__b. nonfiction __e. symbolic
__c. elaborate __f. meaningless

104c

a

pseu do (sü′dō), *adj.* false; sham; pretended: *a pseudo religion.* [< Greek *pseudēs* false]

1. Which words mean the *opposite* of **pseudo**?
    __a. authentic   __d. connoisseur
    __b. real   __e. secular
    __c. actual   __f. true
2. Check the phrase(s) in which **pseudo** is used correctly.
    __a. to give a pseudo answer to a question
    __b. to be a pseudo-intellectual

130a

c

sto ic (stō′ ik)

Some of the other religious groups that followed the **stoic** Pilgrims to the New World were the Puritans, who settled in Massachusetts; the Catholics, who settled in Maryland; and the Quakers, who settled in Pennsylvania.

Write a definition or synonym:

21

173a

col lo qui al (kə lō′ kwē əl)

New York's Governor Alfred E. Smith, running against Herbert Hoover in 1928, spoke in a **colloquial** manner.

Write a definition or synonym:

198a

bour geois (bůr zhwä′, bůr′ zhwä)

Most of the **bourgeois** element were also in favor of the revolution.

Write a definition or synonym:

222c

sar don ic (sär don′ik), *adj.* bitterly sarcastic, scornful, or mocking: *a sardonic outlook.* [< Greek *sardonios,* alteration of *sardanios,* perhaps influenced by *sardonion,* a supposed Sardinian plant that produced hysterical convulsions] —**sar don′i cal ly,** *adv..*

Check the sentence(s) in which **sardonic** is used correctly.
___a. He was a fisherman and had a sardonic smell.
___b. Her gentle brown eyes looked sardonic.
___c. His sardonic smile mocked her.
___d. She had a sardonic manner which many found annoying.
___e. Her sardonic laugh was infectious.

247c

in dis cre tion (in′dis kresh′ən), *n.* 1 a being indiscreet; lack of good judgment; unwiseness; imprudence. 2 an indiscreet act.

An **indiscretion** can be most aptly described as:
___a. illegal
___b. in good taste
___c. thoughtless
___d. a breach of the peace
___e. a breach of good conduct

272b

Having begun their careers in great poverty, some magnates developed a desire for wealth which was so **avid** that it seemed impossible to satisfy.

Avid means:
___a. greedy
___b. inherent
___c. sincere
___d. excruciating

297b

Before her visit to Japan, Lucy thought of the country mainly in terms of mountains, like the famous Mount Fujiyama. She learned that Japan **comprises** four major islands, plus many smaller ones. Japan consists of valleys and broad coastal plains as well as mountain ranges.

Comprise means:
___a. include
___b. exclude
___c. simulate
___d. resemble

22

4b

The **plaintive** sound of the whistle was quite unlike the joyous sound of the excited farewells. It was certainly in direct contrast to Connie's feeling of exhilaration.

Plaintive means:
—**a.** mournful
—**b.** excruciating
—**c.** raucous
—**d.** shrill

---

d

29c

la tent (lāt′nt), *adj.* present but not active; hidden; concealed: *latent germs of disease, latent ability.* [< Latin *latentem* lying hidden] —**la′tent ly,** *adv.*
Syn. Latent, potential mean existing as a possibility or fact, but not now showing itself plainly. **Latent** means actually existing as a fact, but lying hidden, not active or plainly to be seen at the present time: *A grain of wheat has the latent power to grow into a plant.* **Potential** means existing as a possibility and capable of coming into actual existence or activity if nothing happens to stop development: *You have great potential ability in science.*

Check the words that mean about the same as **latent.**
—**a.** dormant   —**d.** rampant
—**b.** component   —**e.** sluggish
—**c.** unused

---

c

54c

co erce (kō ėrs′), *v.t.,* **-erced, -erc ing.** 1 compel; force: *The prisoner was coerced into confessing to the crime.* 2 control or restrain by force or authority. [< Latin *coercere* < *co-* together + *arcere* restrain] —**co erc′er,** *n.* —**co erc′i ble,** *adj.*

1. Which of the following could be used to **coerce** a person?
   —**a.** a moral lesson   —**c.** a show of force
   —**b.** an appeal to authority —**d.** all of these
2. Which of the following is *least* similar to **coerce**?
   —**a.** repress   —**b.** induce   —**c.** implore

---

b, f

80a

pi quant (pē′ kənt)

Many **piquant** stories, poems, and operas have been written about King Arthur's court life.

Write a definition or synonym:

---

a, b,
c, f
b

105a

stat ure (stach′ ər)

After a few months, Linda felt she was doing well in all her classes except one. At first, Linda blamed the **stature** of her instructor.

Write a definition or synonym:

130b

The Pilgrims endured their hardships quietly because of their great religious faith and because they did not believe in displays of emotion. This **stoic** attitude stood them in good stead during that first winter.

A synonym for **stoic** is:
—**a.** self-controlled
—**b.** devout
—**c.** courageous
—**d.** dedicated

a

172c

hack neyed (hak′nēd), *adj.* used too often; commonplace: *"White as snow" is a hack- neyed comparison.* See **commonplace** for synonym study.

1. Check the phrase(s) in which **hackneyed** is used correctly.
   __a. hackneyed bread   __c. hackneyed car
   __b. hackneyed remark
2. Something which is **hackneyed** can *never* be:
   __a. derivative __b. novel __c. unusual

c

197c

pro le tar i at (prō′lə ter′ē ət, prō′lə tar′ē- ət), *n.* 1 the lowest class in economic and social status, including all unskilled laborers, casual laborers, and tramps. 2 (in Europe) the working class, especially as contrasted formerly with slaves and serfs and now with the middle class.

ANALOGY **proletariat : patricians ::**
   __a. annual : centennial
   __b. basement : pinnacle
   __c. canine : scavenger
   __d. liquidate : reimburse
   __e. illiterate : intellectual

222b

Paula was stunned by the chief chimp's expression. The look was amused and at the same time contemptuous of the two visitors. Paula mistakenly assumed that chimps were not intelligent enough to be **sardonic.**

A synonym for **sardonic** is:
   __a. inane
   __b. derisive
   __c. unpleasant
   __d. satirical

247b

It is a grave **indiscretion** for a woman to wander about by herself as Mrs. Cassidy discovered. So many people commented on her lack of good judgment that she hurried back to her hotel to wait for her husband.

Another word for **indiscretion** is:
   __a. imprudence
   __b. impoliteness
   __c. inhibition
   __d. exhibition

, c, d

272a

av id (av′ id)

An **avid** desire for wealth and power often characterized these empire-builders.

Write a definition or synonym:

a, d

297a

com prise (kəm prīz′)

Geographically, Japan **comprises** many elements.

Write a definition or synonym:

24

4c

a

plain tive (plān′tiv), *adj.* expressive of sorrow; mournful; sad. [< Old French *plaintif* < *plaint* plaint] —**plain′tive ly**, *adv.* —**plain′tive ness**, *n.*

Which sounds are most likely to be **plaintive**?
___**a.** a child's laugh
___**b.** a sea gull's cry
___**c.** a tire's squeal
___**d.** a foghorn's signal

30a

a, c

con fi dant (kon′ fə dant′, kon′ fə dant)

None of the security officers had thought to search a plant, particularly the plant of a man who had become the **confidant** of the company director.

Write a definition or synonym:

55a

1. d
2. c

im pel (im pel′)

Impelled by the need to find an ocean route to India and Asia, the Portuguese, in 1498, organized an expedition with Vasco da Gama at its head.

Write a definition or synonym:

80b

The spirit and liveliness of the people who surrounded Arthur and the aura of mystery about King Arthur himself give these tales a fascinating quality that excites the imagination. People everywhere find them **piquant.**

Piquant means:
___**a.** stimulating
___**b.** popular
___**c.** credible
___**d.** legible

105b

Linda was several inches taller than her instructor. She thought the man's slight **stature** made him overly harsh and demanding.

Stature means:
___**a.** image
___**b.** height
___**c.** status
___**d.** attitude

130c

a

sto ic (stō′ik), *n.* **1** person who remains calm, represses his feelings, and is indifferent to pleasure and pain. **2 Stoic**, member of a school of philosophy founded by Zeno. This school taught that virtue is the highest good and that men should be free from passion unmoved by life's happenings. —*adj.* **1** stoical. **2 Stoic**, having to do with the philosophy of the Stoics, or with the followers of this philosophy. [< Latin *stoicus* < Greek *stōikos*, literally, pertaining to a *stoa* portico (especially the portico in Athens where Zeno taught)]

1. A **stoic** person would react to pain:
   ___**a.** readily   ___**b.** with composure
2. A **stoic** person would necessarily always be:
   ___**a.** passionate   ___**c.** exuberant
   ___**b.** virtuous   ___**d.** none of these

25

172b

It is a pleasure to hear a convention speaker who employs fresh and original turns of phrase. More often, unfortunately, one must listen to **hackneyed** political expressions.

Hackneyed means:
__a. worn out
__b. erroneous
__c. unimaginative
__d. habitual

197b

It was not surprising that the **proletariat** welcomed a change in government. Any change would have offered the possibility of an improvement in their social and economic status. Now there was a chance for their children to rise and join the middle class.

Proletariat means:
__a. electorate
__b. general public
__c. lowest class
__d. intelligentsia

222a

c

sar don ic (sär don′ ik)

After favoring the two humans with a **sardonic** smile, the chief chimp led a boarding party to the ship to meet the real owners. In the movie, they assumed Paul and Paula were pets with the ability to mimic the actions of their superiors.

Write a definition or synonym:

247a

c, d

in dis cre tion (in′ dis kresh′ ən)

There are many **indiscretions** possible for the foreigner.

Write a definition or synonym:

271c

b

mag nate (mag′nāt), *n.* an important, powerful, or prominent person: *a railroad magnate.* [< Late Latin *magnatem* < Latin *magnus* great]

A **magnate** is:
__a. "a VIP"
__b. "a cat's paw"
__c. "a bigwig"
__d. "a mogul"
__e. "a good Samaritan"

296c

c

os tra cize (os′trə sīz), *v.t.,* **-cized, -ciz ing.** 1 banish by ostracism. The ancient Greeks ostracized unpopular citizens considered dangerous to the state. 2 shut out from society, favor, privileges, etc. [< Greek *ostrakizein* < *ostrakon* tile, potsherd (because originally potsherds were used in balloting)]

An **ostracized** person is one who is:
__a. "given the silent treatment"
__b. "beating a retreat"
__c. "doing an about-face"
__d. "drummed out"
__e. "missing the mark"

5a

b, d

fa ce tious (fə sē′ shəs)

At first, Mr. Andrade thought the other passengers would be annoyed by the **facetious** remarks made by his students.

Write a definition or synonym:

30b

Once the director began to share his own interest in plants with the missing worker, he made the man his **confidant** and discussed his personal affairs as well. No one ever suspected a man whom the director had confided in. But Sally's hunch led to the solution of the crime.

A **confidant** is:
___**a.** a trusted friend
___**b.** a self-reliant person
___**c.** a courageous friend
___**d.** a trusting person

55b

There is no doubt that the discovery of the ocean route to India would have come about naturally in time. It was certainly hastened, however, by the keen trade competition. The intensity of the rivalry **impelled** the Portuguese to act quickly.

Impel means:
___**a.** drive
___**b.** inspire
___**c.** direct
___**d.** intimidate

80c

a

pi quant (pē′kənt), *adj.* 1 stimulating to the mind, interest, etc.: *a piquant bit of news, a piquant face.* 2 pleasantly sharp; stimulating to the taste: *a piquant sauce.* [< French, pricking, stinging] —**pi′quant ly,** *adv.*

1. Which reaction would result from **piquant** news?
___**a.** raised eyebrows
___**b.** a dark scowl
___**c.** a chuckle
2. Which of the following are **piquant**?
___**a.** ice cream
___**b.** a pickle
___**c.** a lamb chop
___**d.** a spice

105c

b

stat ure (stach′ər), *n.* 1 height: *a man of average stature.* 2 physical, mental, or moral growth; development. [< Latin *statura* < *stare* to stand]

Check the sentence(s) in which **stature** is used correctly.
___**a.** He was a man of dubious moral stature.
___**b.** Achievement tests are given annually to measure the children's academic stature.
___**c.** That mountain has the highest stature of any in this state.
___**d.** The airliner maintained a higher stature during the storm.

LESSON 14

1. b
2. d

Give Me Maine or Give Me Nova Scotia!

Nova Scotia is a province in southeastern Canada. Maine is a state in the northeastern part of the United States. Geographically, they are separated only by the Bay of Fundy—the site of the largest tides on earth. They are separated politically by a national boundary. But the greatest distance between the two areas is in the minds of the vacationers.

172a

a, b

hack neyed (hak′ nĕd)

Political speeches are often full of **hackneyed** expressions.

Write a definition or synonym:

197a

b, c

pro le tar i at (prō′ lə ter′ ē ət, prō′ lə tar′ ē ət)

If there was one reason for the success of the revolution, it was the **proletariat.**

Write a definition or synonym:

221c

c

lu di crous (lü′də krəs), *adj.* causing derisive laughter; amusingly absurd; ridiculous. [< Latin *ludicrus* < *ludus* sport] —**lu′di-crous ly**, *adv.* —**lu′di crous ness**, *n.*

ANALOGY ludicrous : solemn ::
__a. proficient : adept
__b. strata : level
__c. grotesque : beautiful
__d. eradicate : liquidate
__e. laborious : appalling

246c

a

ab sti nence (ab′stə nəns), *n.* 1 an abstaining; partly or entirely giving up certain pleasures, food, drink, etc. 2 Also, **total ab-stinence.** a refraining from drinking any alcoholic liquor.

A person who practices **abstinence**:
__a. "swears off"
__b. "gets out of town"
__c. "gets on the wagon"
__d. "takes the pledge"
__e. "carries the torch"

271b

A man who started life as a nobody could become an industrial **magnate** by means of his wits and ability. Andrew Carnegie, for example, started as a bobbin boy in a cotton factory and rose to become a great steel manufacturer and philanthropist.

A **magnate** is:
__a. a sovereign
__b. a person of importance
__c. an innovator
__d. an autocrat

296b

Lucy was accustomed to the American system of granting special privileges to war veterans. It seemed inexplicable to see a Japanese veteran, perhaps with only one leg, **ostracized** and reduced to begging on the streets.

Ostracize means:
__a. to subject to criticism
__b. to lower in rank
__c. to shut out from society
__d. to cite for bravery

28

5b

Connie and her friends were all happy to be under way and free of the pressures of school. It was natural for them to be **facetious** rather than thoughtful and serious.

Facetious means:
—**a.** exasperating
—**b.** jocular
—**c.** slangy
—**d.** inane

---

a

30c

con fi dent (kon′fə dənt), *adj.* 1 firmly believing; certain; sure. See **sure** for synonym study. 2 sure of oneself and one's abilities. 3 too bold; too sure. —*n.* a close, trusted friend; confidant. —**con′fi dent ly,** *adv.*

ANALOGY confidant : confident ::
—**a.** parent : teacher
—**b.** excuse : excessive
—**c.** personal : personnel
—**d.** friend : friendly
—**e.** stagnant : component

---

a

55c

im pel (im pel′), *v.t.,* **-pelled, -pel ling.** 1 drive or force; cause: *The cold impelled her to go indoors.* See **compel** for synonym study. 2 cause to move; drive forward; push along: *The wind and tide impelled the boat toward the shore.* [< Latin *impellere* < *in-* on + *pellere* to push] —**im pel′ler,** *n.*

Check the sentence(s) in which **impelled** can be correctly substituted for the italicized word.
—**a.** The man *drove* the car away.
—**b.** His financial need *drove* him to study diligently for a scholarship.
—**c.** The robber *forced* the man to turn over his cash.
—**d.** The rapids *drove* the little raft down the river.

---

a
b, d

LESSON

Rock Star Runs from His Roots

Now that Manny Spellbinder has become a famous rock star, many people assume that he has forgotten his humble beginnings back in New York's Greenwich Village. They're right. Manny hates to be reminded of his struggles during his early days as a singer. He never sets foot in the coffeehouses and nightclubs where he played before he hit the big time. This is why....

---

a, b

106a

up braid (up brād′)

It seemed that the instructor found a reason to **upbraid** Linda at least once in every class.

Write a definition or synonym:

131a

moot (müt)

It is a **moot** point whether Maine or Nova Scotia makes the better vacation spot.

Write a definition or synonym:

d

171c

con clave (kon′klāv, kong′klāv), *n.* 1 a private meeting. 2 (in the Roman Catholic Church) a private meeting of the cardinals for the election of a pope. [< Latin, room that can be locked < *com-* with + *clavis* key]

Check the sentence(s) in which **conclave** can be correctly substituted for the italicized word.
__a. The club's officers held a small *meeting*.
__b. The world awaits the result of the Cardinals' *meeting*.
__c. The lovers had a *tryst* at the well.

b

196c

pred e ces sor (pred′ə ses′ər), *n.* 1 person holding a position or office before another: *John Adams was Jefferson's predecessor as President.* 2 thing that came before another. 3 ARCHAIC. ancestor; forefather. [< Late Latin *praedecessor* < Latin *prae-* pre- + *decedere* retire < *de-* from + *cedere* go]

Check the sentence(s) in which a form of **predecessor** is used correctly.
__a. Her will left everything to her predecessors.
__b. The new officer found his predecessor had left everything in good order.
__c. Many of his predecessors fought in the Revolutionary and Civil Wars.
__d. He put his files in order so that his predecessor would have no difficulty.

221b

Sitting in a long, black limousine, just like human beings, the chimps looked so **ludicrous**, Paul began howling with laughter. The chimps began laughing too—it seemed that Paul looked equally ridiculous to them!

Another word for **ludicrous** is:
__a. whimsical
__b. grotesque
__c. laughable
__d. contented

246b

In Ibn Saud's country no alcoholic beverages are permitted. This rule of **abstinence** applies to everyone, Moslem and infidel alike.

A synonym for **abstinence** is:
__a. self-denial
__b. sanctification
__c. religion
__d. franchise

271a

mag nate (mag′ nāt)

During this period, there were a number of industrial **magnates.**

Write a definition or synonym:

296a

1. b
2. b

os tra cize (os′ trə sīz)

Another startling aspect of Japanese culture to Lucy's mind was the tendency to **ostracize** soldiers who had been wounded in the Second World War.

Write a definition or synonym:

5c   **fa ce tious** (fə sē′shəs), *adj.* 1 having the habit of joking; being slyly humorous. 2 said in fun; not to be taken seriously. [< Latin *facetia* jest < *facetus* witty] **—fa ce′tious-ly,** *adv.* **—fa ce′tious ness,** *n.*

Which of the following words mean the *opposite* of **facetious**?
___**a.** melancholy
___**b.** humorous
___**c.** solemn
___**d.** droll

LESSON 4   The American Revolution

The American Revolution began more than 185 years ago, when a small group of Minutemen and British soldiers confronted each other in Lexington, Massachusetts. It was here that the "shot heard 'round the world" was fired. The great struggle that followed had been long in the making.

56a

ca pit u late (kə pich′ ə lāt)

Although this new trade route did have disastrous effects on the Italian monopoly, the Italian merchants did not **capitulate.**

Write a definition or synonym:

81a

pit tance (pit′ ns)

When Manny was a young singer, he shared a tiny apartment in Greenwich Village and managed to live on a **pittance.**

Write a definition or synonym:

106b

For a long while, Linda could do nothing right. Her instructor found fault with her performance and began to **upbraid** her no matter how hard she tried.

Upbraid means:
___**a.** deride
___**b.** punish
___**c.** reprove
___**d.** antagonize

131b

There is certainly something to be said for both sides. Maine offers forests, lakes, and a scenic coast. Nova Scotia possesses comparable attractions. Since there can be no final answer, it is a **moot** point as to which place is more desirable.

Moot means:
___**a.** debatable
___**b.** unspoken
___**c.** popular
___**d.** bewildering

171b

Although the convention as a whole is open to all representatives and alternates, there are also many small **conclaves**. It is during the latter that many important decisions are made.

A **conclave** is:
___a. a committee
___b. a social gathering
___c. a subdivision
___d. a private meeting

196b

Their **predecessor** had been a despot but the new rulers were committed to democracy. They soon announced a general election and many sweeping governmental reforms.

A **predecessor** has:
___a. been preceded
___b. been succeeded
___c. succeeded
___d. superseded

221a

lu di crous (lü′ də krəs)

When Paul and Paula Stargazer landed their spaceship on a remote planet near the edge of the galaxy, they were met by a group of leading citizens. Paul had never seen anything so **ludicrous.** The citizens were all hairy, bow-legged chimps!

Write a definition or synonym:

246a

e

ab sti nence (ab′ stə nəns)

As a devout Moslem, Ibn Saud practices **abstinence.**

Write a definition or synonym:

---

1. c
2. b

LESSON

28

Labor Organizes to Meet Big Business

The uniquely American "rags to riches" success story had its origins in the half-century following the Civil War. Such famous fortunes as those of the Rockefellers, Goulds, and Vanderbilts date from this period, when men could build industrial empires for themselves. In those days, there were no antitrust laws, no income taxes, and labor was only beginning to organize.

---

b

295c **con scrip tion** (kən skrip′shən), *n.*
1 compulsory service of men in the armed forces; draft. 2 act or system of forcing contributions of money, labor, or other service to the government or as the government directs.

1. Which of the following has (have) been **conscripted**?
   ___a. militiaman ___b. draftee ___c. reservist
2. Which of the following words can correctly be applied to **conscription**?
   ___a. voluntary ___b. enforced ___c. optional

6a

a skance (ə skans′)

When the students claimed three tables in the dining car, their waiter looked **askance** at them.

a, c

Write a definition or synonym:

31a

su per sede (sü′ pər sēd′)

The British had decided to **supersede** their old colonial policy with a more effective system.

Write a definition or synonym:

56b

They were adamant in their refusal to **capitulate.** Instead, they devised new trading arrangements with the Middle East and Asia which enabled them to continue the battle.

A synonym for **capitulate** is:
__a. fight
__b. surrender
__c. suspend
__d. compromise

81b

Like many other young artists, singers, and writers, Manny was willing to do without regular meals, expensive clothes, and other material things. He managed to live on a **pittance** in order to pursue his music.

A **pittance** is:
__a. an adequate ration
__b. a contribution
__c. a small amount of money
__d. a tiny donation

106c

c

up braid (up brād′), v.t. find fault with; blame; reprove: *The captain unbraided the guards for falling asleep.* See **scold** for synonym study. [Old English *upbregdan* < *up* up + *bregdan* to weave, braid] —**up braid′-er,** n.

ANALOGY upbraid : praise :: urban :
__a. seethe
__b. harangue
__c. foible
__d. rural
__e. curtail

131c

a

moot (müt), adj. that can be argued; debatable; doubtful: *a moot point.* —v.i. 1 bring forward (a point, subject, case, etc.) for discussion. 2 ARCHAIC. argue, discuss, or debate (a point, subject, case, etc.). [Old English *mōtian* to argue, discuss < *(ge)mōt* meeting]

1. Which word means the *opposite* of **moot**?
  __a. dubious   __c. indisputable
  __b. gullible
2. If a lawyer **moots** a point, he:
  __a. forgets it   __c. states it
  __b. brings it up

171a

con clave (kon′ klāv, kong′ klāv)

During the convention, frequent **conclaves** of delegates are held.

Write a definition or synonym:

196a

pred e ces sor (pred′ ə ses′ ər)

The new rulers were very different from their **predecessor.**

Write a definition or synonym:

LESSON 23 | Planet of the Chimps

For every science fiction film that becomes a box office smash, there are dozens that never quite make it. Some of these losing efforts are so bad they are never released to the public. Here's a review of one of the all-time flops: *Planet of the Chimps.* The producers had one good idea, and one only. They wanted to show a culture in which human beings never develop beyond the point of zoo animals and the dominant species is a group of talking chimpanzees.

245c

op u lent (op′yə lənt), *adj.* 1 having wealth; rich. 2 showing wealth; costly and luxurious: *an opulent home.* 3 abundant; plentiful: *opulent hair.* [< Latin *opulentem* < *ops* power, resources] —**op′u lent ly,** *adv.*

ANALOGY opulent : sumptuous ::
___a. conservative : extravagant
___b. superfluous : temperance
___c. recuperate : rehabilitate
___d. cantankerous : gregarious
___e. naïve : credulous

270c

par a phrase (par′ə frāz), *v.,* **-phrased, -phras ing,** *n.* —*v.t.* state the meaning of (a passage) in other words. —*n.* expression of the meaning of a passage in other words.

1. Which of the following is a **paraphrase**?
___a. a copy
___b. a parody
___c. a restatement
2. A **paraphrase** changes the:
___a. meaning
___b. words
___c. spelling

295b

The Japanese have become a nation of pacifists. The armed forces have had to make do with voluntary enlistments, instead of being able to fill their ranks by means of **conscription.**

A synonym for **conscription** is:
___a. force
___b. draft
___c. guile
___d. coercion

6b

Because the waiter felt the students would annoy the other diners, he looked **askance** whenever he approached their tables. He didn't seem pleased until the students changed trains in Vancouver.

Askance means:
__**a.** skeptically
__**b.** dubiously
__**c.** anxiously
__**d.** disapprovingly

31b

More rigid trade regulations were drawn up to **supersede** the old ones. It was hoped the new regulations would be more effective.

A synonym for **supersede** is:
__**a.** substantiate
__**b.** surpass
__**c.** replace
__**d.** strengthen

---

b

56c

ca pit u late (kə pich′ə lāt), *v.i.,* **-lat ed, -lat ing.** surrender on certain terms or conditions: *The men in the fort capitulated on condition that they be allowed to go away unharmed.* [< Medieval Latin *capitulatum* arranged under headings or chapters < Latin *capitulum* small head < *caput* head] —**ca-pit′u la′tor,** *n.*

Check the sentence(s) in which a form of **capitulate** is used *incorrectly*.
__**a.** I will capitulate my share of the cake.
__**b.** He would die rather than capitulate.
__**c.** Either capitulate or be destroyed.
__**d.** Did you make him capitulate?
__**e.** The general demanded unconditional capitulation.

---

c

81c

pit tance (pit′ns), *n.* 1 a small allowance of money. 2 a small amount or share. [< Old French *pitance* portion of food allotted a monk, piety, pity, ultimately < Latin *pie-tatem* piety]

Which words suggest the *opposite* of a **pittance**?
__**a.** sufficiency   __**d.** excess
__**b.** lack   __**e.** abundance
__**c.** short rations   __**f.** profusion

---

d

107a

ba nal (bā′ nl, bə nal′, ban′ l)

The short instructor asked other students for criticism of Linda's work. He told them that most of their comments were **banal.**

Write a definition or synonym:

---

1. c
2. b

132a

mar i time (mar′ ə tīm)

Nova Scotia is a **maritime** region.

Write a definition or synonym:

b, c

LESSON 18 | Political Conventions

An institution peculiar to the political scene in the United States of America is the presidential nominating convention. Throughout the endless rounds of speechmaking under crowded and disorganized conditions, the convention delegates maintain their interest and spirit.

195c

lan guish (lang'gwish), v.i. 1 become weak or weary; lose energy; droop: *The flowers languished from lack of water.* 2 suffer under any unfavorable conditions: *He languished in prison for twenty years.* 3 grow dull, slack, or less intense: *His vigilance never languished.* 4 long or pine (for): *She languished for home.* 5 assume a soft, tender look for effect. [< Old French *languiss-*, a form of *languir* < Latin *languere*] —**lan'guish er,** n. —**lan'guish ment,** n.

d

1. Which of the following words mean the opposite of **languish?**
—**a.** yearn   —**d.** repent   —**g.** flourish
—**b.** wane   —**e.** intensify   —**h.** heighten
—**c.** thrive   —**f.** flag

2. Which of the following correctly illustrate(s) **languish?**
—**a.** paint flaking from an old picture
—**b.** a love affair coming to an end
—**c.** cornstalks wilting during a drought

220c

im mi nent (im'a nant), *adj.* likely to happen soon; about to occur: *Black clouds show rain is imminent.* See synonym study below.
[< Latin *imminentem* overhanging, threatening] —**im'mi nent ly,** *adv.*
Syn. Imminent, impending mean likely to happen soon. **Imminent** suggests being likely to happen any minute without further warning: *Lyndon Johnson was unaware that his succession to the Presidency was imminent.* **Impending** suggests hanging over one, often indefinitely, and keeping one in suspense: *For weeks I have had a feeling of impending disaster.*

a

ANALOGY **imminent : actual ::**
—**a.** skirmish : battle
—**b.** presentiment : occurrence
—**c.** ordinance : election
—**d.** animation : automation
—**e.** infectious : chronic

245b

Some sheiks enjoy such an **opulent** style of life that they own an entire fleet of luxury cars instead of two or three. When horseback riding is preferred, they choose one of the thoroughbred stallions in their stables. For real speed they use their private jets.

Another word for **opulent** is:
—**a.** idle
—**b.** affluent
—**c.** profuse
—**d.** mobile

270b

"I'd prefer to be quoted verbatim," Linda said. This made my job much easier. It takes time to **paraphrase** a person's statements without changing the meaning of what was actually said.

Paraphrase means:
—**a.** decipher
—**b.** explain
—**c.** reword
—**d.** recite

295a

con scrip tion (kan skrip' shan)
In postwar Japan, **conscription** has been politically unfeasible.

Write a definition or synonym:

b, c

d

6c **a skance** (ə skans′), *adv.* 1 with suspicion or disapproval: *The students looked askance at the suggestion for having classes on Saturday.* 2 to one side; sideways. [origin uncertain]

Check the sentence(s) in which **askance** is used correctly.
__a. She looked askance at her son's untidy room.
__b. He stared askance down the street.
__c. The host gave his guest of honor an askance look.

c

31c **su per sede** (sü′pər sēd′), *v.t.*, **-sed ed, -sed ing.** 1 take the place of; cause to be set aside; displace: *Electric lights have superseded gaslights in most homes.* See **replace** for synonym study. 2 succeed and supplant; replace: *A new governor superseded the old one.* [< Latin *supersedere* be superior to, refrain from < *super-* above + *sedere* sit] —**su′per sed′er,** *n.*

Check the sentence(s) in which a form of **supersede** is used correctly.
__a. Jimmy Carter superseded Gerald Ford as President.
__b. "The superseding announcement will be recorded."
__c. Jets have superseded propeller-type aircraft.

a, e

57a

con sen sus (kən sen′ səs)

The other European countries, especially England and France, began sending out explorers to discover new ocean routes to the Middle East and Asia. The **consensus** was that a new route could be discovered by sailing westward.

Write a definition or synonym:

a, d, e, f

82a

grat is (grat′ is, grā′ tis)

Manny was not only willing to do without money, he was willing to play **gratis** at the Village night spots just so he could share his music with the world.

Write a definition or synonym:

107b

Only one student seemed unafraid to offend the instructor. Linda found his remarks very different from the **banal** observations of the other students. His ideas were not ordinary and commonplace at all.

Banal means:
__a. trite
__b. inhibited
__c. obscure
__d. drab

132b

Nova Scotia's **maritime** locale appeals strongly to vacationers from inland areas. People who have grown up there sometimes take its beaches and fishing for granted.

Maritime means:
__a. on a peninsula
__b. related to shipping
__c. on an island
__d. near the sea

170c

b

ex tol or ex toll (ek stōl′, ek stol′), v.t.,
-tolled, -tol ling. praise highly; commend.
[< Latin *extollere* < *ex-* up + *tollere* to raise]
—ex tol′ler, n. —ex tol′ment, n.

In which of the following is something **extolled**?
—**a.** A student receives 98% on a test.
—**b.** A diner sends compliments to the chef.
—**c.** A critic writes a rave review.

195b

Under a government that allowed no opposition,
there were a great many political prisoners who had
languished in prisons under appalling conditions.
Once released, they were given medical attention
and decent food by the new government.

Another word for **languish** is:
—**a.** dwell
—**b.** labor
—**c.** exist
—**d.** suffer

220b

Ever since they won the prize on the quiz show, Pam
and Tony had thought of little else beyond the
imminent excitement of a honeymoon in Paris. Now
that it was actually beginning, it still seemed too
good to be true.

Imminent means:
—**a.** about to occur
—**b.** possible
—**c.** passing by
—**d.** certain

245a

b, d

op u lent (op′ yə lənt)

The life-style of some of the sheiks can best be
described as **opulent**.

Write a definition or synonym:

270a

b, c,
d, e

par a phrase (par′ ə frāz)

After I thanked Linda for the interview, she asked
me not to **paraphrase** her statements in my article.

Write a definition or synonym:

294c

c

sup plant (sə plant′), v.t. 1 take the place
of; displace or set aside: *Machinery has
supplanted hand labor in making shoes.* See
replace for synonym study. 2 take the place
of by unfair methods or by treacherous
means: *The prince plotted to supplant the
king.* [< Latin *supplantare* trip up < *sub-*
under + *planta* sole of the foot]
—sup′plan ta′tion, n. —sup plant′er, n.

Check the sentence(s) in which a form of **supplant** is
used correctly.
—**a.** The princess supplanted her throne to marry.
—**b.** No one has supplanted Gandhi in the hearts of
the Indians.
—**c.** The employee tried to supplant his boss.

7a

a

squal id (skwol′ id)

Mr. Andrade said the streets of Vancouver made his hometown look **squalid** by comparison.

Write a definition or synonym:

32a

c

sur rep ti tious (sėr′ əp tish′ əs)

The **surreptitious** trade that the Colonists had long practiced with the French West Indies had been discovered.

Write a definition or synonym:

57b

Because the **consensus** of learned men of the time was that the East Indies could be reached by sailing westward, there was no question about the route selected by Columbus in 1492.

A synonym for **consensus** is:
_a. hypothesis
_b. doubt
_c. agreement
_d. surmise

82b

Offering to play **gratis** was no answer. Many nightclub owners refused to let Manny play for nothing and hired well-known singers who demanded large fees. For several months Manny played on the street corners.

Gratis means:
_a. gratefully
_b. free of charge
_c. as a reward
_d. at regular intervals

107c

a

ba nal (bā′nl, bə nal′, ban′l), *adj.* not new or interesting; commonplace; trite. [< French] —**ba′nal ly,** *adv.*

ANALOGY **banal : unusual :: crucial :**
_a. sear
_b. incidental
_c. appalling
_d. grotesque
_e. sterile

132c

d

mar i time (mar′ə tim), *adj.* 1 of the sea; having to do with shipping and sailing; nautical: *maritime law.* 2 on or near the sea: *Boston is a maritime city.* 3 living near the sea: *Many maritime peoples are fishermen.* [< Latin *maritimus* < *mare* sea]

1. Which occupations are **maritime** in nature?
_a. whaling   _c. clamming
_b. lake fishing
2. Which of the following is *not* **maritime**?
_a. Chicago   _c. New York City
_b. San Francisco

294b

The Emperor's Chrysanthemum Throne remains, and Shintoism survives as a religious belief. However, it is no longer the state religion, and many young Japanese do not believe in it, although they have found nothing to supplant it.

A synonym for **supplant** is:
__a. nourish
__b. reinforce
__c. replace
__d. surpass

269c

id i o syn cra sy (id'ē ō sing'krə sē) *n.*, *pl.* -sies. 1 a personal peculiarity of taste, behavior, opinion, etc. 2 (in medicine) a constitutional peculiarity that causes an unusual reaction to a drug, treatment, etc. [< Greek *idiosynkrasia* < *idios* one's own + *synkrasis* temperament]

c

Which of the following are **idiosyncrasies**?
__a. intelligence
__b. wiggling one's ears
__c. eating raw carrots and lettuce for breakfast
__d. an allergy to strawberries
__e. refusing to wear shoes

244c

ac crue (ə krü'), *v.i.* -crued, -cru ing. 1 come as a natural product or result: *Ability to think clearly will accrue to you from good habits of study.* 2 grow or arise as the product of money invested: *accrued interest.* [< Old French *acrue* an increase < *accroistre* to increase < Latin *accrescere* < *ad-* to + *crescere* grow.] —**ac crue'ment**, *n.*

d

Check the sentence(s) in which **accrue** can be correctly substituted for the italicized word.
__a. He taught his dog to *come* to him when he whistled.
__b. Considerable interest will *come to* you from that investment.
__c. Birds *come* back every spring.
__d. Favor will *come to* you for your good deeds.

220a

im mi nent (im' ə nənt)

As their plane neared Orly Field outside Paris a few hours later, Pam and Tony realized their honeymoon in Paris was **imminent**.

b

Write a definition or synonym:

195a

lan guish (lang' gwish)

One of the first things the rebels did was to release the political prisoners who had been **languishing** in jail.

c, e
f, g

Write a definition or synonym:

170b

Although some patients are never satisfied, most patients **extol** the care they receive in hospitals. For the most part, Connie's patients could not speak highly enough of their doctor.

A synonym for **extol** is:
__a. appreciate
__b. commend
__c. esteem
__d. estimate

7b

Mr. Andrade had grown up in a town with neglected buildings and garbage-laden streets. His hometown was **squalid** compared with the clean, prosperous city of Vancouver.

Squalid means:
— **a.** wretched
— **b.** unique
— **c.** dejected
— **d.** despondent

32b

The British tried to prevent the Colonists from trading with the West Indies. The Colonists, however, managed to find **surreptitious** methods of trading which allowed them to continue without being detected.

A synonym for **surreptitious** is:
— **a.** devious
— **b.** profitable
— **c.** secret
— **d.** successful

57c

c

con sen sus (kən sen′səs), *n.* general agreement; opinion of all or most of the people consulted. [< Latin < *consentire*. See CONSENT.]

ANALOGY **consensus : discord ::**
— **a.** pilgrimage : journey
— **b.** celebrity : dignitary
— **c.** issue : revoke
— **d.** silhouette : pictorial
— **e.** crucial : necessary

82c

b

grat is (grat′is, grā′tis), *adv., adj.* for nothing; free of charge. [< Latin, ablative plural of *gratia* favor]

Check the sentence(s) in which **gratis** can be correctly substituted for the italicized word.
— **a.** He decided to let his pet bird go *free*.
— **b.** They were friends of the manager and so were admitted *free*.
— **c.** Americans are determined to keep their country *free*.

108a

b

def er ence (def′ ər əns)

Linda complained about her unfriendly instructor to Mr. Stanton, the director of the academy. He gave her an unusual acting assignment. For the rest of the term, Linda was told to show the greatest possible **deference** to the instructor who was giving her such a hard time!

Write a definition or synonym:

133a

a, c
a

ar a ble (ar′ ə bəl)

For the most part, the land in Nova Scotia is not **arable**.

Write a definition or synonym:

294a

sup plant (sə plant')

c, d

Lucy was surprised to learn that the Emperor was not **supplanted**.

Write a definition or synonym:

269b

Linda smiled as she told me about one of her **idiosyncrasies**. She believes that red is her lucky color and always wears something red on important occasions. She mentioned that she dislikes dresses and prefers slacks, but I didn't think that characteristic was limited to Linda.

An **idiosyncrasy** is:

__a. an aberration
__b. an addiction
__c. a personal peculiarity
__d. an omen

244b

The wealth that had **accrued** to the sheiks from the sale of oil is so great it is almost unimaginable. Some sheiks earn as much in a year as an entire nation does.

Accrue means:

__a. come unexpectedly
__b. be handed down
__c. be donated
__d. come as a result

219c

pro sa ic (prō zā'ik), adj. like prose: matter-of-fact; ordinary; not exciting. —pro-sa'i cal ly, adv.

c

Check the sentence(s) in which **prosaic** can be correctly substituted for the italicized word.

__a. The metal had a *dull* finish.
__b. The housewife became bored with the *dull* details of her daily routine.
__c. The boy was *dull* mentally and could not help being a poor student.
__d. He had a *dull* ache in his head.

194c

an ar chy (an'ər kē), n. 1 absence of a system of government and law. 2 disorder and confusion; lawlessness. 3 anarchism (def. 1). [< Greek *anarchia* < *an-* without + *archos* ruler]

b

During a period of **anarchy**, you might find:

__a. full jails
__b. law and order
__c. looting of shops
__d. martial law
__e. a moral breakdown
__f. plundering
__g. bands of marauders

170a

ex tol (ek stōl', ek stol')

b, c

However, Connie realized that most patients **extol** the quality of hospital care available to the public today.

Write a definition or synonym:

7c squal id (skwol′id), adj. 1 foul through neglect or want of cleanliness; dirty; filthy. 2 morally repulsive or wretched; degraded. [< Latin *squalidus* < *squalere* be filthy] —**squal′id ly**, adv. —**squal′id ness**, n.

a

ANALOGY squalid : elegant :: unlucky :
___a. gifted
___b. blessed
___c. confused
___d. fortunate
___e. dirty

32c sur rep ti tious (sėr′əp tish′əs), adj. 1 stealthy; secret: *a surreptitious glance.* 2 secret and unauthorized; clandestine: *surreptitious meetings.* [< Latin *surrepticius* < *surripere* seize secretly < *sub-* under + *rapere* to snatch] —**sur′rep ti′tious ly**, adv. —**sur′rep ti′tious ness**, n.

c

ANALOGY surreptitious : stealthy ::
___a. humdrum : ordinary
___b. demolition : demure
___c. auditory : visual
___d. breath : bland
___e. delve : raise

58a

c

ep och (ep′ ək, ē′ pok)

The discoveries of Columbus and later explorers began a new **epoch.**

Write a definition or synonym:

83a

b

prod i gy (prod′ ə jē)

At the time Manny lived in Greenwich Village, the streets were filled with musical and artistic **prodigies.**

Write a definition or synonym:

108b

Afterwards, Linda said that Mr. Stanton's assignment was the hardest role she had ever played. Nevertheless, Linda respectfully accepted every criticism her instructor offered and showed **deference** to his every wish.

Deference means:
___a. courteous yielding
___b. concurrence
___c. quiet agreement
___d. fidelity

133b

Much of the land is heavily forested. Where the land has been cleared, it is sandy and loaded with rocks. Thus, **arable** land for cultivation of crops is quite limited.

Arable means:
___a. fit for plowing
___b. arid
___c. available
___d. habitable

169c

a

pique (pēk), n., v., piqued, pi quing. —n. a feeling of anger at being slighted; wounded pride: *In a pique, she left the party.* —v.t. 1 cause a feeling of anger in; wound the pride of: *It piqued her that they should have a secret she did not share.* 2 arouse; stir up: *Our curiosity was piqued by the locked trunk.* 3 **pique oneself on,** feel proud about. [< French < *piquer* to prick, sting]

Check the sentence(s) in which a form of **pique** is used correctly.

__a. She was piqued by a needle.

__b. Piqued at being excluded from the group, she told untrue stories.

__c. Her interest was piqued by the story.

194b

Anarchy is always a danger when a government is overthrown. The chaos of **anarchy** can be avoided if the revolutionary leaders have had the time and foresight to set up in advance a new form of government which can be put into operation at once.

Anarchy means:

__a. bureaucracy

__b. absence of government

__c. military rule

__d. economic depression

219b

The young honeymooners weren't interested in such **prosaic** items as French currency and tips on dry-cleaning their clothing. Instead, they looked up the glamorous tourist attractions such as the Eiffel Tower and the Champs Élysées.

Prosaic means:

__a. necessary

__b. economical

__c. ordinary

__d. monetary

244a

c

ac crue (ə krü′)

Ibn Saud was a wealthy man, but enormous wealth has **accrued** to many other Arab rulers.

Write a definition or synonym:

269a

b

id i o syn cra sy (id′ ē ō sing′ krə sē)

To conclude the interview, I asked Linda if she had any **idiosyncrasies** she would like me to write about.

Write a definition or synonym:

293c

a

ig no min i ous (ig′nə min′ē əs), *adj.* 1 shameful; disgraceful; dishonorable: *an ignominious defeat in warfare.* 2 contemptible. 3 lowering one's dignity; humiliating. —ig′no min′i ous ly, *adv.* —ig′no min′i ous ness, *n.*

Check the word(s) which **ignominious** could correctly describe.

__a. a blessing   __d. a coward

__b. a tree   __e. a hero

__c. a rout

8a

d

pun gent (pun′ jənt)

The group went camping twice as they crossed the western provinces. Connie loved the **pungent** aroma of outdoor cooking.

Write a definition or synonym:

33a

a

sur veil lance (sər vā′ ləns, sər vā′ lyəns)

The British instituted strict **surveillance** of all trade.

Write a definition or synonym:

58b

The **epoch** which followed the great discoveries was characterized by a renewed interest in science and a flourishing of the arts.

A synonym for **epoch** is:
__**a.** learning
__**b.** era
__**c.** knowledge
__**d.** growth

83b

Even a musical or artistic **prodigy** could have a period of struggle before ultimately succeeding. The extraordinary abilities possessed by such individuals do not ensure overnight success.

A **prodigy** is:
__**a.** an individualist
__**b.** a wonder
__**c.** a spectacle
__**d.** a radical

108c

a

def er ence (def′ər əns), *n.* 1 a yielding to the judgment, opinion, wishes, etc., of another. 2 great respect. See **honor** for synonym study. 3 **in deference to,** out of respect for the wishes or authority of.

Check the sentence(s) in which **deference** is used correctly.
__**a.** He graduated with deference.
__**b.** His deference to his grandfather's wishes showed his respect for the older man.
__**c.** The two women had a deference of opinion.
__**d.** She showed a marked deference toward dark-haired men.

133c

a

ar a ble (ar′ə bəl), *adj.* (of land) suitable for producing crops which require plowing and tillage. —*n.* arable land. [< Latin *arabilis* able to be plowed < *arare* to plow]

1. On **arable** land, you would be likely to find:
   __**a.** a fish hatchery   __**c.** skiers
   __**b.** a cornfield   __**d.** a silo
2. Which of the following is (are) noted for being **arable**?
   __**a.** the Everglades   __**b.** the Corn Belt

169b

This type of patient demands constant observation and treatment. Without a doctor's continual attentions, the patient feels ignored and becomes **piqued**. The brunt of this ill-feeling is borne by all who deal with the patient.

Pique means:
___**a.** make angry
___**b.** intimidate
___**c.** humiliate
___**d.** ignore

194a

c, d, e
b

an ar chy (an′ ər kē)

When the revolution unexpectedly succeeded in overthrowing the government, the rebels had to act quickly to prevent **anarchy**.

Write a definition or synonym:

219a

b
b, c

pro sa ic (prō zā′ ik)

Pam and Tony didn't spend much time on the **prosaic** details in the guidebook.

Write a definition or synonym:

243c

c

om nip o tent (om nip′ə tənt), *adj.* 1 having all power; almighty. 2 having very great power or influence. —*n.* the Omnipotent, God. —**om nip′o tent ly,** *adv.*

ANALOGY omnipotent : impotent ::
___**a.** foreboding : undertone
___**b.** boisterous : exuberant
___**c.** omniscient : ignorant
___**d.** vertebrate : invertebrate
___**e.** humility : ignorance

268c

d

plau dit (plô′dit), *n.* Usually, **plaudits,** *pl.* round of applause; enthusiastic expression of approval or praise. [alteration of Latin *plaudite* applaud!]

ANALOGY plaudit : blame ::
___**a.** anarchy : revolution
___**b.** disgrace : renown
___**c.** bauble : carat
___**d.** jargon : vernacular
___**e.** torso : foot

293b

Not only were their largest cities almost completely destroyed, but the Emperor renounced his divinity. This double defeat brought to an **ignominious** end the myth of Japanese racial superiority.

Ignominious means:
___**a.** humiliating
___**b.** terminal
___**c.** belligerent
___**d.** incendiary

8b

The **pungent** flavors and aromas were largely the result of the garlic, onions, and peppers that Mr. Andrade added to each dish he prepared.

Pungent means:
__a. exotic
__b. sharp
__c. fragrant
__d. irritating

33b

The **surveillance** was carried on both by British customs agents in the Colonies and by the British Navy on the coastline. The customs agents could observe goods coming into port, and the navy could keep track of the number and types of ships going to and from the West Indies.

A synonym for **surveillance** is:
__a. reconnaissance
__b. regimen
__c. supervision
__d. interrogation

58c

b

ep och (ep′ək, ē′pok), *n.* 1 period of time; era; age. 2 period of time in which striking things happened. 3 the starting point of such a period: *The invention of the steam engine marked an epoch in the evolution of industry.* 4 one of the divisions of time into which a geological period is divided: *the Recent epoch of the Quaternary period.* 5 (in astronomy) an arbitrarily chosen date or instant of time used as a reference point. [< Greek *epochē* a stopping, fixed point in time < *epechein* to stop < *epi-* up + *echein* to hold]

Which of the following could *not* be called an **epoch**?
__a. breakfast time
__b. the Atomic Age
__c. the Russian Revolution of 1917
__d. the victory of Jimmy Carter in the presidential election of 1976
__e. the Ice Age
__f. middle age
__g. the Middle Ages

83c

b

prod i gy (prod′ə jē), *n., pl.* **-gies.** 1 person endowed with amazing brilliance, talent, etc., especially a remarkably talented child: *a musical prodigy.* 2 a marvelous example: *Samson performed prodigies of strength.* 3 a wonderful sign or omen: *An eclipse of the sun seemed a prodigy to early man.* [< Latin *prodigium* omen]

ANALOGY prodigy : remarkable :: infant :
__a. credible
__b. waif
__c. urchin
__d. ethical
__e. vulnerable

109a

b

scath ing (skā′ ᴛHing)

Whenever her instructor's remarks were unusually **scathing**, Linda would remember the special role she was playing.

Write a definition or synonym:

134a

b, d
b

tor tu ous (tôr′ chü əs)

Many people would say the side roads of the province are **tortuous**.

Write a definition or synonym:

47

b, d

293a

ig no min i ous (ig′ nə min′ ē əs)

The Japanese suffered an **ignominious** defeat in World War II, as Lucy was well aware.

Write a definition or synonym:

268b

Of course, I knew the **plaudits** Linda would receive in my paper would not mean as much as a rave review in one of the big-city papers. But I thought my praise might give Linda some satisfaction.

Plaudit means:
__a. audience
__b. comment
__c. publicity
__d. praise

243b

Because there were no local elected officials, Ibn Saud was virtually **omnipotent** in his domain. All in his sheikdom are governed by his decisions, right or wrong.

The meaning of **omnipotent** is:
__a. having much power
__b. never wrong
__c. having unlimited power
__d. respected and influential

---

a

218c

om ni bus (om′/nə bus), *n.* 1 bus (def. 1). 2 volume of works by a single author or of similar works by several authors. —*adj.* covering many things at once: *an omnibus law.* [< French (*voiture*) *omnibus* (vehicle) for all < Latin *omnibus*]

1. An **omnibus** bill would:
__a. be passed unanimously
__b. contain miscellaneous items
__c. have several authors
2. Which of the following can you do with an **omnibus**?
__a. eat it
__b. ride in it
__c. read it

---

a

193c

fi as co (fē as′kō), *n., pl.* -cos or -coes. a complete or ridiculous failure; humiliating breakdown. [< Italian, literally, flask]

1. Which of the following expressions can be correctly used to describe a **fiasco**?
__a. "with flying colors" __d. "bring to naught"
__b. "gain the day" __e. "drop the ball"
__c. "they blew it"
2. **Fiasco** correctly describes:
__a. a train wreck
__b. a play that closes after one performance
__c. a strike in a large corporation

---

d

169a

pique (pēk)

Connie enjoyed almost all of her patients except for those who became **piqued** for trivial reasons.

Write a definition or synonym:

b

8c

pun gent (pun′jənt), *adj.* **1** sharply affecting the organs of taste and smell: *a pungent pickle, the pungent smell of burning leaves.* **2** sharp; biting: *pungent criticism.* **3** stimulating to the mind; keen; lively: *a pungent wit.* **4** (in biology) piercing; sharp-pointed. [< Latin *pungentem* piercing, pricking < *punctum* point] —**pun′gent ly,** *adv.*

Which of the following words mean the *opposite* of **pungent**?

__a. tart   __d. sweet
__b. mild   __e. harsh
__c. acid

---

c

33c

sur veil lance (sər vā′ləns, sər vā′lyəns), *n.* **1** watch kept over a person: *keep a suspected criminal under close surveillance.* **2** supervision. [< French < *sur-* over + *veiller* to watch]

Check the sentence(s) in which **surveillance** can be correctly used in the blank.
__a. The mother lion's __ of her cubs was constant.
__b. The surveyors made a __ of the land, taking and recording measurements.
__c. The actor made a __ of the audience to see how many people were attending.

---

d, f

59a

het er o ge ne ous (het′ ər ə jē′ nē əs,
               het′ ər ə jē′ ny əs)

The great epoch of exploration had many **heterogeneous** characteristics.

Write a definition or synonym:

---

e

84a

pri va tion (prī vā′ shən)

Manny and many of his friends were devoted to their art. They did not mind **privation** while they worked to achieve their artistic goals.

Write a definition or synonym:

109b

Soon, it seemed as though the instructor's **scathing** criticism was not intended to discourage or humiliate her, but to force her to do her very best work. If he had given her only mild rebukes, Linda might not have tried as hard.

Scathing means:
__a. demolishing
__b. severe
__c. acrid
__d. intermittent

134b

The **tortuous** side roads make for interesting touring. A driver will round a bend and find a quaint old lane with picket fences and cottages. Another sharp turn reveals a meadow full of wild flowers. The next turn will bring an unexpected view of the sea.

Tortuous means:
__a. twisting
__b. in disrepair
__c. dilapidated
__d. deviating

168c

c

ex or bi tant (eg zôr′bə tənt), *adj.* exceeding what is customary, proper, or reasonable; unreasonably excessive: *One dollar is an exorbitant price for a pack of bubble gum.* See **excessive** for synonym study. [< Latin *exorbitantem* going out of the track < *ex-* out of + *orbita* track] —**ex or′bi tant ly,** *adv.*

ANALOGY exorbitant : moderate ::
___**a.** horoscope : humbug
___**b.** apex : delve
___**c.** exotic : expensive
___**d.** great : mediocre
___**e.** scrutinize : ordinance

193b

Government spies assured the leaders that there was no popular support for a revolution. When the people's leaders had been apprehended and executed, the revolutionary armies would throw down their arms and the revolution would become a **fiasco.**

A synonym for **fiasco** is:
___**a.** failure
___**b.** scandal
___**c.** skirmish
___**d.** holocaust

218b

Pam's book contained suggestions on currency exchange, clothing, places to see, meals to order, and even a list of French words and phrases. With such an **omnibus** of information on tourism in France, there was no need to carry an assortment of separate pamphlets and books.

An **omnibus** is a book of:
___**a.** related subjects
___**b.** geographical data
___**c.** general interest
___**d.** statistics

243a

c, d

om nip o tent (om nip′ ə tənt)

To his subjects, an Arab sheik is **omnipotent.** The Cassidys learned this fact within hours after they began instructing the workers on Ibn Saud's building project.

Write a definition or synonym:

268a

, c, d

plau dit (plô′ dit)

Linda said she had received many **plaudits** in the big-city newspapers, although she didn't mention the names of the cities or the newspapers.

Write a definition or synonym:

292c

d

in do lent (in′dl ənt), *adj.* disliking work; lazy; idle. See **idle** for synonym study. —**in′do lent ly,** *adv.*

Which of the following expressions could describe an **indolent** person?
___**a.** "doing an honest day's work"
___**b.** "asleep at the switch"
___**c.** "busy as a bee"
___**d.** "ne'er do well"

9a

b,d

car nage (kär′ nij)

When the group reached Quebec, Connie saw the memorial to Generals Wolfe and Montcalm. It was hard to believe that this quiet scene was the site of such **carnage** during the attack on Quebec.

Write a definition or synonym:

34a

a

in ef fec tu al (in′ ə fek′ chü əl)

The first measures to halt the Colonists' move toward independence were **ineffectual.**

Write a definition or synonym:

59b

The epoch was **heterogeneous** both in terms of the size and wealth of the various participating countries and in their goals. Among the various motives for exploration were nationalism, greed, scientific curiosity, and religious fervor.

A meaning for **heterogeneous** is:
___a. new and different
___b. made up of unlike elements
___c. covering a wide area
___d. having common characteristics

84b

Manny had little desire for the luxuries of life. He was even willing to do without many necessities. **Privation** was a small price to pay for artistic achievement, he felt.

Privation is:
___a. lack of the necessities
___b. bereavement
___c. dispossession
___d. utter seclusion

109c

b

scath ing (skā′ᴛHing), *adj.* bitterly severe: *scathing criticism.* —**scath′ing ly,** *adv.*

Which of the following can correctly be described as **scathing**?
___a. a critic's review of a bad play
___b. a bowl of soup
___c. a winter
___d. a judge's remarks to a habitual criminal
___e. a desert landscape
___f. a child pretending to scold a doll

134c

a

tor tu ous (tôr′chü əs), *adj.* 1 full of twists, turns, or bends; twisting; winding; crooked: *We found the river's course very tortuous.* 2 mentally or morally crooked; not straightforward: *tortuous reasoning.* [< Latin *tortuosus,* ultimately < *torquere* to twist] —**tor′tu ous ly,** *adv.* —**tor′tu ous ness,** *n.*

Check the sentence(s) in which **tortuous** is used correctly.
___a. These tortuous sentences are hard to read.
___b. The dentist straightened her tortuous teeth.
___c. The tortuous testimony of the witness made us doubt his honesty.

168b

Considering the cost of patients' meals and medical supplies, plus the salaries for the hundreds of workers on the hospital staff, Connie felt that the cost of hospital care was not **exorbitant** at all. The expense might be great, but it was within the bounds of reason.

Exorbitant means:
__a. excruciating
__b. negligible
__c. excessive
__d. unusual

193a

d

fi as co (fē as′ kō)

The autocratic government was sure the revolution would be a **fiasco**.

Write a definition or synonym:

218a

c

om ni bus (om′ nə bus)

Tony wondered if he should have planned an elaborate farewell too. However, Pam did not seem envious of the showy couple. After she boarded the plane, Pam began to study an **omnibus** of tourist information, which the people from the quiz show had provided.

Write a definition or synonym:

242c a **o bes i ty** (ō bē′sə tē, ō bes′ə tē), *n.* extreme fatness.

People suffering from **obesity** would be likely:
__a. to be good athletes
__b. to eat sensibly
__c. to keep trying new diets
__d. to need specially made clothes
__e. to be proud of their appearance

267c b **non en ti ty** (non en′tə tē), *n., pl.* **-ties.**
1 person or thing of little or no importance.
2 something that does not exist or that exists only in the imagination.

Which of the following describe(s) a **nonentity**?
__a. "a figment of one's imagination"
__b. "as big as life"
__c. "little fish in a big pond"
__d. "a drop in the ocean"
__e. "one in a million"

292b

Competition in the schools and colleges of Japan, as well as in Japanese industry, is extremely keen. People who wish to get ahead simply cannot afford to be **indolent**. There is little temptation to avoid work.

Indolent means:
__a. indifferent
__b. nonconformist
__c. ingenuous
__d. lazy

9b

Although the losses were heavy on both sides, Mr. Andrade pointed out that the loss of life then was nothing like the **carnage** of modern warfare.

Another word for **carnage** is:
__**a.** marauding
__**b.** slaughter
__**c.** plunder
__**d.** havoc

34b

When they realized that their attempts to restrict trade were **ineffectual,** the British began to pass sterner acts, which they hoped would succeed.

Ineffectual means:
__**a.** irrelevant
__**b.** useless
__**c.** tentative
__**d.** impractical

59c

b

het er o ge ne ous (het′ər ə jē′nē əs, het′ər ə jē′nyəs), *adj.* 1 different in kind or nature; unlike; varied: *a heterogeneous group of people.* 2 composed of unlike parts or elements; miscellaneous: *a heterogeneous collection.* [< Medieval Latin *heterogeneus,* ultimately < Greek *heteros* other + *genos* kind] —**het′er o ge′ne ous ly,** *adv.*

ANALOGY: heterogeneous : diverse ::
__**a.** glutton : greedy
__**b.** eccentric : odd
__**c.** secluded : open
__**d.** arrogant : righteous
__**e.** siesta : afternoon

84c

a

pri va tion (pri vā′shən), *n.* 1 lack of the comforts or of the necessities of life: *Many children were hungry and homeless because of privation during the war.* 2 a being deprived; loss; absence. [< Latin *privationem* < *privatum* deprived]

1. Check the sentence(s) in which **privation** is used correctly.
   __**a.** People in poor countries have never known a life other than one of privation.
   __**b.** It was only after he got home that he discovered the privation of his wallet.
2. If you were living in a state of **privation**, you would be living:
   __**a.** in a lonely place __**b.** on a pittance

110a

a,d

so lic i tous (sə lis′ ə təs)

When her first semester was over, Mr. Stanton called Linda in for a discussion of her work. Linda was pleased that he was so **solicitous.**

Write a definition or synonym:

135a

a, c

som no lent (som′ nə lənt)

Many of the popular tourist spots in the province become **somnolent** little villages during the winter months.

Write a definition or synonym:

53

168a

ex or bi tant (eg zôr′ bə tənt)

Connie often heard the complaint that hospital expenses have become **exorbitant.**

Write a definition or synonym:

192c

des pot (des′pət, des′pot), *n.*   1 monarch having unlimited power; absolute ruler. 2 any person who exercises tyrannical authority; oppressor. [< Greek *despotēs* master]

ANALOGY **despot : power ::**
 __**a.** disciple : pilgrimage
 __**b.** accomplice : crime
 __**c.** felony : probation
 __**d.** billionaire : wealth
 __**e.** patron : conveyance

217c

con jec ture (kən jek′chər), *n., v.,* **-tured, -tur ing.** —*n.* 1 formation of an opinion admittedly without sufficient evidence for proof; guessing. 2 a guess. —*v.t., v.i.* guess. See **guess** for synonym study. [< Latin *conjectura* < *conjicere* discuss, throw together < *com-* together + *jacere* throw] —**con jec′tur a ble,** *adj.* —**con jec′tur er,** *n.*

ANALOGY **conjecture : certainty ::**
 __**a.** imperative : necessary
 __**b.** superimpose : inducement
 __**c.** construction : demolition
 __**d.** amaze : stupefy
 __**e.** annihilate : incriminate

242b

To her surprise and dismay, Irene learned that **obesity** in women seems to be greatly favored. A lady's attractiveness increases with her poundage. Irene had a long way to go before she would win a beauty contest in Ibn Saud's sheikdom.

Obesity means:
 __**a.** extreme fatness
 __**b.** obedience
 __**c.** overeating
 __**d.** stature

267b

Although I was fairly well known in my own town, to her, of course, I was a **nonentity.** However, Linda treated me as if I were a famous reporter during our interview.

A **nonentity** is:
 __**a.** a stupid person
 __**b.** a nobody
 __**c.** a notorious person
 __**d.** a bore

292a

in do lent (in′ dl ənt)

During her two-month visit, Lucy maintains that she never once saw an **indolent** Japanese.

Write a definition or synonym:

9c

car nage (kär′nij), *n.* slaughter of a great number of people. [< Middle French < Italian *carnaggio*, ultimately < Latin *carnem* flesh]

b

Check the adjectives that do *not* apply to the word **carnage.**
_a. wanton   _d. innocent
_b. neat   _e. brutal
_c. savage

34c

in ef fec tu al (in′ə fek′chü əl),   *adj.* 1 without effect; useless. See **useless** for synonym study. 2 not able to produce the effect wanted; powerless. —in′ef fec′tu al ly, *adv.* —in′ef fec′tu al ness, *n.*

b

Check the sentence(s) in which **ineffectual** can be correctly substituted for the italicized word.
_a. She was very *vain* about her appearance.
_b. His efforts to stop the leak were *vain.*
_c. He called in *vain;* they could not hear him.

60a

b

in ces sant (in ses′ nt)

The **incessant** rivalries of the European countries led to many wars.

Write a definition or synonym:

85a

1. a
2. b

vol u ble (vol′ yə bəl)

The only times Manny allowed himself to stop practicing was when he spent an evening at one of the Village coffeehouses filled with other artistic, **voluble** people.

Write a definition or synonym:

110b

Mr. Stanton's **solicitous** attitude made Linda feel as though he cared about her and was really interested in her career. Linda got a C from the unfriendly instructor and an A-plus from Mr. Stanton for her special assignment.

Solicitous means:
_a. philanthropic
_b. abundant
_c. friendly
_d. concerned

135b

With the arrival of the tourists, the **somnolent** little towns awaken and become busy. They remain active until after Labor Day.

Somnolent means:
_a. impassive
_b. isolated
_c. picturesque
_d. sleepy

167c

pa thol o gy (pa thol/ə jē), *n., pl.* **-gies.**
1 study of the causes and nature of diseases, especially the structural and functional changes brought about by diseases. 2 unhealthy conditions and processes caused by a disease, especially changes in the tissues and organs of the body. [< Greek *pathos* disease + English *-logy*]

c

1. A **pathologist** would most likely work with:
   __a. a telescope __b. a microscope __c. fossils
2. Plant **pathology** is:
   __a. the crossbreeding of plants
   __b. the study of plant diseases
   __c. a love of plants

192b

In many ways, the **despot** ruled with benevolence. However, the people preferred to have a voice in their government. They decided to overthrow their absolute ruler and replace the autocracy with rule of the majority.

Another word for **despot** is:
__a. champion
__b. autocrat
__c. monarch
__d. leader

217b

Although it was only a **conjecture,** it turned out to be true. Suddenly a group of well-dressed people ran up and began throwing rice and paper streamers over the couple, laughing loudly and wishing them a long, happy life together.

A synonym for **conjecture** is:
__a. hypothesis
__b. premonition
__c. reference
__d. guess

242a

b, c,

o bes i ty (ō bē′ sə tē, ō bes′ ə tē)

Obesity is rare among the desert sheiks and Ibn Saud was no exception to the general rule.

Write a definition or synonym:

267a

b, d

non en ti ty (non en′ tə tē)

I had feared that Linda might be contemptuous of a **nonentity.**

Write a definition or synonym:

291c

in ex plic a ble (in/ik splik/ə bəl, in-ek/splə kə bəl), *adj.* that cannot be explained, understood, or accounted for; mysterious. **—in′ex plic′a ble ness,** *n.* **—in′ex plic′a bly,** *adv.*

c

ANALOGY **inexplicable : puzzling ::**
   __a. impeccable : diverting
   __b. pretentious : unwitting
   __c. propitious : pleasing
   __d. interminable : thwarting
   __e. communicable : scathing

10a

b, d

im pet u ous (im pech′ ü əs)

Connie and her friends crossed the U.S. border at Niagara Falls. The customs inspector was surprised at the students' **impetuous** behavior.

Write a definition or synonym:

35a

b

un wit ting (un wit′ ing)

In 1765 George Grenville, England's prime minister, approved the Stamp Act. Grenville thus became the **unwitting** cause of even greater unrest in the Colonies.

Write a definition or synonym:

60b

These **incessant** wars weakened France and eventually led to the defeat of the French in North America. England became the dominating power in North America.

A synonym for **incessant** is:
__**a.** intermittent
__**b.** impending
__**c.** infernal
__**d.** continual

85b

Manny's friends tended to be single-minded, vehement, and **voluble**. There was always so much animated conversation at the coffeehouse gatherings that it was often difficult for Manny to get a word into the stream of chatter.

Voluble means:
__**a.** vigorous
__**b.** voluntary
__**c.** overbearing
__**d.** talkative

110c

d

so lic i tous (sə lis′ə təs), *adj.* 1 showing care or concern; anxious; concerned: *Parents are solicitous for their children's progress in school.* 2 desirous; eager: *solicitous to please.* [< Latin *sollicitus* < *sollus* all + *ciere* arouse] —**so lic′i tous ly,** *adv.* —**so lic′i tous ness,** *n.*

Which words mean the *opposite* of **solicitous**?
__**a.** neglectful __**d.** unmindful
__**b.** inaccurate __**e.** careless
__**c.** disinterested __**f.** affectionate

135c

d

som no lent (som′nə lənt), *adj.* 1 sleepy; drowsy. 2 tending to produce sleep. [< Latin *somnolentus* < *somnus* sleep] —**som′no-lent ly,** *adv.*

ANALOGY **somnolent : siesta :: vivacious :**
__**a.** dance
__**b.** epoch
__**c.** edifice
__**d.** crypt
__**e.** apex

167b

In recent years great strides have been made in the field of **pathology.** The study of bacteria and viruses in **pathology** laboratories has resulted in many preventatives and cures.

Pathology is the study of:
__a. medicine
__b. germs
__c. diseases
__d. psychoses

192a

des pot (des′ pət, des′ pot)

The ruler of this Balkan country was what is called "a benevolent **despot.**"

Write a definition or synonym:

217a

con jec ture (kən jek′ chər)

After the couple began to kiss and hug each other, Pam **conjectured** that they, too, were honeymooners.

Write a definition or synonym:

241c

vol a tile (vol′ə təl), *adj.* 1 evaporating rapidly at ordinary temperatures; changing into vapor easily: *Gasoline is volatile.* 2 changing rapidly from one mood or interest to another; fickle; frivolous: *Flighty people often have volatile dispositions.* 3 readily vanishing or disappearing; transient. [< Latin *volatilis* flying < *volare* to fly]

Which of the following are apt to be **volatile**?
__a. perfume __d. milk
__b. a prima donna __e. a cow
__c. alcohol __f. the weather

266c

su per cil i ous (sü′pər sil′ē əs), *adj.* haughty, proud, and contemptuous; disdainful; showing scorn or indifference because of a feeling of superiority: *a supercilious stare.* See **proud** for synonym study. [< Latin *superciliosus* < *supercilium* eyebrow, pride < *super-* above + *-cilium* (< *celare* to cover, conceal)] —**su′per cil′i ous ly,** *adv.* —**su′per cil′i ous ness,** *n.*

Check the sentence(s) in which **supercilious** is used correctly.
__a. She had the typically supercilious manner of a wallflower.
__b. Since she has become famous she has had a supercilious attitude.
__c. He plays a supercilious game of tennis.
__d. He glanced at me in a supercilious manner, as if to say "who are you?"

291b

Lucy's father, like many a baffled American businessman, found the business practices of his Japanese counterparts quite **inexplicable.** At first, he couldn't understand the meaning or importance of these practices.

Inexplicable means:
__a. credible
__b. convenient
__c. mysterious
__d. Asian

10b

Suddenly, all the students seemed to realize that they needed souvenirs of their Canadian journey. There was a headlong rush to take pictures and to buy postcards. The inspector was nearly knocked down by the **impetuous** students.

Impetuous means:
___a. bizarre
___b. sarcastic
___c. impenetrable
___d. impulsive

35b

By this act, Grenville gave an **unwitting** push to the Colonists' move toward independence. The results were not at all what he had intended.

A synonym for **unwitting** is:
___a. unconcerned
___b. unpopular
___c. unintentional
___d. inane

60c

d

in ces sant (in ses′nt), *adj.* never stopping; continued or repeated without interruption; continual: *the incessant noise from the factory.* [< Late Latin *incessantem* < Latin *in-* not + *cessare* cease] —**in ces′sant ly,** *adv.*

Which of the following are most closely associated in meaning with **incessant**?
___a. perpetual   ___d. spasmodic
___b. frequent   ___e. seasonal
___c. perennial   ___f. interminable

85c

d

vol u ble (vol′yə bəl), *adj.* 1 tending to talk much; fond of talking; talkative. See **fluent** for synonym study. 2 having a smooth, rapid flow of speech. 3 (in botany) twining; twisting. [< Latin *volubilis,* originally, rolling < *volvere* to roll] —**vol′u bly,** *adv.*

A **voluble** person would *not* be:
___a. glib   ___d. chatty
___b. reticent   ___e. mute
___c. uncommunicative

a, c, d, e

LESSON

Freedom Is Where You Find It

Only Pete Massey was foolish enough to attempt an escape from the correctional farm near Cooper City. Most of the inmates were model prisoners. That's why they were allowed to pay their debt to society at the clean, comfortable dairy farm run by the state. But as soon as Pete realized there were no stone walls or barbed wire fences separating the convicts from the outside world, he just had to make a break for freedom. Two weeks after his arrival, Pete had worked out an escape plan which he thought was foolproof.

136a

a

pal lid (pal′ id)

There are few **pallid** faces in Nova Scotia.

Write a definition or synonym:

291a

in ex pli a ble (in' ik splik' a bal, in ek' spla ka bal)

Even though she was of Japanese origin, Lucy found many aspects of Japanese culture **inexplicable**.

Write a definition or synonym:

266b

Since I had never met movie stars before, I had supposed that they might be **supercilious** in their relations with unimportant people like me. There was nothing in the manner of this actress, however, to show that she considered me inferior.

Another word for **supercilious** is:

__a. brusque
__b. acrid
__c. disdainful
__d. diffident

241b

Jack knew that **volatile** people are difficult to work with because they are so unpredictable. They may be placid at one moment and wildly excited at the next.

Volatile means:

__a. devious
__b. vociferous
__c. temperamental
__d. taciturn

216c

os ten ta tious (os'ten ta/shas), adj.
1 done for display; intended to attract notice. 2 showing off; liking to attract notice. —os/ten ta'tious ly, adv. —os/ten-ta'tious ness, n.

1. Which of the following is *least* likely to be **ostentatious**?
__a. a stoic
__b. a hermit
__c. an exhibitionist
__d. a comedian

2. Which of the following could correctly be described as **ostentatious**?
__a. a ring
__b. a smile
__c. a gift
__d. a skyscraper
__e. a pile of lumber

b

191c

au toc ra cy (ô tok/ra sē), n., pl. -cies.
1 supreme power of government exerted by one person. 2 country or state characterized by such a centralization of power. 3 supreme control; paramount influence in any sphere or group of persons.

1. People living under an autocracy can be correctly described as:
__a. independent
__b. emancipated
__c. dominated
__d. powerless
__e. tyrannical
__f. overbearing

2. A prominent feature of an autocracy would be:
__a. an electorate
__b. edicts
__c. majority rule

d

167a

pa thol o gy (pa thol' a jē)

As Connie's experience widened, she became convinced that one of the most important departments in any hospital is the department of **pathology**.

Write a definition or synonym:

b,
g,

10c

im pet u ous (im pech′ü əs), *adj.* 1 acting or done with sudden or rash energy; hasty: *Children are more impetuous than adults.* 2 rushing with force and violence: *The dam broke and an impetuous torrent of water swept away the town.* —**im pet′u ous ly,** *adv.* —**im pet′u ous ness,** *n.*

Which of the following words mean the *opposite* of **impetuous**?
_a. calm
_b. rash
_c. sedate
_d. pell-mell
_e. careful

d

35c

un wit ting (un wit′ing), *adj.* not knowing; unaware; unconscious; unintentional. —**un-wit′ting ly,** *adv.*

1. A person who commits an **unwitting** act:
_a. isn't very intelligent
_b. dosen't realize it
_c. doesn't care
_d. would never apologize for it
2. Check the words which mean about the *opposite* of **unwitting.**
_a. hasty   _c. considered
_b. deliberate   _d. impulsive

c

LESSON

7

Joan of Arc

She was a victorious general who defeated the English forces at Orleans, France, while little more than a child. She was thought to be a witch and was burned at the stake about five and a half centuries ago. She was also canonized in 1920 and made a Saint of the Roman Catholic Church. She was Joan of Arc, the Maid of Orleans, the most famous and inspiring woman of her time.

c, f

86a

ab strac tion (ab strak′ shən)

Many evenings were spent arguing endlessly about important-sounding **abstractions.**

Write a definition or synonym:

c, e

111a

ef fron ter y (ə frun′ tər ē)

As far as the older inmates were concerned, Massey's escape plans were sheer **effrontery.**

Write a definition or synonym:

136b

It is rare that you see a **pallid** complexion in the province. The bright sunshine, brisk sea air, and bracing winds remedy this condition quickly.

Pallid means:
_a. plaintive
_b. squalid
_c. pale
_d. unhealthy

b, c

LESSON 30

Roots: The Nakamura Family

Ken Nakamura and his daughter Lucy lived in California where Ken's parents and grandparents had lived before them. When Ken was called to Japan for a business trip, Lucy begged to go with him. She said that many of her friends of African ancestry had become deeply concerned with their roots. Why should a young Japanese-American like herself neglect a chance to explore the Land of the Rising Sun and learn more about her own heritage?

e

266a

su·per·cil·i·ous (sū' pər sil' ē əs)

There was nothing **supercilious** in her attitude.

Write a definition or synonym:

241a

vol·a·tile (vol' ə təl)

Soon after their arrival, the Cassidys realized that Sheik Ibn Saud was a **volatile** man.

Write a definition or synonym:

216b

Both the man and the woman had an **ostentatious** manner, calling attention to themselves through their attire and their actions. It was impossible for Pam and Tony to ignore them.

Ostentatious means:
__a. haughty
__b. pretentious
__c. ornate
__d. unpleasant

191b

Unlike the government of a democracy, where the government rests on the consent of the governed, the Balkan state was an **autocracy** with unlimited powers over its citizens.

An **autocracy** is a government that is:
__a. democratic
__b. socialistic
__c. constitutional
__d. dictatorial

b

166C

poign·ant (poi'nyant), adj. 1 very painful; piercing; poignant suffering. 2 stimulating to the mind, feelings, or passions; keen; intense: a subject of poignant interest. 3 sharp, pungent, or piquant to the taste or smell: poignant sauces. [< Old French, present participle of poindre to prick < Latin pungere]
—poign'ant·ly, adv.

Poignant can be correctly used to describe:
__a. sarcasm
__b. mustard
__c. relaxation
__d. a glance
__e. an automobile
__f. a mood
__g. an experience

LESSON | Profiles of U.S. Presidents

All of the Presidents of the United States of America have shared certain personality traits. However, each President has demonstrated particular traits which we remember him for. For example, Theodore Roosevelt, our twenty-sixth President, loved the outdoors. He toured the western frontier and enjoyed big-game hunting.

36a

vo cif er ous (vō sif′ ər əs)

The reply of the Colonists to the Stamp Act was **vociferous.**

Write a definition or synonym:

61a

ad her ent (ad hir′ ənt)

During her lifetime, Joan of Arc had many **adherents.**

Write a definition or synonym:

86b

In Manny's circle, general ideas and feelings were much more interesting than specific facts or events. Everyone talked about philosophy, the "establishment," and other **abstractions** for hours on end.

An **abstraction** is:
__a. a work of art
__b. a nonconcrete idea
__c. an enigma
__d. an expression of an ideal

111b

The more experienced inmates knew that most escape attempts ended in capture. They tried to convince Massey that his **effrontery** would result in punishment for all of them. Massey laughed impudently at their warnings and continued to plan his daring escape.

Effrontery means:
__a. investigation
__b. disdain
__c. brusqueness
__d. boldness

136c

pal lid (pal′id), *adj.* lacking normal color; wan; pale: *a pallid complexion.* See **pale** for synonym study. [< Latin *pallidum.* Doublet of PALE¹.] —**pal′lid ly,** *adv.* —**pal′lid ness,** *n.*

ANALOGY pallid : convalescent ::
__a. ingenious : celebrity
__b. legitimate : adversary
__c. ravenous : famished
__d. scavenger : urchin
__e. generous : benefactor

290c   **ex pound** (ek spound´), *v.t.* 1 make clear; explain, interpret, etc. 2 set forth or state in detail. [< Old French *espondre* < Latin *exponere* < *ex-* forth + *ponere* put] —**ex-pound´er**, *n.*

Which phrases mean about the same as **expound**?

__a. spell out
__b. show clearly
__c. shed light upon
__d. talk through one's hat
__e. commit to memory

265c   **lu cra tive** (lü´krə tiv), *adj.* yielding gain or profit; profitable. [< Latin *lucrativus* < *lucrum* gain] —**lu´cra tive ly**, *adv.* —**lu´cra-tive ness**, *n.*

ANALOGY lucrative : profitable ::

__a. ingenious : ingenuous
__b. infantry : platoon
__c. infamous : renowned
__d. reveal : recede
__e. arduous : difficult

LESSON 25 | Adventures in Arabia

Jack and Irene Cassidy made an unusual husband-and-wife team. They were both skilled engineers, and they both loved to travel. Last month they received a telegram from the secretary of Sheik Ibn Saud, asking them to report to a remote sheikdom near Saudi Arabia. Ibn Saud was undertaking a massive building project which would create homes and factories where previously there had been only desert sands. It was the kind of work the Cassidys liked best.

216a   **os ten ta tious** (os´ ten tā´ shəs)

Hand in hand, Pam and Tony walked to the entrance gate and took their places in line behind an extremely **ostentatious** couple.

Write a definition or synonym:

191a   **au toc ra cy** (ô tok´ rə sē)

The government of this Balkan state was an **autocracy**.

Write a definition or synonym:

166b

Extremes of emotion may be witnessed daily in a hospital, from irrepressible joy at the birth of a child to **poignant** grief at the loss of a loved one.

Poignant means:

__a. veritable
__b. painful
__c. manifest
__d. incredulous

11a

as tute (ə stüt′, ə styüt′)

President Woodrow Wilson, our twenty-eighth President, was a most **astute** individual.

Write a definition or synonym:

36b

The spokesman for the angry Colonists was Patrick Henry of Virginia. His speeches brought **vociferous** cheers from his excited and sympathetic listeners.

The meaning of **vociferous** is
__a. critical
__b. loud and noisy
__c. nationalistic
__d. vicious

61b

Thousands of Frenchmen became her staunch **adherents**. The purity and courage of the simple peasant girl earned for her the loyalty and devotion of most of her countrymen.

Another word for **adherent** is:
__a. protector
__b. lover
__c. follower
__d. student

86c

b

ab strac tion (ab strak′shən), *n.* 1 an abstract idea, concept, or term: *Whiteness, bravery, and length are abstractions. A line that has no width is only an abstraction.* 2 formation of an abstract idea or concept. 3 a taking away; removal: *the abstraction of iron from ore.* 4 a being lost in thought; absentmindedness. 5 work of abstract art.

Check the sentence(s) in which a form of **abstraction** is used correctly.
__a. They admired the abstractions in the window of the art shop.
__b. She enjoyed gardening because she liked solid abstractions.
__c. Honesty is an abstraction.
__d. The abstraction of water from cactus is sometimes attempted.

111c

d

ef fron ter y (ə frun′tər ē), *n., pl.* **-ter ies.** shameless boldness; impudence; insolence: *My neighbor had the effrontery to say that I talk too much.* [< French *effronterie* < Old French *esfront* shameless < Latin *effrontem* < *ex-* out + *frontem* brow]

ANALOGY **effrontery : shyness ::**
__a. insomnia : audible
__b. affliction : troubles
__c. heritage : centennial
__d. humility : arrogance
__e. exasperate : annoy

137a

e

in gra ti ate (in grā′ shē āt)

Occasionally, summer tourists try to **ingratiate** themselves with the year-round inhabitants.

Write a definition or synonym:

166a

poign ant (poi′ nyənt)

During her year in residence at Mt. Pleasant Hospital, Connie often witnessed scenes of **poignant** emotion.

Write a definition or synonym:

LESSON 20 | A Successful Revolution

I stayed up until two o'clock this morning to finish reading a fictional account of a revolution in one of the small Balkan states shortly after the Second World War. The story concerned several dozen characters who had been caught up in the fight for a new and better government, but the real interest in the story was not the characters but the progress of the revolution itself.

215c

prox im i ty (prok sim′ə tē), *n.* nearness; closeness.

Proximity is described by which of the following?
__**a.** "from cover to cover"
__**b.** "a country mile"
__**c.** "a stone's throw"
__**d.** "a hair's breadth"
__**e.** "up a tree"

240c

im bue (im byü′), *v.t.,* **-bued, -bu ing. 1** fill the mind of; inspire: *The parents imbued their children with the ambition to succeed.* **2** fill with moisture or color; saturate or dye. [< Latin *imbuere*]

Check the sentence(s) in which **imbued** can be correctly substituted for the italicized word.
__**a.** She *filled* his cup with coffee.
__**b.** He returned from church *filled* with missionary zeal.
__**c.** The landscape was *filled* with beautiful shadows.
__**d.** The bathtub was *filled.*

265b

Acting in motion pictures can be **lucrative** for a top star. Linda let me understand that her career was so profitable that she could buy just about anything she wanted.

A synonym for **lucrative** is:
__**a.** remunerative
__**b.** stimulating
__**c.** aesthetic
__**d.** pleasant

290b

After careful study of racial characteristics and other data, some archeologists and anthropologists have **expounded** the theory that the Mayans, Toltecs, and Aztecs were of Mongolian origin. The scientists are able to describe in some detail the possible routes of migration from northern Asia to Alaska and then to Central America.

Expound means:
__**a.** weigh
__**b.** exhibit
__**c.** conjecture
__**d.** set forth

11b

He was **astute** enough to see that the world needed a League of Nations to prevent future wars and that our country must be a member of that League. He didn't believe, as many of his compatriots did, that America could remain isolated from the rest of the world.

A synonym for **astute** is:
__a. diplomatic
__b. scholarly
__c. shrewd
__d. prejudiced

---

b

36c

vo cif er ous (vō sif′ər əs), *adj.* loud and noisy; shouting; clamoring: *a vociferous person, vociferous cheers.* —**vo cif′er ous ly,** *adv.* —**vo cif′er ous ness,** *n.*

1. A person engaged in **vociferous** action would be:
   __a. calm   __c. unreasonable
   __b. aroused __d. subdued
2. You are likely to hear a **vociferous** crowd at:
   __a. a library __c. a football game
   __b. a movie   __d. a church service

---

c

61c

ad her ent (ad hir′ənt). *n.* a faithful supporter or follower: *an adherent of the conservative party. Our church has many adherents.* See **follower** for synonym study. —*adj.* sticking fast; attached. —**adher′ent ly,** *adv.*

Adherent can be used to describe which of the following?
__a. water   __e. disciple
__b. elder of the Church __f. party worker
__c. registered voter __g. resident
__d. glue

---

c, d

87a

staid (stād)

One evening, a rather **staid** man walked in. He sat down at Manny's table and began asking questions.

Write a definition or synonym:

---

d

112a

ab duct (ab dukt′)

However, Massey was not easily discouraged. After Massey's cellmate refused to go along, Massey threatened to **abduct** him.

Write a definition or synonym:

137b

In their efforts to **ingratiate** themselves, these tourists may put on an act of being "just plain folks" or they may leave tips which are far too lavish. Getting on the good side of the residents in this way rarely is effective.

Ingratiate means:
__a. show gratitude
__b. bring oneself into favor
__c. show superiority
__d. be friendly

165c

de cry (di krī′), *v.t.,* **-cried, -cry ing.**
1 express strong disapproval of; condemn; denounce: *The pacifist decried all forms of violence.* 2 make little of; try to lower the value of by slighting statements; disparage: *The lumber dealer decried the use of concrete for houses.* [< French *decrier* < *de-* + *crier* to cry] **—de cri′er,** *n.*

a

Check the sentence(s) in which **decried** can be used correctly in place of the italicized word(s).
__a. The prisoner was *condemned* to death.
__b. The editorial *condemned* the corruption in the city government.
__c. He *made little* of his injury.

190c

to pog ra phy (tə pog′rə fē), *n., pl.* **-phies.**
1 the accurate and detailed description or drawing of places or their surface features. 2 the surface features of a place or region, including hills, valleys, streams, lakes, bridges, tunnels, roads, etc. [< Greek *topos* place + *graphein* write]

b

Check the sentence(s) in which **topography** is used correctly.
__a. The topography of the state of Colorado shows great variety.
__b. He took great care of his topography, cultivating and weeding it regularly.
__c. They hired an expert at topography to work on the new atlas.
__d. She had a beautiful topography.

215b

Tony explained that their flight would be announced very shortly. He said the lack of **proximity** of the shopping area to the boarding zone might not allow them to shop and board their flight on time. Pam was tempted to argue, but she didn't want to spoil the honeymoon, either.

Proximity means:
__a. nearness
__b. attention
__c. admission
__d. hastening

240b

As usual, she didn't believe her parents when they praised her for her good work. The sight of her father cheering for the stars of the show **imbued** her with the desire to be even better than the rest. It was only when Roseann promised herself that she would triumph over everyone else that she began to feel happy.

Another word for **imbue** is:
__a. inspire
__b. fortify
__c. motivate
__d. impel

265a

b, c

lu cra tive (lü′ krə tiv)

Linda admitted that her work was often very **lucrative.**

Write a definition or synonym:

290a

b, c

ex pound (ek spound′)

Several theories have been **expounded** concerning the origins of these jungle empires.

Write a definition or synonym:

11c

as tute (ə stüt′, ə styüt′), *adj.* shrewd, especially with regard to one's own interests; crafty; sagacious. See **shrewd** for synonym study. [< Latin *astutus* < *astus* sagacity] —**as tute′ly**, *adv.* —**as tute′ness**, *n.*

Which of the following would help one become more **astute**?
__a. to pay less attention to what others do
__b. to concentrate on what you are doing
__c. to be observant
__d. to believe everything you are told

c

37a

1. b
2. c

vul ner a ble (vul′ nər ə bəl)

The Stamp Act placed a tax on such items as newspapers, legal documents, almanacs, and other articles. The Colonists then began to boycott the very **vulnerable** British commerce by adopting nonimportation agreements.

Write a definition or synonym:

62a

o, d,
e, f

in gen u ous (in jen′ yü əs)

Was Joan really as **ingenuous** as she seemed?

Write a definition or synonym:

87b

The scene at the coffeehouse could hardly be called dignified or conventional. The **staid** man in his business suit didn't fit in at all.

Staid means:
__a. sedate
__b. neurotic
__c. pompous
__d. inhibited

112b

The escape plan would go more smoothly if more than one inmate broke out. Massey was so determined to take someone with him, he told his cellmate he would **abduct** him unless the man came along willingly.

To **abduct** means:
__a. to taunt
__b. to threaten
__c. to kidnap
__d. to abandon

137c

b

in gra ti ate (in grā′shē āt), *v.t.,* -at ed, -at ing. bring (oneself) into favor; make (oneself) acceptable: *He tried to ingratiate himself with the teacher by giving her presents.* [ultimately < Latin *in gratiam* into favor] —**in gra′ti at′ing ly**, *adv.* —**in gra′ti a′tion**, *n.*

Trying to **ingratiate** oneself means about the same as:
__a. "riding roughshod" over someone
__b. "waiting on (someone) hand and foot"
__c. "putting on airs"
__d. "polishing the apple"
__e. "rolling out the red carpet"

165b

When they receive their medical degrees, all doctors take the Hippocratic Oath to uphold the code of medical ethics. Good doctors **decry** any lapse from this oath by a colleague. This censure from colleagues is even more damning than public condemnation would be.

Decry means:
__a. condemn
__b. forbid
__c. deride
__d. indict

190b

The **topography** of any city contributes to its beauty or lack of it. A city like Rome, with its seven hills and the Tiber River running through it, cannot help but be more beautiful than a city on a flat plain.

Topography means:
__a. climatic conditions
__b. natural surface features
__c. geographical location
__d. historical significance

215a

1. a
2. b

prox im i ty (prok sim′ ə tē)

Fortunately, the weight of the bags was just under the limit allowed. Pam wondered if they would have time to send postcards announcing the start of their honeymoon. Tony wondered about the **proximity** of the airport shopping area to the boarding zone.

Write a definition or synonym:

240a

a, d

im bue (im byü′)

When Roseann met her parents in the lobby after the final act, she was **imbued** with envy and hard feelings toward her fellow performers.

Write a definition or synonym:

264c

d

im pec ca ble (im pek′ə bəl), *adj.* 1 free from fault; irreproachable: *impeccable manners, an impeccable appearance.* 2 not capable of or liable to sin. [< Latin *impeccabilis* < *in-* not + *peccare* to sin] —**im pec′ca bly,** *adv.*

Check the sentence(s) in which **impeccable** is used correctly.
__a. She scrubbed the kitchen floor until it was impeccable.
__b. He would have been poor material for a blackmailer, because his record was impeccable.
__c. The critics raved about his impeccable performance.
__d. The mountain scenery was impeccable.

289c

b

a grar i an (ə grer′ē ən), *adj.* 1 having to do with farming land, its use, or its ownership: *agrarian laws.* 2 for the support and advancement of farmers and farming: *an agrarian movement.* 3 agricultural. —*n.* person who favors a new or more equitable division of rural land. [< Latin *agrarius* < *ager* field]

Which of these can be described as **agrarian**?
__a. A rich landowner passes out Christmas presents to his tenants.
__b. A legislature enacts a law breaking up large estates into small farms.
__c. Farmers attend a Grange meeting.

12a

c

can tan ker ous (kan tang′ kər əs)

Andrew Jackson, the hero of the Battle of New Orleans, and our seventh President, was said to have been very **cantankerous.**

Write a definition or synonym:

37b

The nonimportation agreements of the Colonists were intended to reduce the amount of commerce between England and the Colonies. Just how **vulnerable** this trade was could not be concealed: it decreased drastically.

A synonym for **vulnerable** is:
___a. overbearing
___b. susceptible
___c. important
___d. vacillating

62b

Her supporters contend that she was indeed the **ingenuous** country maiden she claimed to be. Others, however, believe that she was an extremely cunning opportunist.

A synonym for **ingenuous** is:
___a. provincial
___b. visionary
___c. rustic
___d. naïve

87c

a

staid (stād), *adj.* 1 having a settled, quiet character; sober; sedate. 2 settled; unchanging; fixed. —*v.* ARCHAIC. a pt. and a pp. of **stay**¹. [originally past participle of *stay*¹ in sense of "restrain"] —**staid′ly**, *adv.* —**staid′ness**, *n.*

Who would be most likely to be **staid**?
___a. a master of ceremonies
___b. a bishop
___c. a teen-ager
___d. a cheerleader
___e. the president of a large bank

112c

c

ab duct (ab dukt′), *v.t.* 1 carry off (a person) by force or by trickery; kidnap. 2 pull (a part of the body) away from its normal position, as to raise an arm upward and outward. [< Latin *abductum* led away < *ab-* away + *ducere* to lead] —**ab duc′tion**, *n.*

Check the sentence(s) in which a form of **abduct** is used correctly.
___a. The expressway abducts traffic from the city.
___b. To treat an injured shoulder, the arm is abducted from the side.
___c. A small child was abducted last night.
___d. The flood abducted the stream from its former course.

138a

d, e

in sa tia ble (in sā′ shə bəl)

The mammoth tides along the beaches which face the Bay of Fundy are one attraction for which tourists in Novia Scotia have an **insatiable** appetite.

Write a definition or synonym:

71

165a

b

de cry (di krī′)

Dedicated doctors **decry** unethical medical practices.

Write a definition or synonym:

190a

c
a, b

to pog ra phy (tə pog′ rə fē)

Rome's **topography** adds immeasurably to its beauty.

Write a definition or synonym:

214c

b

me tic u lous (mə tik′yə ləs), *adj.* extremely or excessively careful about small details. [< Latin *meticulosus* fearful, timid < *metus* fear] —**me tic′u lous ly**, *adv.*

1. A **meticulous** person would:
 __**a.** "split hairs"
 __**b.** "ride rough-shod"
 __**c.** "be namby-pamby"
2. Of the three, a **meticulous** person would be best suited as:
 __**a.** a farmer
 __**b.** an auditor
 __**c.** a football player

239c

d

tran scend (tran send′), *v.t.* 1 go beyond the limits or powers of; exceed; be above: *The grandeur of Niagara Falls transcends description.* 2 be higher or greater than; surpass; excel. 3 (of God) be above and independent of (the physical universe). —*v.i.* be superior or extraordinary. [< Latin *transcendere* < *trans-* beyond + *scandere* to climb]

Which of the following words mean about the same as **transcend**?
 __**a.** surmount __**d.** outstrip
 __**b.** ascend __**e.** overshoot
 __**c.** diminish

264b

Impeccable was the word for Linda that morning. Even though she was not wearing her usual makeup, her hair was done so carefully that not one strand was out of place. Her clothing was in the very latest style. Even her fingernails were absolutely perfect.

Another word for **impeccable** is:
 __**a.** inimitable
 __**b.** exotic
 __**c.** conscientious
 __**d.** faultless

289b

The Toltecs lived off the land and developed agriculture to a high level. The Mayans, on the other hand, despite their impressive technical and artistic achievements, were unable to develop a satisfactory **agrarian** system.

Agrarian means:
 __**a.** peaceful
 __**b.** agricultural
 __**c.** legislative
 __**d.** financial

12b

Many of Jackson's frontier friends felt he wasn't **cantankerous** at all but very good-natured and even friendly in many ways. He was misjudged by many only because of his brusque, direct manner.

A synonym for **cantankerous** is:
- __a. impassive
- __b. ill-natured
- __c. vehement
- __d. impetuous

---

b

37c

vul ner a ble (vul′nər ə bəl), *adj.* 1 that can be wounded or injured; open to attack: *Achilles was vulnerable only in his heel.* 2 sensitive to criticism, temptations, influences, etc.: *Most people are vulnerable to ridicule.* 3 (in contract bridge) in the position where penalties and premiums are increased. [< Late Latin *vulnerabilis* < Latin *vulnerare* to wound < *vulnus* wound] —**vul′ner ably,** *adv.*

Check the sentence(s) in which **vulnerable** is used correctly.
- __a. She is a sweet girl, always vulnerable to the wishes of others.
- __b. Our opponents in the bridge game would incur bigger penalties now that they were vulnerable.
- __c. Texas' location makes it vulnerable to hurricanes.

---

d

62c

in gen u ous (in jen′yü əs), *adj.* 1 free from restraint or reserve; frank and open; sincere. 2 simple and natural; innocent; naïve. [< Latin *ingenuus,* originally, native < *in-* in + *gignere* beget] —**in gen′u ous ly,** *adv.* —**in gen′u ous ness,** *n.* ➜ See ingenious

1. Which of the following could be **ingenuous**?
   - __a. a manner __c. a smile
   - __b. an invention __d. a blackmailer
2. Check the sentence(s) in which **ingenuous** can be correctly substituted for the italicized word.
   - __a. *Candid* camera shots are usually more entertaining than posed pictures.
   - __b. The reporters were disarmed by the starlet's *candid* manner.

---

b, e

88a

flip pant (flip′ ənt)

Manny had just played his guitar for six hours at a Village party. He was feeling good and his answers to the man's questions were often **flippant.**

Write a definition or synonym:

---

b, c

113a

fet id (fet′ id, fē′ tid)

In spite of Massey's threats, none of the men would accompany him in the garbage truck which left the farm twice weekly. The **fetid** odor of the truck was too much for the men to take.

Write a definition or synonym:

138b

Once they have seen the huge tides—the largest in the world—they feel they have to see them again and again. Their appetite for the fifty-foot tides is **insatiable.**

Insatiable means:
- __a. that cannot be satisfied
- __b. extremely rude
- __c. out of the ordinary
- __d. that cannot be repressed

289a

a grar i an (a grer' ē an)

The ancient Toltecs were a peaceful and industrious people whose economy was **agrarian.**

Write a definition or synonym:

c, d

264a

im pec ca ble (im pek' a bal)

As our interview progressed, I could not help being impressed by Linda's **impeccable** grooming.

Write a definition or synonym:

b, c, d, f

239b

Unfortunately for Roseann, the singer was in good voice that night. Several of his songs were excellent, and one **transcended** all the others in the sheer beauty of its melody. After the show, Roseann's father claimed the singer's performance was the best he had ever seen.

Transcend means:
__a. depreciate
__b. affect
__c. rival
__d. surpass

214b

The **meticulous** clerk overlooked nothing, however trivial. He even discovered that one of Pam's bags was unlocked and suggested that she lock it as a precaution against theft.

Meticulous means:
__a. overly polite
__b. extremely careful
__c. civil
__d. subservient

b

189c

ec cle si as ti cal (i klē'zē as'ti kal), adj. of or having to do with the church or the clergy. —ec cle'si as'ti cal ly, adv.

1. Check the word closest in meaning to **ecclesiastical.**
__a. provincial
__c. clerical
__b. parochial

2. **Ecclesiastical** can be correctly used to describe:
__a. robes
__c. bells
__b. duties

b

164c

char la tan (shär'la tan), n. person who pretends to have more knowledge or skill than he really has; quack. [< French < Italian *ciarlatano* < *cerretano* person from Cerreto (di Spoleto), town in Italy where street hucksters were common in the Middle Ages]

ANALOGY charlatan : fraud :: seethe :
__a. furtive
__b. boil
__c. gala
__d. assess
__e. bogus

d

b

12c

can tan ker ous (kan tang′kər əs), *adj.*
hard to get along with because of a nature
that is ready to make trouble and oppose
anything suggested; ill-natured; quarrelsome.
[Middle English *contecker* contentious person < *conteck* strife, quarreling < Anglo-
French]   —**can tan′ker ous ly,**   *adv.*
—**can tan′ker ous ness,** *n.*

A **cantankerous** person would probably:
—**a.** be unintelligent
—**b.** be slow at making decisions
—**c.** have few friends
—**d.** be easy to talk with

38a

b, c

suc cumb (sə kum′)

The English eventually recognized that the Colonies
would not **succumb** to their efforts to impose these
taxes.

Write a definition or synonym:

63a

a, c
b

cred i ble (kred′ ə bəl)

Joan's story did not seem **credible** to
King Charles VII of France.

Write a definition or synonym:

88b

Manny's **flippant** replies did not come from a desire
to be impudent or disrespectful. Manny just couldn't
take the staid visitor seriously.

Flippant means:
—**a.** irrelevant
—**b.** inept
—**c.** disgraceful
—**d.** impertinent

113b

Massey claimed that freedom would smell so good, it
would make the men forget the **fetid** smell of the
garbage in which they would hide themselves.
However, the hiding place was too unclean and
unhealthy for anyone but Pete Massey to tolerate.

Fetid means:
—**a.** savory
—**b.** disconcerting
—**c.** stinking
—**d.** present everywhere

---

a

138c

in sa tia ble (in sā′shə bəl), *adj.* that cannot
be satisfied; extremely greedy: *an insatiable
appetite.*   —**in sa′tia ble ness,** *n.*   —**in-
sa′tia bly,** *adv.*

Check the sentence(s) in which **insatiable** is used
correctly.
—**a.** The lawn was insatiable after the drought.
—**b.** The insatiable employer was always finding
fault with the clerk's work.
—**c.** She had an insatiable thirst for knowledge.

288c

caste (kast), *n.* 1 one of the social classes into which Hindus are divided. By tradition, a Hindu is born into the caste of his father and cannot rise above it. 2 an exclusive social group; distinct class. 3 a social system having distinct classes separated by differences of birth, rank, wealth, or position. 4 the position which caste confers: *renounce caste.* 5 lose caste, lose social rank, status, or position. [< Portuguese *casta* race, class, animal species; perhaps < Germanic]

b

Check the sentence(s) in which **caste** is used correctly.
__a. The habits of social caste are still strong among the people of India.
__b. The Republican caste was voted out of office.
__c. The scandal resulted in his losing caste.
__d. Wealth can move a person to a higher caste.

263c

mod u late (moj'ə lāt), *v.,* -lat ed, -lat ing. —*v.t.* 1 regulate or adjust so as to tone down; soften. 2 alter (the voice) in pitch, tone, or volume for expression. 3 in music: a attune (sounds, etc.) to a certain pitch or key. b cause to change from one key to another. 4 (in electronics) to vary the amplitude, frequency, or phase of (the carrier wave) in accordance with the sound wave or other signal being sent. —*v.i.* undergo modulation. [< Latin *modulatum* regulated, ultimately < *modus* measure] —**mod'u la'tor,** *n.*

d

In which of the following would you use **modulation?**
__a. writing a novel
__b. composing a symphony
__c. tuning a piano
__d. building a radio
__e. coaching football
__f. acting in a play

239a

tran scend (tran send')

Roseann had to admit the young man's voice **transcended** all the descriptions of it. She hoped her parents wouldn't care for his performance that much.

a

Write a definition or synonym:

214a

me tic u lous (ma tik' ya las)

Tony was tempted to argue, but he had no wish to spoil the honeymoon. Nevertheless, he looked rather worried as their baggage was weighed and stamped by a **meticulous** baggage clerk.

1. d
2. a

Write a definition or synonym:

189b

Since the home and heart of the Roman Catholic Church are located in Rome, it is natural that **ecclesiastical** matters would have prominence in this city.

b

Ecclesiastical means:
__a. concerned with government
__b. pertaining to the church
__c. pertaining to the Bible
__d. covering a wide area

164b

In a good modern hospital, a well-trained and skilled physician is soon recognized, just as a **charlatan** is quickly exposed. False credentials cannot long disguise a lack of knowledge.

A **charlatan** is:
__a. a blunderer
__b. a drone
__c. a criminal
__d. an impostor

13a

c

char ac ter ize (kar′ ik tə rīz′)

John F. Kennedy, the thirty-fifth President of the United States, was a difficult man to **characterize**.

Write a definition or synonym:

38b

In time, the British government had no choice but to **succumb** to public opinion. Reluctantly, they revoked the Stamp Act.

A synonym for **succumb** is:
___**a.** assent
___**b.** defer
___**c.** yield
___**d.** adhere

63b

It did not seem **credible** to the king that this young girl believed she could save France. However, her fervor and sincerity finally won him over: perhaps it was true that she had a divine mission.

Credible means:
___**a.** practical
___**b.** possible
___**c.** preposterous
___**d.** believable

88c

d

flip pant (flip′ənt), *adj.* smart or pert in speech or manner; not respectful; impertinent; saucy: *a flippant answer.*

Which words mean the *opposite* of **flippant**?
___**a.** mannerly   ___**d.** rude
___**b.** cheeky   ___**e.** courteous
___**c.** polite   ___**f.** pompous

113c

c

fet id (fet′id, fē′tid), *adj.* smelling very bad; stinking. [< Latin *foetidus* < *foetere* to stink] —**fet′id ly**, *adv.* —**fet′id ness**, *n.*

1. Check the words that mean about the same as **fetid.**
   ___**a.** pungent   ___**d.** reeking
   ___**b.** aromatic   ___**e.** scented
   ___**c.** malodorous
2. **Fetid** can be correctly used to describe:
   ___**a.** an illegal act
   ___**b.** a garbage dump
   ___**c.** burnt toast

139a

c

pre text (prē′ tekst)

Most people need no **pretext** for taking a vacation in Maine or Nova Scotia.

Write a definition or synonym:

164a

c, d

char la tan (shär′ lə tən)

As Connie became more experienced, she often said that **charlatans** have no place in modern medicine.

Write a definition or synonym:

189a

c, d

ec cle si as ti cal (i klē′ zi as′ tə kəl)

Ecclesiastical matters are of great importance in Rome.

Write a definition or synonym:

213c

c

dis suade (di swād′), *v.t.,* **-suad ed, -suad ing.** 1 persuade not to do something. 2 advise against. [< Latin *dissuadere* < *dis-* against + *suadere* to urge]

1. Which of the following people would be hardest to **dissuade**?
   __a. one who vacillates   __c. a compromiser
   __b. a young child   __d. a fanatic
2. **Dissuading** is most like:
   __a. coaxing   __d. forcing
   __b. arguing   __e. bullying
   __c. preventing

238c

b

pro té gé (prō′tə zhā), *n.* person who has been taken under the protection or kindly care of a friend or patron. [< French]
pro té gée (prō′tə zhā), *n.* a woman protégé. [< French]

ANALOGY **protégé : patron ::**
   __a. baby : mother
   __b. tenant : landlord
   __c. schooner : captain
   __d. congregation : minister
   __e. sally : guerilla

263b

An actress learns to **modulate** her voice to a pleasing pitch and intensity. Linda's voice during our interview was quite different from the one she used on the stage.

Another word for **modulate** is:
   __a. enhance
   __b. amplify
   __c. simulate
   __d. adjust

288b

Highest in the Mayan social order was the priesthood. Ranking just below the priests were the nobles. The craftsmen and farmers made up the lower **castes.**

A **caste** is:
   __a. a segment
   __b. a social class
   __c. an organization of workers
   __d. a subject

13b

Writers who have **characterized** John F. Kennedy have all agreed that he was a vigorous and idealistic individual.

A synonym for **characterize** is:
___**a.** describe
___**b.** impersonate
___**c.** evaluate
___**d.** visualize

---

c

38c

suc cumb (sə kum′), *v.i.* 1 give way; yield: *succumb to temptation.* 2 die. —*v.t.* **succumb to,** die of. [< Latin *succumbere* < *sub-* down + *-cumbere* to lie]

1. Which of the following is *least* similar to **succumb**?
   ___**a.** weaken ___**c.** resist
   ___**b.** compromise ___**d.** err
2. Check the synonyms for **succumb**.
   ___**a.** quarrel ___**c.** advance
   ___**b.** submit ___**d.** give in

---

d

63c

cred i ble (kred′ə bəl), *adj.* worthy of belief; believable; reliable. [< Latin *credibilem* < *credere* believe] —**cred′i ble ness,** *n.* —**cred′i bly,** *adv.*
➜ **Credible, creditable,** and **credulous** are sometimes confused. *Credible* means believable: *The story is hardly credible; how could all that happen to one person? Creditable* means bringing honor or praise: *He turned in a creditable performance, though his heart was no longer in his acting. Credulous* means too ready to believe: *Credulous people are easily fooled and often swindled.*

Check the sentence(s) in which **credible** is used correctly.
___**a.** He was a credible person, easily deceived by glib talkers.
___**b.** She won no medals, but did a credible job as an army officer.
___**c.** His story had too many loopholes to be credible.
___**d.** Her success came too quickly to be credible.

---

c, e

89a

in nate (i nāt′, in′ āt)

The conversation took a more serious turn when the man stated that he was prepared to manage Manny's career. Oddly enough, he said he thought Manny had little **innate** talent.

Write a definition or synonym:

---

c, d
b

114a

in fec tious (in fek′ shəs)

Massey's cellmate pointed out that the bacteria in the garbage was highly **infectious.**

Write a definition or synonym:

139b

Some people, however, will just not admit their reasons for acting as they do. They need one **pretext** or another to explain their behavior.

A **pretext** is:
___**a.** an apology
___**b.** a pretense
___**c.** a hypothesis
___**d.** a façade

163c

d

em a nate (em′ə nāt), v., -nat ed, -nat ing. —v.i. originate from a person or thing as a source; come forth; spread out: *The rumor emanated from Chicago.* See **issue** for synonym study. —v.t. send out; emit. [< Latin *emanatum* flowed out < *ex-* out + *manare* to flow]

Check the sentence(s) in which a form of **emanate** is used correctly.
__a. A growing boy emanates from his clothes.
__b. In an emergency, emanate from the city!
__c. The orders emanated from Washington.
__d. An odor emanated from the closet.

188c

c

sump tu ous (sump′chü əs), *adj.* lavish and costly; magnificent; rich: *a sumptuous banquet.* [< Latin *sumptuosus* < *sumptus* expense < *sumere* spend] —**sump′tu ous ly,** *adv.* —**sump′tu ous ness,** *n.*

Sumptuous can be correctly used to describe which of the following?
__a. jungle foliage
__b. price of theater tickets
__c. evening gown
__d. palace furnishings
__e. ice cream soda
__f. new bicycle

213b

Tony wanted to keep at least one hundred dollars in reserve for an emergency. But Pam told him they would probably visit Paris only once. She would not be **dissuaded** from using all of their funds to enjoy the trip fully.

To **dissuade** is to:
__a. effect a compromise
__b. surrender an opinion
__c. divert by persuasion
__d. give advice

238b

The producer had noticed the singer's talent and offered to help him. As the producer's **protégé**, the singer received additional voice training, publicity, and a starring role in the show. Roseann envied him greatly.

A **protégé** is a person who is:
__a. a stand-in for another
__b. under the care of another
__c. under the jurisdiction of another
__d. the constant companion of another

263a

b, c

mod u late (moj′ ə lāt)

After Linda had been talking for fifteen minutes or so about her early struggles to become a great star, I noticed what a well-**modulated** voice she had.

Write a definition or synonym:

288a

b, g

caste (kast)

In the Mayan society there were rigid lines between the **castes**.

Write a definition or synonym:

a

13c

char·ac·ter·ize (kar′ik tə rīz′), *v.t.,* **-ized,
-iz·ing.** 1 describe the special qualities or
features of (a person or thing); describe. 2 be
a characteristic of; distinguish: *A camel is
characterized by the hump on its back and its
ability to go without water for several days.*
3 give character to: *The author characterized
his heroine in a few short paragraphs.*

1. Almost all people would like to **characterize**
   themselves as:
   ___**a.** belligerent   ___**c.** cantankerous
   ___**b.** inept   ___**d.** affable
2. If you were to **characterize** your friend, you
   would:
   ___**a.** write to him   ___**b.** tell about him

c
b, d

39a

har·ass (har′ əs, hə ras′)

The British repealed the Stamp Act, but then passed
other acts which also **harassed** the Colonists.

Write a definition or synonym:

c, d

64a

dis·sent (di sent′)

In the fifteenth century severe penalties were
imposed upon those who **dissented.**

Write a definition or synonym:

89b

The man quickly explained that real success did not
depend on **innate** talent. Diligent study and practice
could replace an inborn natural ability. The man was
convinced that Manny's drive and good looks could
take him right to the top. Manny began to listen
closely.

Innate means:
___**a.** congenial
___**b.** inborn
___**c.** internal
___**d.** ordinary

114b

Many **infectious** diseases are spread by bacteria
in decaying refuse. If Massey did not come down
with some illness himself, the chances were good
that he would spread the illness to someone else.

Infectious means:
___**a.** unhealthy
___**b.** virile
___**c.** causing infection
___**d.** in jeopardy

b

139c

pre·text (prē′tekst), *n.* a false reason con-
cealing the real reason; misleading excuse;
pretense: *He did not go, on the pretext of
being too tired.* [< Latin *praetextum,* literally,
woven in front, alleged as an excuse < *prae-*
pre- + *texere* to weave]

Which of the following can be described as a
pretext?
___**a.** a note written to explain a pupil's absence
___**b.** going to a party in a costume
___**c.** claiming to have laryngitis in order to avoid
       singing in a concert
___**d.** a fox lying in wait for a rabbit

287c c

ven·e·rate (ven'ə rāt'), v.t., -rat·ed, -rat·ing. regard with deep respect; revere: *He venerates his father's memory.* [< Latin *veneratum* revered < *Venus* Venus, original-ly, love] —ven'e·ra'tor, n.

If you **venerate** something, you:

___a. pay homage to it
___b. salute it
___c. scorn it
___d. observe it
___e. dishonor it
___f. remember it
___g. commemorate it

262c c

a·me·na·ble (ə mē'nə bəl, ə men'ə bəl), adj. 1 open to influence, suggestion, advice, etc.; responsive; submissive: *amenable to persua-sion.* 2 accountable or answerable to some jurisdiction or authority: *People living in a country are amenable to its laws.* [< Middle French *amener* lead to < *a-* to + *mener* to lead] —a·me'na·ble·ness, n. —a·me'-na·bly, adv.

Check the sentence(s) in which **amenable** is used correctly.

___a. If you continue to act that way, you will be amenable to criticism.
___b. Every adult is amenable to society for his or her actions.
___c. She is a well-behaved child, amenable to the advice of her elders.

238a a, b

pro·té·gé (prō'tə zhā)

The lead singer in the show was the **protégé** of the show's producer.

Write a definition or synonym:

213a b, d

dis·suade (di swād')

Tony tried in vain to **dissuade** his bride from using all their money for food, entertainment, and shopping.

Write a definition or synonym:

188b

The Pope's **sumptuous** vestments are a symbol of his princely status. It is thought fitting that the leader of the Church should be richly adorned.

Sumptuous means:

___a. extravagant
___b. patrician
___c. magnificent
___d. celestial

163b

Connie's years of experience gave her an air of assurance. The confidence that **emanated** from her as she made her rounds often had a beneficial effect on her patients.

Emanate means:

___a. characterize
___b. evoke
___c. infuse
___d. come forth

14a

dis creet (dis krēt')

Among our recent Presidents, Harry S. Truman may have been the least **discreet.**

Write a definition or synonym:

39b

Some of these laws **harassed** the Colonists by denying them any voice in the government to which they paid taxes. More and more Colonists were troubled by these attacks on their economic well-being.

A synonym for **harass** is:
__a. flaunt
__b. regiment
__c. restrict
__d. plague

64b

The Church in the fifteenth century exacted strict obedience from the people. Those who **dissented** in word or deed were subjected to severe punishment.

Dissent means:
__a. cause to appear different
__b. become a collaborator
__c. refuse to conform
__d. oppose strenuously

b

89c

in nate (i nāt', in'āt), *adj.* 1 existing in a person from birth; natural; inborn; native. 2 existing naturally in anything; inherent. [< Latin *innatum* < *in-* in + *nasci* be born] —**in nate'ly,** *adv.* —**in nate'ness,** *n.*

ANALOGY **innate : acquired ::**
__a. unique : special
__b. component : part
__c. barracks : houses
__d. essential : trivial
__e. superfluous : extra

c

114c

in fec tious (in fek'shəs), *adj.* 1 spread by infection: *Measles is an infectious disease.* 2 causing infection. 3 apt to spread from one to another: *an infectious laugh.* —**in fec'tious ly,** *adv.* —**in fec'tious ness,** *n.*

ANALOGY **infectious : infection ::**
__a. chronic : habitual
__b. dynamic : slothful
__c. colleague : medical
__d. project : projection
__e. spasm : transfusion

c

140a

o vert (ō' vėrt, ō vėrt')

Other tourists are willing to make their sentiments **overt.**

Write a definition or synonym:

287b

It is now believed that the pyramids are actually temples dedicated to the sun. One archeologist has theorized that the temples were built by people who came before the Aztecs, and who also **venerated** the sun.

Venerate means:
- __a.__ fear
- __b.__ personify
- __c.__ revere
- __d.__ praise

262b

In fact, Linda was more than **amenable.** She was eager to start at the beginning of her career and provide me with every detail of her triumphs.

Another word for **amenable** is:
- __a.__ compelling
- __b.__ hospitable
- __c.__ responsive
- __d.__ affable

237c

a

prow·ess (prou'is), *n.* 1 bravery; daring, 2 brave or daring acts. 3 unusual skill or ability. [< Old French *proece* < *prod* valiant]

Check the sentence(s) in which a form of **prowess** is used correctly.
- __a.__ His prowess permitted many victories.
- __b.__ The Vikings were men of prowess.
- __c.__ They used to celebrate the prowess of their boats.
- __d.__ Her prowess caused her to shrink from him.
- __e.__ He was a prowessed acrobat.

212c

d

al·lo·cate (al'ə kāt), *v.t.,* **-cat·ed, -cat·ing.** 1 set or lay aside for a special purpose: assign, allot, or apportion: *The Ford Foundation allocated millions of dollars among colleges and hospitals.* 2 locate. [< Medieval Latin *allocatum* located < Latin *ad-* to, at + *locus* place]

In which of the following is something **allocated?**
- __a.__ The head of a company decides how to distribute stock.
- __b.__ A real estate developer decides on the sites for some houses she plans to build.
- __c.__ A boy finds a number in a telephone directory.
- __d.__ A department manager plans her budget for the year.

188a

b

sump·tu·ous (sump' chü əs)

In some of his public appearances, the Pope is garbed in **sumptuous** robes.

Write a definition or synonym:

163a

a, b

em·a·nate (em' ə nāt)

Nevertheless, as Connie completed her last year of study, her parents noticed that an air of quiet confidence began to **emanate** from their daughter.

Write a definition or synonym:

14b

President Truman was a candid, plain-speaking man who made his feelings known clearly. He could be **discreet** when necessary, but he preferred to be direct.

A synonym for **discreet** is:
__a. decisive
__b. cautious
__c. infallible
__d. critical

---

d

39c

har ass (har′əs, hə ras′), v.t. 1 trouble by repeated attacks; harry: *Pirates harassed the villages along the coast.* 2 distress with annoying labor, care, misfortune, etc.; disturb; worry; torment. See **worry** for synonym study. [< French *harasser* < Old French *harer* set a dog on < *hare* a shout to excite dogs to attack] —**har′ass ment,** n.

ANALOGY **harass : assist :: detract :**
__a. specialist
__b. help
__c. beautify
__d. enhance
__e. spurn

---

c

64c

dis sent (di sent′), v.i. 1 think differently; disagree: *Two of the judges dissented from the decision of the other three.* 2 withhold consent. 3 refuse to conform to the rules and beliefs of an established church. —n. 1 difference of opinion; disagreement. 2 declaration of disagreement of opinion about something. 3 refusal to conform to the rules and beliefs of an established church. [< Latin *dissentire* < *dis-* apart + *sentire* think, feel]

ANALOGY **dissent : rift :: agreement :**
__a. scavenger
__b. perception
__c. ardor
__d. consensus
__e. chaos

---

d

90a

de ride (di rīd′)

All the rest is now ancient history. After three performances at a popular nightclub, Manny was offered a recording contract. Manny's Village friends, who lived only for their art, were quick to **deride** Manny's sudden success.

Write a definition or synonym:

115a

rib ald (rib′ əld)

The inmates' conversation was **ribald** as they discussed Massey's escape plan and described the way he would look and smell. Nevertheless, Massey planned to escape during his third week on the state farm.

Write a definition or synonym:

---

d

140b

They make their feelings evident by returning to Maine (or to Nova Scotia) each year. If questioned, they make their reasons **overt.** "Nova Scotia (or Maine) is the best place in the world for a summer vacation!"

Overt means:
__a. permissible
__b. authentic
__c. manifest
__d. candid

162c

hag gard (hag′ərd), *adj.* looking worn from pain, fatigue, worry, hunger, etc.; careworn; gaunt. [perhaps < Old French *hagard*] —**hag′gard ly**, *adv.* —**hag′gard ness**, *n.*

d

Check the phrase(s) in which **haggard** is used correctly.
__a. a haggard expression
__b. a haggard child
__c. haggard clothes
__d. a haggard appetite

187c

hal lowed (hal′ōd; *in church use, often* hal′ō id), *adj.* 1 made holy; sacred; consecrated: *A churchyard is hallowed ground.* 2 honored or observed as holy.

b

ANALOGY **hallowed : bewitched ::**
__a. spring : geyser
__b. faithful : heathen
__c. telescope : apprentice
__d. superficial : trivial
__e. rove : wander

212b

Pam wanted to **allocate** half their money for food and entertainment and half for shopping. Tony was against her plan for dividing up all of their funds.

A synonym for **allocate** is:
__a. determine
__b. compile
__c. segregate
__d. assign

237b

A dancer of **prowess** stands out in a troupe of average performers. Her advancement from chorus to starring part is usually rapid.

Another word for **prowess** is:
__a. ability
__b. stature
__c. ambition
__d. experience

262a

b, d, e, f

a me na ble (ə mē′ nə bəl, ə men′ ə bəl)

Rather nervously, I suggested we begin talking about her first role in motion pictures. Linda was **amenable** to my request.

Write a definition or synonym:

287a

c, d

ven e rate (ven′ ə rāt)

Archeologists originally believed that the Aztecs constructed pyramids to **venerate** the moon as well as the sun.

Write a definition or synonym:

b

14c

dis creet (dis krēt′), adj. very careful and sensible in speech and action; having or showing good judgment; wisely cautious. [< Old French discret < Late Latin discretus discerning < Latin discernere discern] —dis creet′ly, adv. —dis creet′ness, n.

ANALOGY discreet : reckless ::
___a. wary : prudent
___b. honest : cautious
___c. firm : careful
___d. terrible : horrible
___e. hidden : revealed

d

40a

in al ien a ble (in ā′ lyə nə bəl, in ā′ lē ə nə bəl)

The continuation of these British acts led to the Revolution. To sum it up, we can say the Colonists felt they had certain **inalienable** rights for which the British showed little or no respect.

Write a definition or synonym:

d

65a

her e tic (her′ ə tik)

Joan of Arc was tried as a **heretic.**

Write a definition or synonym:

90b

Of course, many artists who have used their talents for popular or commercial success are subjected to ridicule and mockery. Because Manny couldn't stand being **derided** by his old friends, he moved away from the Village. However, Manny never stopped asking himself whether he had sold out his art for quick success.

Deride means:
___a. ignore completely
___b. make an example of
___c. treat humorously
___d. ridicule contemptuously

115b

In fact, Massey paid no attention to the other inmates. Coarse remarks and vulgar jokes were common in the **ribald** speech of the convicts. They could be as gross as they wanted. Massey would soon be a free man.

Ribald means:
___a. destitute
___b. untutored
___c. gregarious
___d. indelicate

c

140c

o vert (ō′vèrt′, ō vèrt′), adj. open or public; evident; not hidden: Hitting someone is an overt act. [< Old French, past participle of ovrir to open < Latin aperire. Related to APERTURE.] —o′vert ly, adv.

Which do *not* describe **overt** behavior?
___a. He contemplated leaving the country.
___b. She flew to Europe.
___c. The florist arranged a beautiful bouquet.
___d. He kept his love for her a secret.
___e. She wanted to ask for a salary increase.

162b

Connie's **haggard** expression was the result of long hours of study, exhausting work, and the tension and pressure inherent in the school routine. Her parents thought she was more in need of rest than some of the patients.

Haggard means:
___a. impassive
___b. disheveled
___c. irritated
___d. careworn

187b

St. Peter's stands on the site of the Circus of Nero, where many Christians were martyred. Here St. Peter is generally believed to have been buried after his crucifixion. In the eyes of the world's Catholics, these events have **hallowed** the ground.

Hallowed means:
___a. made memorable
___b. consecrated
___c. idealized
___d. dedicated

212a

c, d

al lo cate (al′ ə kāt)

Tony made the suggestion that they **allocate** their money ahead of time.

Write a definition or synonym:

237a

b, d

prow ess (prou′ is)

Because of her **prowess**, the young dancer was the focus of all eyes. Roseann became convinced that her parents wouldn't even notice their daughter when she moved out onto the stage with the rest of the chorus.

Write a definition or synonym:

261c

c

in cog ni to (in kog′nə tō, in′kog nē′tō), *adj., adv., n., pl.* **-tos.** —*adj., adv.* with one's real name, character, rank, etc., concealed: *The prince traveled incognito to avoid crowds and ceremonies.* —*n.* 1 person who is incognito. 2 a disguised condition. [< Italian < Latin *incognitus* unknown < *in-* not + *cognitus* known < *co-* (intensive) + *gnoscere* know]

Which of the following would you be likely to employ if you wish to be **incognito**?
___a. your checkbook   ___d. dark glasses
___b. a wig   ___e. an assumed name
___c. a forger   ___f. false eyebrows

286c

b

ef fi gy (ef′ə jē), *n., pl.* **-gies.** 1 image or statue, usually of a person: *The dead man's monument bore his effigy.* 2 **burn in effigy** or **hang in effigy**, burn or hang an image of a person to show hatred or contempt. [< Latin *effigies* < *effingere* to fashion < *ex-* out + *fingere* to form]

Which of the following is an **effigy**?
___a. a portrait of George Washington
___b. Lincoln's head on a penny
___c. a voodoo doll
___d. a bust of Napoleon
___e. a cartoon

15a

e

ex tem po ra ne ous (ek stem′ pə rā′ nē əs)

President Franklin D. Roosevelt, the only man ever to serve more than two terms as President, was known as a very good **extemporaneous** speaker.

Write a definition or synonym:

40b

They called "life, liberty, and the pursuit of happiness" their **inalienable** rights, and were willing to die to prove no one could take these rights away.

An **inalienable** right is one:
__a. that is completely legal
__b. that is traditional; historical
__c. that cannot be taken away
__d. that is justly earned

65b

There were codes of war which protected her from a military trial, so the English occupying forces decided to have her tried as a **heretic**. In those days, people who opposed important Church doctrines were regarded as **heretics**.

Another word for **heretic** is:
__a. dissenter
__b. insurrectionist
__c. heathen
__d. atheist

90c

d

de ride (di rīd′), *v.t.*, **-rid ed, -rid ing.** make fun of; laugh at in scorn. See **ridicule** for synonym study. [< Latin *deridere* < *de-* + *ridere* to laugh] **—de rid′er,** *n.* **—de rid′ing ly,** *adv.*

Check the sentence(s) in which a form of **deride** is used correctly.
__a. The clown's antics were so amusing that no one could help deriding him.
__b. They derided as the loser walked out of the ring.
__c. He walked out when they derided his attempt to act.
__d. Do not deride something you do not understand.

115c

d

rib ald (rib′əld), *adj.* offensive in speech; coarsely mocking; irreverent; indecent; obscene: *a ribald story, a ribald party.* [< Old French *ribauld*]

Check the sentence(s) in which **ribald** can be correctly substituted for the italicized word.
__a. His *coarse* features belied his gentle nature.
__b. The man's *coarse* humor offended his host.
__c. Writers sometimes use *indelicate* situations for emphasis.
__d. His *gross* body was the direct result of overeating.

d, e

LESSON 15

Secrets of the Pyramids

The Great Pyramids of Egypt have been "discovered" dozens of times since they were constructed several thousand years ago. Unfortunately, most of the discoverers were bandits who specialized in robbing ancient graves. It was not until the last century that archeologists and other scientists began to preserve the last remaining treasures of ancient Egypt.

286b

The elaborately carved robes of the **effigies** indicate that they represent either priests or rulers.

An **effigy** is:
- **a.** a vestige
- **b.** a statue
- **c.** a mummy
- **d.** a memento

261b

I thought it would be difficult for Linda to remain **incognito** when she was a movie star. Someone would be sure to recognize a celebrity no matter what name she used or how she dressed. Linda said no one ever recognized her without her makeup.

Incognito means:
- **a.** solitary
- **b.** obscure
- **c.** disguised
- **d.** invisible

286c

pre co cious (pri kō/shəs), *adj.* I developed earlier than usual in knowledge, skill, etc.: *This very precocious child could read well at the age of four.* 2 developed too early; occurring before the natural time. [< Latin *praecocem* < *praecoquere* to mature or ripen early < *prae-* pre- + *coquere* ripen] —pre co/cious ly, *adv.* —pre co/cious ness, *n.*

Precocious correctly describes which of the following?
- **a.** a prediction at the half as to which team will win
- **b.** a child of three who can play the piano
- **c.** a plant which first bears leaves, then flowers
- **d.** a fourteen-year-old world chess champion

211c

af flu ent (af/lü ənt), *adj.* I having an abundance of money, property, etc.; wealthy; rich. 2 abundant; plentiful. 3 flowing freely. —*n.* stream flowing into a larger stream or body of water; tributary. [< Latin *affluentem* flowing out < *ad-* + *fluere* to flow] —af/flu ent ly, *adv.*

Check the sentence(s) in which **affluent** is used correctly.
- **a.** That large river is an affluent of the little stream we just passed.
- **b.** Her affluent inventiveness was much admired.
- **c.** His elegant clothes gave him an affluent appearance.
- **d.** Her bankbook did not substantiate the impression she tried to give of affluent circumstances.

187a

hal lowed (hal/ōd, hal/ō id)

The great cathedral of St. Peter's is a **hallowed** spot in the Vatican City.

Write a definition or synonym:

162a

hag gard (hag/ ərd)

When Connie returned home during vacations from medical school, she frequently looked **haggard**.

Write a definition or synonym:

15b

Most people listening to Roosevelt were impressed with the organization and clarity of his **extemporaneous** speeches. Many thought these talks even better than those he had thought about and planned for weeks.

A synonym for **extemporaneous** is:
— **a.** organized
— **b.** contrived
— **c.** premeditated
— **d.** impromptu

c

40c

in al ien a ble (in ā′lyə nə bəl, in ā′lē ə nə-bəl), *adj.* that cannot be given or taken away; that cannot be transferred to another: *an inalienable right.* Also, **unalienable.** —**in al′ien a bly,** *adv.*

If something is **inalienable:**
— **a.** it can be taken only on the consent of the owner
— **b.** it cannot be taken under any conditions
— **c.** it can be given away
— **d.** none of these

a

65c

her e tic (her′ə tik), *n.* 1 member of a church who adopts religious doctrines or opinions contrary to the established beliefs of his church. 2 person who maintains opinions or doctrines on any subject contrary to those generally accepted as authoritative. —*adj.* heretical.

Match each statement with the group that would consider it **heretical.**
a. "A four-day week is just around the corner."
b. "Professionals should compete for national amateur championships."
c. "Hurrah for the Taft-Hartley Act."
d. "This country needs socialized medicine."
___ labor unions   ___ management
___ doctors' organizations   ___ amateur athletes

c, d

LESSON 10 | Small-Town Scandal

After three years without a vacation, Sergeant Leo Salinger decided to take a break from the demands of police work. He drove to the lake country for some fishing and boating. Hours after he arrived, Salinger was involved in the most bizarre case of his career. Lucy Bast, the mayor's wife, had just been arrested for the murder of her husband Leonard. The authorities were convinced Mrs. Bast had poisoned her husband. Gradually, Salinger became convinced she was innocent.

116a

b, c

rai ment (rā′ mənt)

Unfortunately, Massey was trapped in one of the garbage containers for over nine hours before he was tossed out onto the city dump and half-buried in garbage. When he finally crawled free, his biggest obstacle was his **raiment.**

Write a definition or synonym:

141a

aes thet ic (es thet′ ik)

When they begin to excavate the tombs and cities of the distant past, archeologists normally unearth many objects of **aesthetic** value.

Write a definition or synonym:

161c af·fin·i·ty (ə fin/ə tē), n., pl. -ties. 1 a natural attraction to a person or liking for a thing: If you have an affinity for mathematics, you will probably enjoy physics. 2 relation; connection. 3 relationship by marriage. 4 resemblance between species, genera, etc., that makes a common ancestry probable. 5 force that attracts certain chemical elements to others and keeps them combined. [< Latin affinitatem relation < affinis related, bordering on < ad- on + finis border]

Check the sentence(s) in which a form of **affinity** is used correctly.

__a. The affinity of oxygen for hydrogen makes water a stable substance.
__b. Spanish and French have an affinity.
__c. They were affinitied by marriage.

186c ma ca bre (mə kä/brə, mə kä/bər), adj. causing horror; gruesome; horrible; ghastly. [< French] —ma ca/bre ly, adv.

ANALOGY macabre : vampire :: inspiring :

__a. amphitheater
__b. crypt
__c. edifice
__d. orifice
__e. cathedral

211b

It might seem that Pam and Tony "had it made." However, only their travel and hotel expenses were paid. Their own limited funds would have to cover meals and any shopping they hoped to do. Pam and Tony weren't **affluent** by any means.

Affluent means:

__a. exuberant
__b. expensive
__c. wealthy
__d. jovial

236b

Barely sixteen, this **precocious** girl was already one of the finest dancers on stage. Roseann couldn't help wishing that she herself had begun dancing earlier.

Precocious means:

__a. extremely ambitious
__b. developed early
__c. very beautiful
__d. unusually muscular

261a in cog ni to (in kog' nə tō)

Write a definition or synonym:

When I met Linda Superstar in the restaurant of her hotel, I saw a rather ordinary-looking young woman. She was attractive enough, but she certainly wasn't the most beautiful woman alive. "That's because I'm traveling **incognito**," Linda told me.

286a ef fi gy (ef' ə jē)

Write a definition or synonym:

Among the statuary uncovered, archeologists have found **effigies**.

b

a

d, e

15c ex tem po ra ne ous (ek stem′pə rā′nē- əs), *adj.* 1 spoken or done without prepara- tion; offhand. 2 made for the occasion: *an extemporaneous shelter against a storm.* 3 (of a speech) carefully prepared, though usually not written out and never committed to memory. [< Late Latin *extemporaneus* < Latin *ex tempore* on the spur of the mo- ment] —ex tem′po ra′ne ous ly, *adv.* —ex tem′po ra′ne ous ness, *n.*

One would be acting **extemporaneously** if:
—**a.** one studied a problem before replying.
—**b.** one failed to respond to a question.
—**c.** one reacted immediately to any question.
—**d.** one sought shelter under an awning when caught in the rain.

LESSON 5 | The City of the Future

Over a century ago, before automobiles were invented, people had already begun leaving the small towns and farms to live in the rapidly growing cities. A woman named Linda Banner devoted her time to setting aside large sections of land for use as parks. She asked land owners to sell their property to the city because there would soon be a great need for public parks. Most people thought Linda was a little mad.

66a

re pu di ate (ri pyü′ dē āt)

The French king and his ministers **repudiated** her.

Write a definition or synonym:

91a

sci on (sī′ ən)

Mayor Leonard Bast, who was well known and widely respected, had been the **scion** of the town's oldest family.

Write a definition or synonym:

116b

For one thing, Massey's shirt and trousers and shoes smelled unbelievably bad. It was impossible to stay at even a cheap hotel or to hitchhike. Massey and his **raiment** smelled so disgusting, no one would have anything to do with him.

Raiment is:
—**a.** habitat
—**b.** characteristic
—**c.** penalty
—**d.** clothing

141b

Many objects are valuable because they provide information about the culture that created them. Some objects, like pots or weapons, are valuable because they are useful. But many statues, vases, jewelry, and other objects of art go beyond simple utility. Their delicate colors and fine craftsmanship give them an **aesthetic** value.

Aesthetic means pertaining to:
—**a.** monetary value
—**b.** primitive man
—**c.** beauty
—**d.** history

93

—

285c   **wreak** (rēk), *v.t.* 1 give expression to; work off (feelings, desires, etc.): *The cruel boy wreaked his bad temper on his dog.* 2 inflict (vengeance, punishment, etc.). [Old English *wrecan*]

To wreak one's vengeance is to:
—a. "bury the hatchet."
—b. "give an eye for an eye"
—c. "look a gift horse in the mouth."
—d. "get even with"
—e. "get back at."

LESSON 27

An Interview with Linda Superstar

To tell the truth, I had never even heard of an actress named Linda Superstar when her press agent called the newspaper office. After about ten minutes of listening, I knew that Linda was the greatest thing to hit the screen since talking pictures. I also learned that her latest picture was sure to win an Academy Award. Then I learned that Ms. Superstar would be available for an exclusive interview at ten the next morning. Since the reporter who usually handles celebrity interviews was on vacation, I had no choice but to go.

236a   **pre co cious** (pri kō′ shəs)

Roseann knew the lead dancer was better than she was. The dancer was precocious too.

Write a definition or synonym:

211a   **af flu ent** (af′ lü ənt)

When Pam and Tony arrived at the airport to begin their honeymoon, they felt affluent for the first time in their lives.

Write a definition or synonym:

186b   To some visitors, the displays of the bones of long-dead Christians have an aesthetic as well as a religious significance. To others, the displays, with their emphasis on death and suffering, are macabre.

Macabre means:
—a. gruesome
—b. intimidating
—c. ominous
—d. fraudulent

161b   Because of Connie's affinity for healing, neighborhood children brought their ailing pets to her attention. When Connie's natural interest was combined with years of diligent study and practice, she became a skilled physician.

Affinity means:
—a. strange occurrence
—b. natural inclination
—c. natural phenomenon
—d. fortunate situation

b

g
b,

a
b

16a

gre gar i ous (grə ger′ ē əs, grə gar′ ē əs)

President Lyndon Baines Johnson, the thirty-sixth President, was a very **gregarious** man.

Write a definition or synonym:

41a

ver dant (vėrd′ nt)

"We need a park on this land," Linda explained to the group of business leaders. "If our city continues to grow, this land will someday seem like a **verdant** oasis."

Write a definition or synonym:

66b

When the King of France saw that Joan of Arc was more interested in France than in his personal interests, he **repudiated** her. He left her to the mercy of the English invaders.

Repudiate means:
__a. repulse
__b. reject
__c. reprove
__d. deride

91b

The Bast family had been prominent for more than two hundred years. Leonard's forbears had served with distinction in every American war. Leonard himself was the **scion** of John Bast, a Revolutionary War hero.

Another word for **scion** is:
__a. pride
__b. antecedent
__c. descendant
__d. mainstay

116c

rai ment (rā′mənt), *n.* clothing; garments. [short for *arraiment* < *array*]

1. Check the words that mean about the same as **raiment**.
   __a. attire   __d. garb
   __b. coat   __e. boots
   __c. vestments
2. Check the things that would *not* be considered part of one's **raiment**.
   __a. eyeglasses   __d. coat
   __b. hair style   __e. sweater
   __c. shirt

141c

aes thet ic (es thet′ik), *adj.* 1 based on or determined by beauty rather than by practically useful, scientific, or moral considerations. 2 having or showing an appreciation of beauty in nature or art. 3 showing good taste; artistic. Also, **esthetic.** [< Greek *aisthētikos* sensitive, perceptive < *aisthanesthai* perceive] —**aes thet′i cal ly**, *adv.*

ANALOGY aesthetic : distasteful :: beautiful :
   __a. practical
   __b. extravagant
   __c. righteous
   __d. repulsive
   __e. abominable

161a

af fin i ty (ə fin′ ə tē)

Connie Franklin showed an **affinity** for health care while she was still in high school.

Write a definition or synonym:

186a

ma ca bre (mə kä′ brə, mə kä′ bər)

Some of the displays in the catacombs outside Rome might be considered **macabre.**

Write a definition or synonym:

LESSON 22

All Expenses Paid!

When Pam and Tony entered the TV quiz show for young couples who were engaged to be married, they assumed they might win a set of matching luggage or even a new set of furniture. They never dreamed they would win the grand prize: a honeymoon trip to Paris with all expenses paid!

235c **pir ou ette** (pir′ü et′), *n., v.,* **-et ted, -et ting.** —*n.* a whirling about on one foot or on the toes, as in dancing. —*v.i.* whirl in this way. [< Middle French, spinning top]

1. Which of the following can **pirouette**?
   __a. the hands of a clock
   __b. a figure skater
   __c. the earth on its axis
2. You would be most likely to witness a **pirouette** at:
   __a. the ballet
   __b. a swimming meet
   __c. a parade

260c **re miss** (ri mis′), *adj.* 1 careless or slack in doing what one has to do; neglectful; negligent: *be remiss in one's duty.* 2 characterized by carelessness, negligence, or inattention. [< Latin *remissum* remitted] —**re miss′ly,** *adv.* —**re miss′ness,** *n.*
re mis si ble (ri mis′ə bəl), *adj.* that can be remitted.

Which of the following words mean the *opposite* of **remiss**?
__a. conscientious   __e. stoic
__b. painstaking   __f. scrupulous
__c. unmindful   __g. meticulous
__d. indifferent

285b

The Aztecs **wreaked** punishment on their marauding enemy by destroying Spanish bridges and dikes. Their acts of vengeance were swift and thorough.

Wreak means:
__a. desire
__b. inflict
__c. seek
__d. return

96

16b

Johnson's **gregariousness** extended to all types of people. He enjoyed being with people from all walks of life and was particularly happy when surrounded by crowds.

A synonym for **gregarious** is:
—**a.** contemptuous of others
—**b.** fond of being with others
—**c.** democratic in manner
—**d.** extremely talkative

41b

The business leaders looked out at the tall trees covered with fresh, new leaves and at the thick grass of the meadows. The scene of **verdant** beauty made little impression.

Verdant means:
—**a.** green
—**b.** exotic
—**c.** vigorous
—**d.** luxuriant

66c

b

re pu di ate (ri pyü′dē āt), *v.t.,* **-at ed, -at ing.** 1 refuse to accept; reject: *repudiate a doctrine.* 2 refuse to acknowledge or pay: *repudiate a debt.* 3 cast off; disown: *repudiate a son.* 4 put away by divorce. [< Latin *repudiatum* divorced < *repudium* divorce] —**re pu′di a′tion,** *n.* —**re pu′di a′tor,** *n.*

Check the sentence(s) in which **repudiated** can be used correctly.
—**a.** He __ his debts when he left the country.
—**b.** She __ the policies of the new government and resigned her post.
—**c.** They hoisted the sails and __ the anchor.
—**d.** She __ her hostess's offer of tea.
—**e.** The publisher __ the manuscript with a short note of thanks.

91c

c

sci on (sī′ən), *n.* 1 bud or branch cut for grafting. 2 descendant; heir. Also, **cion.** [< Old French *cion*]

Check the sentence(s) in which a form of **scion** is used correctly.
—**a.** A nurseryman works with scions.
—**b.** The scions exploded in the middle of the night.
—**c.** In many towns, the scions of the founders are the prominent citizens of today.
—**d.** As a member of the younger generation, I enjoy parties with all my scions.

117a

a, c,
d

a, b

gar ish (ger′ ish, gar′ ish)

For several hours, Massey wandered along the waterfront, hoping to find a source of money or clean clothing. He avoided the **garish** lights of the taverns and bars.

Write a definition or synonym:

142a

de fin i tive (di fin′ ə tiv)

When archeologists first uncovered the tombs of Egyptian Pharaohs, they were reluctant to make **definitive** statements regarding their findings.

Write a definition or synonym:

LESSON 17 | My Daughter, the Doctor

a, c

Connie Franklin's mother was a registered nurse and her father was a pharmacist. Both parents had once had dreams of attending medical school but had been financially unable to do so. When Connie announced her intention of becoming a physician, her parents were delighted. They each waited for the day when they could say "my daughter, the doctor."

---

a

185c

pa·tri·cian (pə·trish/ən), *n.* 1 member of the nobility of ancient Rome, composed of the families descended from the original body of Roman citizens. 2 person of noble birth; noble; aristocrat. —*adj.* 1 of the patricians. 2 of high social rank; aristocratic. 3 suitable for an aristocrat. [< Latin *patricius* of the *patres* (senators), literally, fathers) at Rome]

Check the sentence(s) in which **patrician(s)** can be correctly substituted for the italicized word.

___ a. It is a *noble* gesture to try to save the life of another.
___ b. The *nobles* attended the coronation ceremonies.
___ c. His *noble* features belied his lowly status.
___ d. St. Mark's Cathedral is a *noble* edifice.

---

b

210c

vi·car·i·ous (vī·ker/ē·əs, vi·ker/ē·əs), *adj.* 1 done or suffered for others: *vicarious work.* 2 felt by sharing in others' experience: *The invalid received vicarious pleasure from reading travel stories.* 3 taking the place of another; doing the work of another: *a vicarious agent.* 4 delegated: *vicarious authority.* 5 (in physiology) denoting the performance by or through one organ of functions normally discharged by another. [< Latin *vicarius* < *vicis* turn, change, substitution. Doublet of VICAR.] —vi·car/i·ous·ly, *adv.* —vi·car/i·ous·ness, *n.*

Check the sentence(s) in which a form of **vicarious** is used correctly.

___ a. The deputy mayor used his vicarious authority wisely.
___ b. They were so devoted that it was said that one suffered vicariously when the other was ill.
___ c. Margarine is often vicariously substituted for butter.
___ d. They were extremely vicarious and never had a serious quarrel.

285b

It took Roseann many years of practice to learn to do a **pirouette** without becoming dizzy. The secret is to keep the eyes focused on one particular spot each time you turn.

A **pirouette** is:

___ a. a whirling about
___ b. a back flip
___ c. an acrobatic act
___ d. a somersault

260b

It would be **remiss** to celebrate Van Gogh's enormous drive to create, while neglecting Theodor's contributions. Without his brother's love and assistance, it is unlikely that Van Gogh would have created his magnificent paintings.

Remiss means:

___ a. neglectful
___ b. inadvertent
___ c. justifiable
___ d. negligible

285a

a

wreak (rēk)

The Aztecs **wreaked** vengeance on the Spaniards.

Write a definition or synonym:

16c

b

gre gar i ous (grə ger′ē əs, grə gar′ē əs), *adj.* 1 living in flocks, herds, or other groups: *Sheep and cattle are gregarious, raccoons are not.* 2 fond of being with others: *Hermits are not gregarious.* 3 of or having to do with a flock or crowd. [< Latin *gregarius* < *gregem* flock] **—gre gar′i ous ly,** *adv.* **—gre gar′i ous ness,** *n.*

Which of the following would be likely to be **gregarious**?

__**a.** a circus clown   __**d.** a religious mystic
__**b.** a wounded lion   __**e.** a salesperson
__**c.** a mining prospector   __**f.** an actor

41c

a

ver dant (verd′nt), *adj.* 1 green: *verdant hills, verdant grass.* 2 inexperienced. [< *verdure*] **—ver′dant ly,** *adv.*

Which of the following are **verdant**?

__**a.** emeralds   __**d.** airports
__**b.** fall foliage   __**e.** orchards
__**c.** recruits

67a

a, b

pre sen ti ment (pri zen′ tə mənt)

Joan of Arc was burned at the stake. An English soldier watching had a **presentiment**.

Write a definition or synonym:

92a

a, c

con vene (kən vēn′)

Court **convened** to hear Mrs. Bast's defense only two days after her arrest. Salinger thought that was unusual.

Write a definition or synonym:

117b

The **garish** orange and red neon lights made a sharp contrast to the dimly lit alleys where Massey hid. The bright glare of the light "screamed" the presence of cheap, tastelessly decorated taverns. Was this the freedom that Massey had been yearning for? It seemed as unattractive as it was dangerous.

Garish means:
__**a.** ornate
__**b.** elegant
__**c.** expensive
__**d.** gaudy

142b

The contents of many of the pyramids had been so ravaged by looters and by the passage of time that it was difficult to complete an analysis of what remained. The scientists could not supply **definitive** statements until they had studied and analyzed all available information.

Definitive means:
__**a.** decisive
__**b.** infallible
__**c.** momentous
__**d.** dogmatic

160c

a

prag mat ic (prag mat′ik), *adj.* 1 concerned with practical results or values; viewing things in a matter-of-fact way. 2 of or having to do with pragmatism: *a pragmatic philosophy.* [< Latin *pragmaticus* < Greek *pragmatikos* efficient, ultimately < *prassein* do] —**prag mat′i cal ly,** *adv.*

Check the sentence(s) in which **pragmatic** is used correctly.
__a. His pragmatic ways made him a nuisance.
__b. The pragmatic youth was a dreamer.
__c. He was a pragmatic individual who never listened to the opinions of others.

185b

Engrossed as they were in running the government and priesthood of ancient Rome, the **patricians** had little or no contact with the common people.

A **patrician** is:
__a. an aristocrat
__b. a Roman senator
__c. a bureaucrat
__d. an elected official

210b

It's human to dream of revenge on those we feel are taking advantage of us. If we can't triumph directly, we can at least get **vicarious** pleasure from seeing someone else accomplish what we can't accomplish ourselves. That's why almost everyone loves Penny Dreadful.

Vicarious means:
__a. on a small scale
__b. felt by sharing others' experience
__c. having common characteristics
__d. serving to gain vengeance

235a

c

pir ou ette (pir′ ü et′)

Roseann managed to look at her parents as the lead dancer went into a graceful **pirouette.** When she saw how ecstatic her father looked, Roseann felt a twinge of jealousy.

Write a definition or synonym:

260a

, e,
, g

re miss (ri mis′)

In a discussion of Van Gogh's greatness, it would be **remiss** not to acknowledge his brother's emotional and financial support.

Write a definition or synonym:

284c

a

fo ray (fôr′ā, for′ā), *n.* a raid for plunder. —*v.t.* lay waste; plunder; pillage. [< Old French *forrer* to forage]

ANALOGY **foray : pillage ::**
__a. pilgrimage : worship
__b. scrutinize : discover
__c. rove : carnage
__d. quest : verify
__e. sojourn : havoc

17a

e, f

em broil (em broil′)

It has been said that John Adams, our second President, **embroiled** even the most friendly people in arguments.

Write a definition or synonym:

42a

c, e

ed i fice (ed′ ə fis)

The men listened politely while Linda explained the need for a large park within the city limits. The idea really didn't make much sense, they thought. After all, the nearest **edifice** was almost a mile away.

Write a definition or synonym:

67b

As she raised her cross and died, this soldier had a **presentiment** that the tide of battle had turned in France's favor. Events that followed proved her to be correct.

Presentiment means:
__**a.** foreboding
__**b.** admonition
__**c.** message
__**d.** hallucination

92b

Because the judge was punctual, the court **convened** promptly at 10:00 A.M. The courtroom was crowded and noisy as the judge rapped his gavel for attention.

Convene means:
__**a.** adjourn
__**b.** sojourn
__**c.** recess
__**d.** assemble

117c

d

gar ish (ger′ish, gar′ish), *adj.* 1 excessively bright; glaring: *a garish yellow.* 2 obtrusively bright in color; gaudy: *a garish suit.* 3 adorned to excess. [ultimately < obsolete *gaure* to stare] —**gar′ish ly,** *adv.* —**gar′ish ness,** *n.*

Check the sentence(s) in which **garish** is used correctly.
__**a.** My friend speaks in a garish manner.
__**b.** The interior decoration of their home is garish.
__**c.** What a garish bracelet she is wearing!
__**d.** The starlight is garish tonight.
__**e.** We were startled by his garish voice.

142c

a

de fin i tive (di fin′ə tiv), *adj.* 1 that decides or settles a question; conclusive; final: *She appealed to the Supreme Court for a definitive answer.* 2 authoritative; completely reliable. 3 limiting; defining. —**de fin′i tive ly,** *adv.* —**de fin′i tive ness,** *n.*

Check the sentence(s) in which **definitive** is used correctly.
__**a.** *This* is a definitive when it precedes a noun.
__**b.** The day has a definitive feeling of autumn.
__**c.** I waited in vain for a definitive reply.

284b

Cortez's soldiers made **forays** on the Aztec settlements in Mexico, taking food as well as priceless art objects. This, eventually, led to retaliation by the Aztecs.

Foray means:
- __a. a raid for plunder
- __b. an exploration
- __c. a skirmish
- __d. a sojourn

259c

fis cal (fis′kəl), *adj.* 1 of or having to do with financial matters; financial. See **financial** for synonym study. 2 having to do with public finance: *the government's fiscal policy.* [< Latin *fiscalis* < *fiscus* purse] —**fis′cal-ly,** *adv.*

d

Which of the following are concerned with **fiscal** matters?
- __a. football teams
- __b. Federal Reserve Banks
- __c. U.S. State Department
- __d. Bureau of Weights and Measures
- __e. U.S. Treasury
- __f. investment bankers
- __g. accounting departments

234c

ap a thy (ap′ə thē), *n., pl.* **-thies.** 1 lack of interest in or desire for activity; indifference. See **indifference** for synonym study. 2 lack of feeling. [< Greek *apatheia* < *a-* without + *pathos* feeling]

c

ANALOGY **apathy : interest ::**
- __a. pulverize : saturate
- __b. fallacy : error
- __c. misery : ecstasy
- __d. turmoil : trouble
- __e. insomnia : vigil

210a

vi car i ous (vī ker′ē əs, vi ker′ē əs)

a, b

Just before his cartoons became famous, Tim told me that people always feel **vicarious** pleasure in seeing the underdog win.

Write a definition or synonym:

185a

pa tri cian (pə trish′ən)

1. b
2. b

Visiting the ancient amphitheater, the Circus Maximus, one can almost see the **patricians** of ancient Rome.

Write a definition or synonym:

160b

The writers of the Constitution were not impractical romanticists but men of a **pragmatic** turn of mind. This is substantiated by the fact that the Constitution has remained a workable document for governing a nation.

A synonym for **pragmatic** is:
- __a. practical
- __b. fastidious
- __c. prodigious
- __d. ethereal

17b

During Adams' term in office the legislative and executive offices frequently seemed to be **embroiled** in struggles over one issue or another. During subsequent administrations, the various branches of the government were able to keep their functions better separated.

A synonym for **embroil** is:

___**a.** exclude
___**b.** entangle
___**c.** engross
___**d.** outlaw

42b

"Our city is growing too fast," Linda said. "If we continue to build at this rate, there will be no trees left in a few years. All the land will be covered with your stately homes, your huge factories, and similar **edifices**."

The meaning of **edifice** is:

___**a.** a new structure
___**b.** an imposing building
___**c.** a private residence
___**d.** a domed church

---

a

67c

pre sen ti ment (pri zen′tə mənt), *n.* a feeling or impression that something, especially something evil, is about to happen; vague sense of approaching misfortune; foreboding.

Check the sentence(s) in which a form of **presentiment** is used correctly.

___**a.** One may feel a presentiment for no apparent reason.
___**b.** He came bearing presentiments.
___**c.** When a plane is overdue, airport personnel may have a presentiment.
___**d.** The dark clouds were a presentiment of an approaching hurricane.

---

d

92c

con vene (kən vēn′), *v.*, **-vened, -ven ing.** —*v.i.* meet for some purpose; gather together; assemble: *Congress convenes in the Capitol at Washington, D.C., at least once a year.* —*v.t.* call together (members of an organization, etc.). [< Latin *convenire* < *com-* together + *venire* come] —**con ven′er,** *n.*

Which of the following words mean the *opposite* of **convene**?

___**a.** dissent   ___**d.** dissuade
___**b.** disperse   ___**e.** disband
___**c.** dissolve   ___**f.** dissect

---

b, c

118a

lon gev i ty (lon jev′ ə tē)

Before his escape plans backfired, Massey had been confident that he would achieve **longevity**.

Write a definition or synonym:

---

a, c

143a

de fray (di frā′)

In some cases universities or governments **defrayed** the expenses of excavating the pyramids.

Write a definition or synonym:

160a

prag mat ic (prag mat′ ik)

The Constitution has proved to be a **pragmatic** instrument of government.

Write a definition or synonym:

b, c

184c

i tin e rar y (ī tin′ə rer′ē, i tin′ə rer′ē), *n.,* *pl.* **-rar ies,** *adj.* —*n.* **1** route of travel; plan of travel. **2** record of travel. **3** guidebook for travelers. —*adj.* **1** of traveling or routes of travel. **2** itinerant.

b

1. You would be likely to have an **itinerary** if you were:
   __**a.** on your way to school
   __**b.** on a shopping trip
   __**c.** in a track meet
2. Which of the following has an **itinerary** job?
   __**a.** temporary Christmas employee
   __**b.** traveling salesman
   __**c.** typist

209c

sub ser vi ent (səb sėr′vē ənt), *adj.* **1** slavishly polite and obedient; tamely submissive; servile. **2** useful as a means to help a purpose or end; serviceable. —**sub ser′vi ent ly,** *adv.*

c

Check the sentence(s) in which a form of **subservient** is used correctly.
__**a.** Her subservient manner thinly disguised her contempt for them.
__**b.** In societies where there is a caste system, many are forced to be subservient.
__**c.** He was hired as a subservient clerk in the store.
__**d.** Her subservients came to attention and saluted as she entered the room.

234b

Apathy in an audience can make the most enthusiastic performers lose heart. A responsive audience, on the other hand, will make the performers work even harder to please.

Another word for **apathy** is:
__**a.** somnolence
__**b.** animosity
__**c.** indifference
__**d.** anesthesia

259b

Van Gogh received substantial **fiscal** assistance from his brother Theodor. Without Theodor's gifts of money and his numerous loans, Van Gogh would not have been able to survive.

Fiscal means:
__**a.** pragmatic
__**b.** affluent
__**c.** commercial
__**d.** financial

284a

fo ray (fôr′ ā, for′ ā)

In the Aztec ruins of Mexico, evidence of Spanish **forays** has been found.

Write a definition or synonym:

b, c
a, b

b

17c

em broil (em broil′), v.t. 1 involve (a person, country, etc.) in a quarrel. 2 throw (affairs, etc.) into a state of confusion. [< French *embrouiller* < *en-* in + *brouiller* to broil] —em broil′ment, n.

In which of the following is one likely to become **embroiled**?
_a. a friendly discussion
_b. an argument
_c. a minister's sermon
_d. a fund-raising speech

---

b

42c

ed i fice (ed′ə fis), n. a building, especially a large or impressive one, such as a cathedral, palace, or temple. See **building** for synonym study. [< Old French < Latin *aedificium* < *aedificare* build < *aedis* a dwelling, temple + *facere* make]

Which of the following buildings might correctly be termed **edifices**?
_a. Empire State Building
_b. Washington Monument
_c. Grand Central Station
_d. St. Patrick's Cathedral
_e. Golden Gate Bridge
_f. a bungalow

---

a, c

68a

ret ro spect (ret′ rə spekt)

In **retrospect**, it is obvious that Joan of Arc was endowed with special qualities.

Write a definition or synonym:

---

c, e

93a

caus tic (kô′ stik)

Salinger noticed that the prosecuting attorney made **caustic** remarks about Mrs. Bast every chance he could get.

Write a definition or synonym:

118b

As he shivered in the alley, Massey's thoughts turned to his hopes for **longevity**. He smiled bitterly at his optimism, wondering now whether he would survive the night.

Longevity means:
_a. good health
_b. virility
_c. moderation
_d. long life

143b

In other cases, private individuals hired the engineers, workmen, and scientists and **defrayed** the expense of their wages themselves.

Defray means:
_a. determine
_b. liquidate
_c. pay
_d. repay

283c

a

e rode (i rōd'), v., e rod ed, e rod ing.
—v.t. 1 eat away gradually; eat into: *Running water erodes soil and rocks.* 2 form by a gradual eating or wearing away: *The stream eroded a channel in the solid rock.*
—v.i. be worn away or eaten out. [< Latin *erodere* < *ex-* away + *rodere* gnaw]

1. Which of the following might be eroded?
__a. an apple __b. a hillside __c. a statue

2. Which of the following was (were) created by erosion?
__a. the Grand Canyon
__b. the White Cliffs of Dover
__c. the faces of Presidents on Mt. Rushmore

259a

c, d

fis cal (fis' kəl)

Van Gogh was plagued by **fiscal** problems all of his life.

Write a definition or synonym:

234a

b, c

ap a thy (ap' ə thē)

There was certainly no **apathy** in the audience.

Write a definition or synonym:

209b

Many of Tim's most enthusiastic readers are adults. Like Penny, they dream of rising above forces which keep them in **subservient** positions. They, too, would like to use their wits to become the equal of those who consider them subordinate.

Subservient means:
__a. destitute
__b. impassive
__c. submissive
__d. indebted to

184b

The Victor Emmanuel Monument is included in all the guided tours of Rome. Regardless of your **itinerary**, you may expect to see it.

The meaning of **itinerary** is:
__a. financial condition
__b. route of travel
__c. place of origin
__d. individual taste

159c

c

de riv a tive (di riv'ə tiv), *adj.* coming from a source; not original; derived. —*n.* 1 something derived. 2 word formed by adding a prefix or suffix to another word. 3 a chemical substance obtained from another by modification or by partial substitution of components: *Acetic acid is a derivative of alcohol.* 4 (in mathematics) the instantaneous rate of change of a function with respect to its variable. —de riv'a tive ly, *adv.*

Check the sentence(s) in which a form of **derivative** is used correctly.
__a. We are the derivatives of our offspring.
__b. Aniline, used in making dyes, is a derivative of coal tar.
__c. *Girlish* is a derivative of *girl.*

18a

b

mag nan i mous (mag nan′ ə məs)

Thomas Jefferson, the drafter of the Declaration of Independence, and our third President, was very **magnanimous**.

Write a definition or synonym:

43a

e, d

her biv or ous (hėr′ biv′ ər əs)

"And what about the animals?" Linda continued. "Did you ever stop to think that most of our wild animals are **herbivorous**?"

Write a definition or synonym:

68b

Judgements made in **retrospect** are likely to be more rational than those made in the heat of the moment. In the case of Joan of Arc, 500 years passed before she was officially dignified by the Church.

Retrospect means:
__a. looking inward
__b. looking back
__c. looking beyond
__d. looking forward

93b

The prosecutor's contemptuous sneer matched his **caustic** remarks. Salinger felt this attitude was uncalled for.

Caustic means:
__a. sarcastic
__b. erroneous
__c. deceitful
__d. aggressive

118c

d

lon gev i ty (lon jev′ə tē), *n.* 1 long life. 2 length or duration of life. [< Late Latin *longaevitatem* < *longaevus* long-lived < *longus* long + *aevum* age]

In which sentence(s) is **longevity** used correctly?
__a. Longevity the Queen!
__b. The family is known for longevity among its members.
__c. I wish you longevity.
__d. The longevity of the party made the hostess very tired.

143c

c

de fray (di frā′), *v.t.* pay (costs or expenses): *The expenses of national parks are defrayed by the taxpayers.* [< Middle French *desfraier* < *de-* out + *frais* costs] —**de fray′a ble,** *adj.* —**de fray′er,** *n.*

Check the sentence(s) in which **defray** can be correctly substituted for the italicized word.
__a. He could not *pay* for the groceries.
__b. Her parents offered to *pay* the expenses of her trip.
__c. The criminal had to *pay* the extreme penalty.

283b

Many of the carvings found above ground have been so badly **eroded** by wind and rain that their decorations and inscriptions are barely distinguishable.

Erode means:

___a. wear away
___b. obliterate
___c. suffuse
___d. change in nature

258c

ar·chive (är′kīv), n. Usually, **archives,** pl. 1 place where public records or historical documents are kept. 2 the public records or historical documents kept in such a place. [< Latin *archivum* < Greek *archeia* < *arché* government]

b

Which of the following probably would be most interested in **archives?**

___a. disc jockey
___b. historian
___c. reporter
___d. F.B.I. agent
___e. gym teacher

233c

tac·i·turn (tas′ə tėrn′), adj. speaking very little; not fond of talking. See silent for synonym study. [< Latin *taciturnus* < *taci-tum* unspoken, tacit] —**tac′i·turn′ly,** adv.

d

A **taciturn** person would probably *not* make a good:

___a. librarian
___b. politician
___c. salesperson
___d. secret service agent
___e. monk

209a

sub ser vi ent (sab sėr′ vē ənt)

At first, Tim expected Penny to be a heroine to children her own age. Like Penny, young children are often expected to play a **subservient** role.

Write a definition or synonym:

b, c

184a

i tin e rar y (ī tin′ ə rer′ ē, i tin′ ə rer′ ē)

Almost every **itinerary** of Rome includes the Victor Emmanuel Monument.

Write a definition or synonym:

c, e,
3, h

159b

The constitutions of some European countries are **derivatives.** Their authors borrowed many of the principles originated by the founders of the Constitution of the United States.

Derivative means:

___a. repetition
___b. reminiscent expression
___c. something not original
___d. identical object

18b

The noble ideas and deeds that Jefferson fostered will always impel us to think of him as one of our most **magnanimous** Presidents. He was seldom selfish or petty in word or in action.

A synonym for **magnanimous** is:
__a. indispensable
__b. trustworthy
__c. high-minded
__d. astute

43b

"How can the **herbivorous** animals survive without leaves and grasses to eat?" Linda demanded. "We can't let animals and grass stand in the way of progress!" one of the men declared.

Herbivorous means:
__a. living on flesh
__b. eating herbs and spices
__c. feeding on grass and plants
__d. belonging to a group of animals

68c

b

ret ro spect (ret′rə spekt), *n.* 1 survey of past time, events, etc.; thinking about the past. 2 **in retrospect,** when looking back. —*v.t.* think of (something past). [< Latin *retro-* back + *specere* to look]

1. Check the words that mean about the same as **retrospect.**
   __a. oblivion   __d. anticipation
   __b. hindsight   __e. afterthought
   __c. foresight   __f. review
2. You are seeing something in **retrospect** when you are:
   __a. focusing   __c. reminiscing
   __b. contemplating

93c

a

caus tic (kô′stik), *n.* substance that burns or destroys flesh; corrosive substance. —*adj.* 1 that burns or destroys flesh; corrosive. Lye is caustic soda or caustic potash. 2 very critical or sarcastic; stinging; biting: *The coach's caustic remarks made the football players angry.* [< Latin *causticus* < Greek *kaustikos* < *kaiein* to burn] —**caus′ti cal ly,** *adv.*

1. A **caustic** would be useful for which of the following?
   __a. removing grease from one's hands
   __b. cleaning a clogged drain
   __c. washing laundry
   __d. cleaning an oven
2. **Caustic** comments might be found in:
   __a. a syndicated newspaper column
   __b. a bedtime story
   __c. a political satire

119a

b, c

lim bo (lim′ bō)

After midnight the streets became deserted and the sounds of the city died away. Massey began to think he was trapped in a **limbo**.

Write a definition or synonym:

144a

b

de funct (di fungkt′)

Near the Valley of the Kings, where many of the ancient Pharaohs were laid to rest, several **defunct** villages were discovered in the shifting sands.

Write a definition or synonym:

159a

de riv a tive (di riv′ə tiv)

The U.S. Constitution is not a derivative.

Write a definition or synonym:

1. b
2. a
3. d
4. c

183c

dec a dence (dek′ə dəns, di kād′ns), *n.* a falling off; growing worse; decline; decay: *The decadence of morals was one of the causes of the fall of Rome.* [< Middle French *décadence* < Medieval Latin *decadentia* < Latin *de-* + *cadere* to fall]

c

Which words mean the *opposite* of **decadence**?

___ **a.** enhancement   ___ **e.** improvement
___ **b.** deterioration   ___ **f.** resurrection
___ **c.** restoration   ___ **g.** revival
___ **d.** devastation   ___ **h.** rejuvenation

208c

im po tent (im′pə tənt), *adj.* 1 not having power; helpless: *We were impotent against the force of the tornado.* 2 (of males) incapable of having sexual intercourse. —im′po tent ly, *adv.*

a

Check the sentence(s) in which **impotent** is used correctly.

___ **a.** The invalid could take only toast and impotent tea.
___ **b.** The ruler proved impotent when a crisis arose.
___ **c.** When I lose my temper, I become impotent with fury.

233b

Taking the part of a **taciturn** individual suited the comedian perfectly. His facial expressions were so funny he did not have to say a word to get laughs from the audience.

Taciturn means:

___ **a.** sardonic
___ **b.** ludicrous
___ **c.** staid
___ **d.** silent

258b

Archives serve both a legal and historical service for a community. Without them, many important documents would be lost or inaccessible.

Archives means:

___ **a.** history of a town
___ **b.** place for public records
___ **c.** safe-deposit vault
___ **d.** ancient building

283a

e rode (i rōd′)

The surfaces of many archaeological finds have been badly **eroded.**

c, d

Write a definition or synonym:

18c

c

mag nan i mous (mag nan′ə məs), *adj.*
1 noble in soul or mind; generous in forgiving; free from mean or petty feelings or acts;
unselfish. 2 showing or arising from a generous spirit: *a magnanimous attitude toward a
conquered enemy.* [< Latin *magnanimus*
< *magnus* great + *animus* spirit] —**mag-
nan′i mous ly,** *adv.* —**mag nan′i mous-
ness,** *n.*

Which of the following does one need in order to be
magnanimous?
__a. wealth
__b. sense of humor
__c. education
__d. high ideals

43c

c

her biv or ous (hėr′biv′ər əs), *adj.*
1 feeding on grass or other plants. 2 of or
belonging to the herbivores. [< New Latin
herbivorus < Latin *herba* herb + *vorare*
devour]

ANALOGY herbivorous : carnivorous ::
__a. limousine : livery
__b. malicious : evil
__c. deer : cat
__d. apprehend : understand
__e. sublime : superficial

69a

b, e,
f
c

sanc ti fy (sangk′ tə fī)

It is generally recognized now that the sacrifices and
noble deeds of Joan of Arc had **sanctified** her life.

Write a definition or synonym:

94a

b, d
a, c

al lege (ə lej′)

Salinger also noticed that the **alleged** murderess
sat quietly through the trial with her hands folded in
her lap.

Write a definition or synonym:

119b

Massey had found a place where he was unknown
and unnoticed. But even if he lasted the night in this
limbo, cast aside and forgotten like the trash
and debris around him, he would have been better
off back on the prison farm.

Limbo means:
__a. safe shelter
__b. place for forgotten people and things
__c. state of physical deterioration
__d. dangerous place, as a jungle, etc.

144b

A **defunct** village or two did not interest the
local government. These ruins had been dead and
buried for ages, and they were too poor to contain
any treasure.

Defunct means:
__a. dead
__b. nonexistent
__c. passé
__d. deferred

b

158c   **par a gon** (par′ə gon), *n.* model of excellence or perfection. [< Middle French, comparison < Italian *paragone* touchstone < Greek *parakonan* to whet < *para*-¹ + *akonē* whetstone]

Each of the people in the first column can be considered a **paragon** of one item in the second column.

1. __ Helen of Troy	**a.**	eloquence
2. __ Patrick Henry	**b.**	beauty
3. __ Nathan Hale	**c.**	inventiveness
4. __ Thomas Edison	**d.**	patriotism

183b

According to some historians, the decline of ancient Rome was partly caused by moral **decadence**. This softening of morality contributed to the eventual downfall of the empire, making it easy prey for the armies of toughened, disciplined barbarians.

Decadence means:
__**a.** code
__**b.** status
__**c.** decay
__**d.** condition

208b

The pleasure Penny's readers take in seeing her triumph over her enemies is the age-old joy of witnessing the weak render the strong **impotent**. We laugh with Penny to see her enemies deprived of their power to hurt her.

A synonym for **impotent** is:
__**a.** helpless
__**b.** entangled
__**c.** snared
__**d.** enraged

233a

a, c

tac i turn (tas′ ə tėrn)

A very funny comedian played the role of a **taciturn** old man. Standing in the wings, Roseann could see her parents laughing heartily.

Write a definition or synonym:

258a

, c, g

ar chive (är′ kīv)

Vincent's letters to his brother Theodor are part of the Van Gogh **archives**.

Write a definition or synonym:

282c   **ves tige** (ves′tij), *n.* **1** a slight remnant; trace; mark: *Ghost stories are vestiges of a former widespread belief in ghosts.* See **trace**¹ for synonym study. **2** (in biology) a part, organ, etc., that is no longer fully developed or useful but performed a definite function in an earlier stage of the existence of the same organism or in lower preceding organisms. **3** RARE. footprint or track. [< French < Latin *vestigium* footprint]

d

Which of the following can correctly be called **vestiges**?
__**a.** the human appendix
__**b.** the Statue of Liberty
__**c.** Indian arrowheads
__**d.** ashes of a dead fire
__**e.** the League of Nations

19a

pro cras ti nate (prō kras′ tə nāt)

All in all, the U.S. Presidents have been men who did not **procrastinate** in the performance of their constitutional duties.

d

Write a definition or synonym:

44a

lan guid (lang′ gwid)

Linda thought the demeanor of most of the businessmen was disappointingly **languid**.

c

Write a definition or synonym:

69b

In 1920, the Roman Catholic Church **sanctified** Joan. Long before this official act, however, countless people had considered Joan a truly holy person.

Sanctify means:
__a. sacrifice
__b. cite
__c. consecrate
__d. reward

94b

Since Mrs. Bast had not been proven guilty, the prosecutor could only **allege** that she had poisoned her husband. Unfortunately, the local newspapers treated the **alleged** crime as though it had been established as fact.

Allege means:
__a. surmise
__b. claim
__c. infer
__d. hope

119c

b

lim bo (lim′bō), *n.* 1 Often, **Limbo.** (in Roman Catholic theology) a place for those who have not received the grace of Christ while living, and yet have not deserved the punishment of willful and impenitent sinners. 2 place for persons and things forgotten, cast aside, or out of date: *The belief that the earth is flat belongs to the limbo of outworn ideas.* 3 prison; jail; confinement. [< Latin *(in) limbo* (on) the edge]

Which of the following is (are) likely to be in **limbo** (or **Limbo**)?
__a. a habitual criminal
__b. angels
__c. a baby who died before being baptized
__d. an enterprising businessman
__e. the theory that the sun revolves around the earth
__f. a dope addict

144c

a

de funct (di fungkt′), *adj.* no longer in existence; dead; extinct. [< Latin *defunctum* finished < *de-* + *fungi* perform]

Which words mean the *opposite* of **defunct**?
__a. extinguished   __e. vital
__b. exterminated   __f. primeval
__c. obsolete   __g. existing
__d. animated   __h. somnolent

158b

The Constitution was such a **paragon** that many European countries, including France, followed it in setting forth the objectives of democratic government.

Paragon means:
__**a.** an object of renown
__**b.** a model of perfection
__**c.** a good imitation
__**d.** a precedent

183a

b, e
a

dec a dence (dek′ ə dəns, di kād′ ns)

The history books speak of the **decadence** of ancient Rome.

Write a definition or synonym:

208a

a, d,
e, f

im po tent (im′ pə tənt)

Without exception, Penny's enemies are left raging or **impotent**.

Write a definition or synonym:

232c

b

par o dy (par′ə dē), *n., pl.* **-dies,** *v.,* **-died, -dy ing.** —*n.* 1 a humorous imitation of a serious writing. A parody follows the form of the original, but often changes its sense to nonsense in order to ridicule the writer's characteristics. 2 a poor imitation. 3 a musical composition making fun of another. —*v.t.* 1 ridicule by imitating; make a parody on. 2 imitate poorly. [< Greek *parōidia* < *para-¹* + *ōidē* song]

Check the sentence(s) in which a form of **parody** is used correctly.
__**a.** Hemingway's clipped prose is often parodied by humorists.
__**b.** The forgery was an exact parody of the original painting.
__**c.** The author merely parodied real people in his inept writings.

257c

b

festoon (def. 1)

fes toon (fe stün′), *n.* 1 a string or chain of flowers, leaves, ribbons, etc., hanging in a curve between two points: *The bunting was draped on the wall in colorful festoons.* 2 a carved or molded ornament like this on furniture, pottery, architectural work, etc. —*v.t.* 1 decorate with festoons. 2 form into festoons; hang in curves. [< French *feston* < Italian *festone*]

Something that is **festooned** would be:
__**a.** stark   __**e.** made fun of
__**b.** adorned   __**f.** inane
__**c.** ornamented   __**g.** ornate
__**d.** concealed

282b

Throughout the world are scattered monuments which stand alone and mysterious, offering only a hint of the culture that gave them being. The giant sculptures on Easter Island, for example, are **vestiges** of a lost civilization.

A **vestige** is:
__**a.** an artifact
__**b.** a symbol
__**c.** a hypothesis
__**d.** a trace

114

19b

The office of President is not one in which a person can **procrastinate**. Decisions must often be made promptly in order to be effective.

A synonym for **procrastinate** is:
—**a.** decide
—**b.** refuse
—**c.** delay
—**d.** vacillate

44b

Linda tried to capture the interest of the businessmen. She appealed to their better natures, their sense of responsibility, and their reputation as progressive leaders. They merely nodded and yawned politely, regarding Linda with bored, **languid** eyes.

Languid means:
—**a.** without anger
—**b.** indifferent
—**c.** insensible
—**d.** impassive

69c

c

sanc ti fy (sangk′tə fī), v.t., -fied, -fy ing. 1 make holy; make legitimate or binding by a religious sanction: *sanctify a marriage.* 2 set apart as sacred; observe as holy: *"Lord, sanctify this our offering to Thy use."* 3 make right; justify or sanction. [< Latin *sanctificare* < *sanctus* holy + *facere* to make. See SAINT.] —**sanc′ti fi′er,** n.

ANALOGY sanctify : saint :: ordain :
—**a.** replica
—**b.** minister
—**c.** isthmus
—**d.** envoy
—**e.** accomplice

94c

b

al lege (ə lej′), v.t., -leged, -leg ing. 1 state positively; assert; declare. 2 assert without proof; claim. 3 give or bring forward as a reason, argument, or excuse. [< Latin *allegare* to cite < *ad-* to + *legare* to commission] —**al lege′a ble,** adj. —**al leg′er,** n.

Check the sentence(s) in which a form of **allege** is used correctly.
—**a.** The man alleged his innocence.
—**b.** She alleged that illness had caused her absence.
—**c.** One witness says he can allege his alibi.
—**d.** A biographer alleges his or her sources in a bibliography.

120a

a, c,
e, f

ig no ble (ig nō′ bəl)

As Massey thought about the morning and his almost certain discovery, his attempt to escape began to seem more and more **ignoble**.

Write a definition or synonym:

145a

e, g

come ly (kum′ lē)

Objects like the statue of the **comely** face of Queen Nefertiti were of interest to everyone. The small statue of the ancient queen is perhaps the most famous piece of ancient Egyptian sculpture in the world.

Write a definition or synonym:

282a

e

ves·tige (ves′tij)

After this initial discovery, other **vestiges** of ancient cultures were found.

Write a definition or synonym:

257b

There was a time when the inner walls of many buildings were decorated with bands of sculptured garlands that linked one wall with the next. These **festoons** often appeared in the paintings of the earlier nineteenth century.

A **festoon** is:

___a. a bouquet of flowers
___b. a hanging curved decoration
___c. an outmoded style
___d. a theme or motif

232b

In this **parody**, a plot and cast of characters typical of the nineteen-twenties were used. Everything was exaggerated just enough to be ludicrous. Serious lines brought chuckles, and "asides" to the audience brought howls of laughter.

A **parody** is:

___a. a musical show
___b. a burlesque
___c. a replica
___d. a melodrama

207c

a

ex·tri·cate (ek′stra kāt), v.t., -cat·ed, -cat·ing. set free (from entanglements, difficulties, embarrassing situations, etc.); re-lease: *He extricated his younger brother from the barbed-wire fence.* [< Latin *extricatum* freed from perplexities < *ex*- out of + *tricae* perplexities] —ex/tri·ca'tion, n.

From which of the following can one be extricated?

___a. a dilemma
___b. an illness
___c. water
___d. a predicament
___e. a wrecked automobile
___f. financial debt
___g. one's backyard

182c

a

raze (rāz), v.t., razed, raz·ing. tear down; destroy completely; demolish. [< Middle French *raser* to scrape, ultimately < Latin *radere*]

1. Which of the following can be razed?
___a. a lawn
___b. a forest
___c. a point
___d. a beard
___e. a house
___f. a hem

2. A synonym for raze is:
___a. devastate
___b. nullify
___c. erode

158a

c

par·a·gon (par′a gon)

Once finished, the Constitution was a **paragon** among documents of its kind.

Write a definition or synonym:

19c

c

pro cras ti nate (prō kras′tə nāt), v.i., v.t., -nat ed, -nat ing. put things off until later; delay, especially repeatedly. [< Latin *procrastinatum* postponed, ultimately < *pro-* forward + *cras* tomorrow] —pro cras′ti na′tion, n. —pro cras′ti na′tor, n.

Which might cause one to **procrastinate**?
___a. a medical checkup
___b. paying the bills
___c. buying the groceries
___d. writing a letter
___e. answering the telephone

44c

b

lan guid (lang′gwid), adj. 1 without energy; drooping; weak; weary: *A hot, sticky day makes a person feel languid.* 2 without interest or enthusiasm; indifferent; listless. 3 not brisk or lively; sluggish; dull. [< Latin *languidus* < *languere* be faint] —lan′guid ly, adv. —lan′guid ness, n.

Check the sentence(s) in which a form of **languid** is used correctly.
___a. The actors were roundly panned by the critics for their languid performances.
___b. This tea is too languid.
___c. The model strolled languidly about the showroom.
___d. My coat is languid.

70a

b

post hu mous (pos′ chə məs)

Joan of Arc was given **posthumous** recognition.

Write a definition or synonym:

95a

a, b

vin di cate (vin′ də kāt)

Salinger was a little disappointed at the efforts of the defense attorney to **vindicate** Mrs. Bast. Salinger began to think he was the only person who was convinced of her innocence.

Write a definition or synonym:

120b

Finally, Massey walked into a bar and tried to surrender to the police. No one looking at his filth and misery would believe he had the strength or will to have committed a crime or escaped from prison. It was an **ignoble** end to Massey's dream of freedom. He and his dream had been degraded and made contemptible.

Ignoble means:
___a. incurable
___b. vulgar
___c. dishonorable
___d. ignorant

145b

Not all the statues and wall-drawings depict faces with a pleasant appearance. However, the small statue of Nefertiti has been duplicated and exhibited in museums around the world. Almost everyone responds to her **comely** features.

Comely means:
___a. vivid
___b. aesthetic
___c. symmetrical
___d. attractive

157c

ha·rangue (hə rang´), n., v., -rangued,
-rangu·ing. —n. 1 a noisy, vehement
speech. 2 a long, pompous, formal speech.
—v.t. address (someone) with a harangue.
—v.i. deliver a harangue. [< Middle French]
—ha·rangu´er, n.

ANALOGY harangue : converse ::
__a. scrimmage : reimburse
__b. narrate : tell
__c. enthrall : interest
__d. scrutinize : resemble
__e. biology : dissect

182b

Italy lost many of its most priceless antiquities
when bombs razed the towns of the Italian
countryside. Beautiful buildings, statues, and other
works of art were smashed and reduced to rubble.

Raze means:
__a. demolish
__b. plunder
__c. dismantle
__d. strike

207b

It doesn't matter what kind of a mess Penny gets
herself into. If someone else can't be tricked into
setting her free from her difficulties, Penny can
always manage to extricate herself.

Extricate means:
__a. disentangle
__b. escape
__c. sever
__d. excavate

232a

par·o·dy (par´ə dē)

Roseann's first show was a parody of the
old-fashioned musical comedies. The lead singers
and dancers were top stars. Even the boys and girls
in the chorus with Roseann were first-rate.

Write a definition or synonym:

257a

fes·toon (fe stün´)

Van Gogh never used devices such as the
festoons that were traditional in earlier
nineteenth-century art.

Write a definition or synonym:

281c

in·de·ter·mi·nate (in/di ter/mə nit), adj.
1 not determined; not definite or fixed; indefinite; vague. 2 having flowers which arise
from axillary buds so that the tip continues to
grow forming new bracts and flowers; race-
mose. —in/de·ter/mi·nate·ly, adv.
—in/de·ter/mi·nate·ness, n.

ANALOGY indeterminate : certain ::
__a. titanic : abject
__b. gauche : awkward
__c. tutelage : collegiate
__d. describe : characterize
__e. obscure : enlighten

20a

c, e

in ter mi na ble (in tėr′ mə nə bəl)

The work of a President seems **interminable**.

Write a definition or synonym:

45a

a, c

ad mon ish (ad mon′ ish)

Finally, one of the men **admonished** Linda for her dream of a huge park within the city limits.

Write a definition or synonym:

70b

Many people attain only **posthumous** fame. Society is often too late in recognizing and rewarding greatness.

Posthumous means:
__a. short-lived
__b. after proof
__c. belated
__d. after death

95b

Salinger realized that Mrs. Bast must be completely **vindicated** by the jury. If there was the slightest suggestion of doubt about her innocence, she would never again be accepted by the townspeople.

Another word for **vindicate** is:
__a. corroborate
__b. prove
__c. avenge
__d. clear

120c

c

ig no ble (ig nō′bəl), *adj.* 1 without honor; disgraceful; base: *To betray a friend is ignoble.* 2 not of noble birth or position; humble. [< Latin *ignobilis* < *in-* not + *nobilis* noble] —**ig no′ble ness**, *n.* —**ig no′bly**, *adv.*

1. Which of the following words mean about the *opposite* of **ignoble**?
    __a. intelligent   __d. humble
    __b. estimable   __e. magnanimous
    __c. depraved
2. Which of the following can be considered **ignoble**?
    __a. failing an examination
    __b. forgetting to deliver a message
    __c. cheating on an examination

145c

d

come ly (kum′lē), *adj.*, **-li er**, **-li est.** 1 pleasant to look at; attractive. 2 fitting; suitable; proper. [Old English *cȳmlic*]

1. Check the word that is closest in meaning to **comely**.
    __a. elegant   __d. fascinating
    __b. gorgeous   __e. beautiful
    __c. pretty
2. Which might be described as **comely**?
    __a. a sunset   __b. a child   __c. a deed

157b

Members **harangued** each other on occasion. Voices would rise dramatically when it came to deciding on the powers to be given to the President, for this was a subject about which there was much disagreement.

The meaning of **harangue** is:
___**a.** interrupt frequently
___**b.** address in a noisy speech
___**c.** reprove
___**d.** show contempt for

182a

, d

raze (rāz)

Unlike some of the surrounding areas, Rome was not **razed** during World War II.

Write a definition or synonym:

207a

, d

ex tri cate (ek′ strə kāt)

No matter what the danger is, Penny always manages to **extricate** herself in the nick of time.

Write a definition or synonym:

231c **dif fi dent** (dif′ə dənt), *adj.* lacking in self-confidence; shy. [< Latin *diffidentem* < *dis-* + *fidere* to trust] —**dif′fi dent ly,** *adv.*

c

A **diffident** person would probably be:
___**a.** reticent   ___**e.** haughty
___**b.** voluble   ___**f.** hesitant
___**c.** vociferous   ___**g.** vacillating
___**d.** shameless   ___**h.** bored

256c **vo lup tu ous** (və lup′chü əs), *adj.* 1 caring much for the pleasures of the senses. 2 giving pleasure to the senses: *voluptuous music, voluptuous beauty.* [< Latin *voluptuosus* < *voluptas* pleasure] —**vo lup′tu ous ly,** *adv.* —**vo lup′tu ous ness,** *n.*

b

ANALOGY **voluptuous : senses ::**
___**a.** wary : cautious
___**b.** relevant : pertinent
___**c.** intellectual : mind
___**d.** pseudo : false
___**e.** prodigy : bigot

281b

The **indeterminate** origin of the stone (or stele) led to considerable speculation. Some saw in the design a resemblance to artwork found in the Pacific islands. Others said that the designers were members of one of the lost tribes of Israel, or even survivors from the legendary Atlantis.

Indeterminate means:
___**a.** indefinite
___**b.** dubious
___**c.** ultimate
___**d.** primeval

120

20b

A President must have a great deal of energy, since the tasks of the office are virtually **interminable.** From the beginning to the end of a four-year term, the work is never-ending.

A synonym for **interminable** is:
__**a.** unrewarding
__**b.** complex
__**c.** insoluble
__**d.** endless

45b

In turn, Linda **admonished** the city leaders for being selfish and shortsighted. While she was scolding them, she urged them not to forget their duty to future generations of city dwellers.

Admonish means:
__**a.** stipulate
__**b.** reprove
__**c.** intimidate
__**d.** orient

70c

d

post hu mous (pos′chə məs), *adj.*
1 happening after death: *posthumous fame.*
2 published after the death of the author: *a posthumous book.* 3 born after the death of the father: *a posthumous daughter.* [< Late Latin *posthumus,* variant of Latin *post-umus* last born, originally superlative of *posterus* coming after] —**post′hu mous ly,** *adv.*

Which of the following is most likely to be **posthumous**?
__**a.** award to a policeman who had been shot through the heart while chasing a robber
__**b.** an award for good behavior
__**c.** a first novel
__**d.** the second of three sons
__**e.** a compost pile
__**f.** good citizenship award

95c

d

vin di cate (vin′də kāt), *v.t.,* **-cat ed, -cat ing.** 1 clear from suspicion, dishonor, a hint or charge of wrongdoing, etc.: *The verdict of "Not guilty" vindicated him.* 2 defend successfully against opposition; uphold; justify: *The heir vindicated his claim to the fortune.* 3 assert a claim to; establish possession of. [< Latin *vindicatum* defended, avenged < *vindex* defender, avenger] —**vin′di ca′tor,** *n.*

1. If a law has been **vindicated**, it has been:
__**a.** repealed
__**b.** upheld
__**c.** vetoed
2. The *opposite* of **vindicate** is:
__**a.** suppress
__**b.** condemn
__**c.** liberate

b, e
c

LESSON 13 | The American Experiment

It is sometimes difficult to believe that a country as large and powerful as the United States of America has existed for less than four hundred years. When you remember that some nations, such as Egypt or China, go back several thousand years in history, the year 1607 does not seem very long ago. That year marked the first permanent English settlement in America—in Jamestown, Virginia.

146a

1. c
2. b

o ri fice (ôr′ ə fis, or′ ə fis)

The pyramids are fortress-like monuments with artfully hidden **orifices**.

Write a definition or synonym:

1. d
2. b

a

d

157a

ha rangue (hə rang′)

Sometimes during their work on the document, the founding fathers would **harangue** each other.

Write a definition or synonym:

181c

so journ (*v.* sō′jėrn′, sō jėrn′; *n.* sō′jėrn′), *v.i.* stay for a time: *The Israelites sojourned in the land of Egypt.* —*n.* a brief stay. [< Old French *sojorner*, ultimately < Latin *sub* under + *diurnus* of the day] —**so′journ′-er**, *n.*

1. At which of the following places would one **sojourn**?
   __**a.** one's place of employment
   __**b.** a friend's summer house
   __**c.** the college of one's choice
   __**d.** a vacation resort
   __**e.** in the bathtub
2. The word most applicable to **sojourn** is:
   __**a.** unexpected __**b.** temporary __**c.** unlimited

206c

guile (gīl), *n.* crafty deceit; sly tricks; cunning: *By guile the fox got the cheese from the crow.* See **deceit** for synonym study. [< Old French; of Germanic origin. Related to WILE.]

Which of the following correctly illustrate(s) the meaning of **guile**?
__**a.** A thief breaks into an empty house.
__**b.** A man persuades a rich widow to buy shares of nonexistent stock.
__**c.** A magician performs a trick in which he appears to saw a woman in half.
__**d.** An unscrupulous youth talks his grandfather into making him his sole heir.

231b

When she visited her parents back home, Roseann usually felt quite confident and worldly. Now that her parents were sitting in the audience, Roseann felt **diffident**. It was almost like having stagefright!

Another word for **diffident** is:
__**a.** disinterested
__**b.** provincial
__**c.** shy
__**d.** different

256b

Van Gogh gave such physical beauty and sensual impact to his landscapes that their shape and color are truly **voluptuous.**

Voluptuous means:
__**a.** of world-wide renown
__**b.** pleasing to the senses
__**c.** regarded as ideal
__**d.** unbelievably beautiful

281a

in de ter mi nate (in′ di tėr′ mə nit)

In 1839 a tall and richly carved slab of stone of **indeterminate** origin was discovered in the jungles of Honduras.

Write a definition or synonym:

d

20c

in ter mi na ble (in tėr′mə nə bəl), *adj.*
1 never stopping; unceasing; endless. 2 so long as to seem endless; very long and tiring.
—in ter′mi na bly, *adv.*

ANALOGY interminable : limited ::
___a. local : neighboring
___b. lengthy : brief
___c. time : space
___d. clothing : fashion
___e. final : middle

---

b

45c

ad mon ish (ad mon′ish), *v.t.* 1 advise against something; warn: *admonish a person of danger.* 2 scold gently; reprove: *admonish a student for careless work.* 3 urge strongly; advise earnestly; exhort: *admonish one to be more careful.* 4 recall to a duty overlooked or forgotten; remind. [< *admonition*] —ad-mon′ish er, *n.* —ad mon′ish ment, *n.*

Check the sentence(s) in which **admonished** is used correctly.
___a. His father admonished him to remember his obligation to his family.
___b. She was admonished by the size of the crowd.
___c. He admonished the child that it was time for dinner.
___d. The supervisor admonished the workers for arriving late.

---

a

LESSON

The Age of Chivalry

According to the old tales, King Arthur ruled the people of England back in the sixth century. Arthur and his knights of the Round Table were the finest expression of the ideal of chivalry. While Arthur was away from his kingdom, however, his villainous nephew, Mordred, led a group of rebels against him. Arthur succeeded in killing Mordred, although he was severely wounded himself, and was carried away to the island of Avalon to recover. Whether Arthur recovered or not, he never returned to England, and the values and dreams of chivalry became part of the legendary past.

---

1. b
2. b

96a

vin dic tive (vin dik′ tiv)

On the second day of the trial the prosecution attempted to show that Mrs. Bast was a **vindictive** person. After the session, Salinger found a mysterious note in his car.

Write a definition or synonym:

121a

ac cli mate (ə klī′ mit, ak′ lə māt)

It was difficult for the settlers to **acclimate** themselves to Jamestown.

Write a definition or synonym:

146b

The pyramids were designed as tombs to protect the kings buried in them. To achieve this end, **orifices** ending in blind alleys were constructed to discourage tomb robbers.

An **orifice** is:
___a. an aperture
___b. an enclosure
___c. an edifice
___d. a capsule

LESSON 29

The Lost Civilizations of Ancient America

Long before America was discovered by Europeans, the great civilizations of the Aztecs, the Toltecs, and the Mayans flourished in the area we now call Latin America. We still have much to learn about how advanced and how complex these cultures actually were. For example, we still do not know where these peoples came from or why the empires of the Toltecs and the Mayans came to an end.

256a

vo lup tu ous (va lup' chū as)

Some of the fields and meadows in Van Gogh's paintings can only be called **voluptuous.**

Write a definition or synonym:

b

231a

dif fi dent (dif' a dant)

Roseann felt rather **diffident** the night her parents drove into town to watch her perform on Broadway.

Write a definition or synonym:

206b

Most readers enjoy watching Penny as she plays sly, crafty jokes on her opponents. Penny is so cunning she can always rely on **guile** rather than force to win the day.

Guile means:
__a. intelligence
__b. effrontery
__c. secrecy
__d. trickery

181b

Many travelers in Italy have given up planned visits to other Italian cities in order to make a **sojourn** in Rome. They realized that one or two days is simply not enough time to appreciate the Eternal City.

Sojourn means:
__a. a brief stay
__b. a short rest
__c. a pleasant experience
__d. an evening

156c

cor re late (kôr'a lāt, kor'a lāt), v., -lat ed, -lat ing. —v.t. place in or bring into proper relation with one another; show the connection or relation between: *Try to correlate your knowledge of history with your knowledge of geography.* —v.i. be related one to the other; have a mutual relation: *The diameter and the circumference of a circle correlate.*

1. Which of the following subjects correlate least?
__a. history and government
__b. science and math
__c. nursing and home economics
__d. art and physical education
2. Check the word closest in meaning to correlate.
__a. resemble   __b. interrelate   __c. conclude

a

LESSON 3

The Spy Who Loved Plants

Sally Kimball knew the Tektron Research Lab had won an important contract to produce a communications device for the space program. Like any good reporter, Sally was curious about the top secret program at Tektron. However, until an employee disappeared with some secret plans, Sally was not able to secure an interview.

46a

a, d

re it e rate (rē it′ ə rat′)

When Linda felt she had scolded the men enough, she **reiterated** her request.

Write a definition or synonym:

71a

dub (dub)

Most of the knights of the Round Table were **dubbed** by King Arthur.

Write a definition or synonym:

96b

That note stated that Mrs. Bast was far from being **vindictive**. She carried no grudges and would readily have forgiven the people who believed her guilty of murder.

Vindictive means:
___**a.** violent
___**b.** revengeful
___**c.** justified
___**d.** bigoted

121b

The weather, the swamps, and the hostility of the Indians made it difficult for the settlers to **acclimate** themselves to this New World. Some, who found this new life intolerable, returned to England.

Acclimate means:
___**a.** conquer fear or fears
___**b.** be an integral part of
___**c.** accustom to new conditions
___**d.** feel affection for

146c

a

o ri fice (ôr′ə fis, or′ə fis), *n.* an opening or hole; mouth: *the orifice of a tube.* [< Latin *orificium* < *os, oris* mouth + *facere* make]

Orifice can be used to describe which of the following?
___**a.** a volcano's crater ___**d.** a cave entrance
___**b.** a well ___**e.** a bowl
___**c.** a sieve ___**f.** the Grand Canyon

280c

in·trin·sic (in trin/sik), adj. 1 belonging to a thing by its very nature; essential; inherent: *The intrinsic value of a dollar bill is the cost of the paper it is printed on.* 2 originating or being inside the part on which it acts: *the intrinsic muscles of the larynx.* [< Late Latin *intrinsecus* internal < Latin, inwardly] —in·trin/si·cal·ly, *adv.*

b

1. A quality that is **intrinsic** cannot be:
__a. inborn   __c. native
__b. acquired   __d. learned
2. Which of the following can be called **intrinsic**?
__a. the popularity of a rock singer
__b. the sweetness of sugar

255c

suf·fuse (sə fyüz/), *v.t.,* -fused, -fus·ing. overspread (with a liquid, dye, etc.): *eyes suffused with tears. At twilight the sky was suffused with color.* [< Latin *suffusum* poured under < *sub-* under + *fundere* to pour]

c

Check the sentence(s) in which a form of **suffuse** is used correctly.
__a. The toast was suffused with jam.
__b. The choking man's face became suffused with color.
__c. The painter suffused the walls with green paint.
__d. My thoughts were suffused with fear.

LESSON 24   Green Eyes

?, e

Rosann Peters was a good-looking actress of twenty-three who had just won a part in the chorus line of the newest hit on Broadway. As usual, she was miserable about her good fortune. She envied the stars in the show. What was wrong with her, she thought. Why hadn't she made it all the way to the top? Rosann was just as jealous of the lead singers. Her voice was a good one. Why hadn't she been recognized and given a solo to sing? The night her parents attended the show Rosann was most dissatisfied.

206a

guile (gīl)

?, c

Guile is one of Penny's most noticeable characteristics.

Write a definition or synonym:

181a

so·journ (v. sō/ jėrn/, sō jėrn/; n. sō/ jėrn/)

Very few travelers to Italy neglect a sojourn in Rome.

Write a definition or synonym:

156b

By examining ideas and experiments of the past, the authors of the Constitution could select valuable principles and correlate them with the requirements of their own situation.

Correlate means:
__a. bring into relation
__b. make a comparison
__c. make equal to
__d. change drastically

21a

af fi da vit (af′ ə dā′ vit)

Sally was not surprised to learn that an **affidavit** of loyalty was required of each employee at the Tektron plant.

Write a definition or synonym:

46b

Each time one of the men tried to put her off, Linda **reiterated** her original request. She was determined to keep asking all afternoon if she had to. Gradually, some of the men began to warm up to the idea of a park in the middle of the city.

Reiterate means:
___**a.** corroborate
___**b.** announce
___**c.** retract
___**d.** repeat

71b

To be selected for knighthood was a great honor. In King Arthur's court, those nobles who qualified were **dubbed** in a ceremony of pomp and splendor. After the ceremony they took their places as knights at the Round Table with quiet pride.

To **dub** means:
___**a.** to be designated
___**b.** to be knighted
___**c.** to be nominated
___**d.** to be consecrated

96c

vin dic tive (vin dik′tiv), *adj.* 1 feeling a strong tendency toward revenge; bearing a grudge: *He is so vindictive that he never forgives anybody.* 2 showing a strong tendency toward revenge: *Vindictive acts rarely do much good.* [< Latin *vindicta* revenge < *vindex* avenger] —**vin dic′tive ly,** *adv.* —**vin dic′tive ness,** *n.*

ANALOGY vindictive : forgiving ::
___**a.** contemporary : passé
___**b.** demure : shy
___**c.** reverie : dream
___**d.** festive : gala
___**e.** elongate : stretch

b

121c

ac cli mate (ə klī′mit, ak′lə māt), *v.t., v.i.,* **-mat ed, -mat ing.** accustom or become accustomed to a new climate, surroundings, or conditions. —**ac cli ma tion** (ak′lə-mā′shən), *n.*

Check the sentence(s) in which a form of **acclimate** is used correctly.
___**a.** She had been acclimated for years to having a soft-boiled egg for breakfast.
___**b.** It is possible that people will some day become acclimated to life on one of the planets.
___**c.** He liked the acclimate so much he decided to stay.

c

147a

chat tel (chat′ l)

The tombs of the ancient Egyptian kings contained many of their **chattels.**

Write a definition or synonym:

b, d

156a

a

cor re late (kôr′ə lāt, kor′ə lāt)

The founding fathers **correlated** past experience with their present circumstances.

Write a definition or synonym:

LESSON 19 — Rome, the Eternal City

The city of Rome, located on the banks of the Tiber River, is more than the capital of Italy; it is one of the world's oldest and most beautiful cities. Once the heart of the Roman Republic and later, of the great Roman Empire, the Eternal City is now the site of Vatican City, the heart of the Roman Catholic Church. There is no city quite like Rome.

205c

d

in trep id (in trep′id), *adj.* very brave; fearless; dauntless; courageous. [< Latin *intrepidus* < *in-* not + *trepidus* alarmed] —in trep′id ly, *adv.*

If you are **intrepid**, you are:

__a. "resting on your oars"
__b. "bold as a lion"
__c. "standing by your guns"
__d. "keeping your ear to the ground"
__e. "risen from the ranks"

230c

b

prop a gate (prop′ə gāt) *v.*, **-gat ed, -gat ing.** —*v.i.* produce offspring; reproduce: *Pigeons propagate at a fast rate.* —*v.t.* 1 increase in number or intensity; multiply: *Trees propagate themselves by seeds.* 2 cause to increase in number by the production of young: *Cows and sheep are propagated on farms.* 3 spread (news, knowledge, etc.); extend: *Don't propagate unkind reports.* 4 pass on; send further: *Sound is propagated by vibrations.* [< Latin *propagatum* propagated, originally (of plants) multiplied by slips or layering < *pro-* forth + *pangere* fasten, plant with] —prop′a ga′tor, *n.*

Which of the following words mean the same as **propagate?**

__a. breed   __e. transmit
__b. dissolve   __f. refrain
__c. publish   __g. divide
__d. enlarge

255b

Many painters before Van Gogh took pride in painting sunlight realistically. Van Gogh attempted to capture the experience of being soaked through with sunlight. Many of his paintings are so **suffused** with sunlight that everything seems tinged with gold.

Suffuse means:

__a. illuminate
__b. silhouette
__c. overspread
__d. reveal

280b

The corrupt practices of a few individuals can give either management or labor a bad reputation even though there is no **intrinsic** evil in either one. Giant corporations and giant labor unions are not, by their nature, either good or bad.

Intrinsic means:

__a. manifest
__b. inherent
__c. extreme
__d. latent

21b

Since the research at Tektron was classified as "top secret," it was not enough for the employees simply to say that they were loyal and trustworthy. An **affidavit** to this effect was taken and checked carefully before anyone could be hired.

Affidavit means:
- __a. typed paper
- __b. summary
- __c. sworn statement
- __d. testimonial

46c

d

re it e rate (rē it′ə rāt′), *v.t.*, **-rat ed, -rat ing.** say or do several times; repeat (an action, demand, etc.) again and again: *The teacher reiterated her command.* See **repeat** for synonym study. **—re it′e ra′tion,** *n.*
re it e ra tive (rē it′ə rā′tiv), *adj.* repetitious. **—re it′e ra′tive ly,** *adv.*

Check the sentence(s) in which **reiterate** can be correctly substituted for **repeat**.
- __a. The teacher told the student to repeat after him.
- __b. They did not care to repeat the experience.
- __c. The defense counsel repeated her objections until the judge silenced her.
- __d. A repeat performance was planned.

71c

b

dub¹ (dub), *v.t.*, **dubbed, dub bing. 1** give a title or nickname to; name; call. **2** make (a man) a knight by striking his shoulder lightly with a sword. **3** make smooth by cutting, rubbing, or scraping. [Old English *dub-bian*]
dub² (dub), *v.t.*, **dubbed, dub bing.** add music, voices, or other sounds to (a motion-picture film, a radio or television broadcast, a recording, etc.). [short for *double*]
dub³ (dub), *n., v.,* **dubbed, dub bing. —n.** SLANG. a clumsy, unskillful person. **—v.t., v.i.** do or play awkwardly; bungle. [perhaps < *dub¹*]

ANALOGY **dub : sword :: shave :**
- __a. knight
- __b. beard
- __c. barber
- __d. razor
- __e. smooth

97a

a

ret i cence (ret′ ə səns)

Salinger was absent when the court convened for the third day of the trial. By this time, the evidence weighed heavily against Mrs. Bast. However, she showed no **reticence** when she took the witness stand.

Write a definition or synonym:

122a

b

a cu men (ə kyü′ mən)

Fortunately for the settlers, their leader was a man of **acumen**.

Write a definition or synonym:

147b

The theory was that the king, though dead, was still a king. If he chose to reanimate his body for participation in the afterworld, he would need certain **chattels**. Ornaments, food, weapons, and trusted servants were buried with him.

Chattel means:
- __a. companion
- __b. movable possession
- __c. necessity of life
- __d. comfort

155c

em bod y (em bod′ē), *v.t.,* **-bod ied,
-bod y ing.** 1 put into a form that can be
seen; express in definite form: *A building
embodies the idea of an architect.* 2 bring
together in a single book, law, system, etc.;
include; organize. 3 make part of an organized book, law, system, etc.; incorporate:
embody suggestions in a revised plan.

b

Each of the items on the left **embodies** one item on
the right. Write in the correct letter for each.

__ Miss America   **a.** state driving regulations

__ a driver's manual   **b.** a bathing suit

                 c. an ideal of beauty

                 d. ability to drive

180c

cul mi nate (kul′mə nāt), *v.i.,* **-nat ed,
-nat ing.** reach its highest point; reach a
climax: *The Christmas party culminated in
the distribution of the presents.* [< Late Latin
culminatum crowned, topped < Latin *culmi-
nem* top]

c

Check the sentence(s) in which a form of **culminate**
is used correctly.

__**a.** Romance often culminates in marriage.

__**b.** My afternoon of washing culminated in clean
     clothes.

__**c.** The prom culminated in the crowning of a
     queen.

__**d.** Two plus two culminates in four.

205b

Penny reminds readers of adults who remain
intrepid in the face of all dangers or obstacles.
Penny is smaller or weaker than all her adversaries,
but she always stands her ground.

Intrepid means:

__**a.** impassive

__**b.** unconcerned

__**c.** reticent

__**d.** courageous

230b

This terrible movie ended with a shot of Paul and
Paula being led away with thousands of other
omnivorous humans. The chimps were determined to
prevent the humans from **propagating**. And the
quickest way to prevent them from creating more of
their kind was to make them extinct.

Propagate means:

__**a.** eat

__**b.** reproduce

__**c.** expire

__**d.** become tame

255a

suf fuse (sə fyüz′)

The paintings Van Gogh created outdoors in the
south of France are **suffused** with sunlight.

, b

Write a definition or synonym:

280a

in trin sic (in trin′ sik)

, d

There is no **intrinsic** evil in either big
corporations or big labor organizations.

Write a definition or synonym:

21c

c

af fi da vit (af′ə dā′vit), *n.* statement written down and sworn to be true, usually before a notary public or other authorized official. [< Medieval Latin, he has stated on oath]

In which of the following situations might an **affidavit** be needed?
__a. deed transfer
__b. wedding ceremony
__c. civil service application
__d. bankruptcy action
__e. hospital admission

47a

c

e ques tri an (i kwes′ trē ən)

"What about the **equestrians**?" one man asked. "What place will they have in this park of yours?"

Write a definition or synonym:

72a

d

am i ty (am′ ə tē)

The institution of the Round Table helped preserve **amity** among the knights.

Write a definition or synonym:

97b

Reticence does not usually win juries. A witness who is voluble impresses them much more favorably. While guilt must be proved, innocence must be stated and stated well.

A synonym for **reticence** is:
__a. placidness
__b. ingenuousness
__c. reserve
__d. simplicity

122b

A man lacking John Smith's **acumen** would not have been able to see their problems as clearly or to make such sound decisions concerning them.

Acumen means:
__a. proficiency
__b. repute
__c. jurisdiction
__d. insight

147c

b

chat tel (chat′l), *n.* 1 piece of property that is not real estate; any movable possession. Furniture, automobiles, and animals are chattels. 2 slave or bondman. [< Old French *chatel* < Latin *capitale*, neuter of *capitalis*. Doublet of CAPITAL¹, CATTLE.]

Check the things that would be considered **chattels**.
__a. sheep   __e. country house
__b. jewels   __f. sense of humor
__c. office equipment   __g. lawn furniture
__d. station wagon   __h. duck pond

279c

met a mor pho sis (met'ə môr'fə sis), *n.*, *pl.* -ses (-sēz'). 1 a marked change in the form, and usually the habits, of an animal in its development after the embryonic stage. Tadpoles become frogs by metamorphosis; they lose their tails and grow legs. 2 change of form, structure, or substance by or as if by witchcraft; transformation. 3 form, shape, substance, etc., resulting from any such change. 4 a noticeable or complete change of character, appearance, circumstances, etc. [< Greek, ultimately < *meta*- after + *morphē* form]

Which of the following can be called a **metamorphosis**?

- __a. Ebenezer Scrooge's change of heart on Christmas morning
- __b. a few grey hairs
- __c. a newly emerged butterfly
- __d. the change from caterpillar to moth
- __e. the passing of time

132

254c

ab er ra tion (ab'ə rā'shən), *n.* 1 a deviating from the right path or usual course of action. 2 an abnormal structure or development. 3 a temporary mental disorder. 4 failure of a lens or mirror to bring to a single focus the rays of light coming from one point. Aberration causes a blurred image or an image with a colored rim. 5 a slight periodic variation in the apparent position of a heavenly body, caused by the movement of the earth while the light from the heavenly body travels through the telescope. [< Latin *aberrationem* < *ab*- away + *errare* wander]

Check the sentence(s) in which a form of **aberration** is used correctly.

- __a. The package of seeds produced healthy plants except for one aberration.
- __b. The temporary aberrations of adolescence are part of growing up.
- __c. The clear image was a perfect example of aberration.

230a

prop a gate (prop'ə gāt)

"Go and collect all the captive humans," the chief chimp ordered. "Now that we know their true nature, we cannot allow them to **propagate!**"

Write a definition or synonym:

205a

in trep id (in trep'id)

The **intrepid** Penny Dreadful is always the winner in the cartoons.

Write a definition or synonym:

180b

Before the final roll call, nomination followed nomination as various candidates were brought before the convention. Discussion, argument, and balloting ensued, **culminating** in the party's nomination for the U.S. Presidency.

Culminate means:

- __a. reach a stalemate
- __b. come to a turning point
- __c. reach a climax
- __d. make an affirmation

155b

It is one thing for a group of men to discuss principles of government, but to **embody** them in a document for conducting the government requires precise, clear, and highly organized writing.

The meaning of embody is:

- __a. preserve for posterity
- __b. express in definite form
- __c. make legible
- __d. make public

22a

dog mat ic (dôg mat′ ik, dog mat′ ik)

The personnel manager at Tektron assured Sally in a very **dogmatic** manner that every precaution had been taken to guard against theft or espionage.

Write a definition or synonym:

47b

Linda knew that many of the wealthy families were proud of being skilled **equestrians**. "I plan to have many bridle paths," Linda said quickly, "and we'll have a fine stable where the horses will receive the best of care. Your wives and children will be able to go riding every day without leaving the city."

An **equestrian** is:
__**a.** a sportsman
__**b.** a thoroughbred horse
__**c.** an entertainer
__**d.** a horseback rider

72b

Legend says that the Round Table was made round so there would be no arguments among the knights as to seating position. In this way, **amity** was maintained around the marble Round Table.

Amity means:
__**a.** equity
__**b.** peaceful relations
__**c.** proper behavior
__**d.** retribution

97c

ret i cence (ret′ə səns), *n.* tendency to be silent or say little; reserve in speech.

You would expect **reticence** from a person who is:
__**a.** shy   __**d.** withdrawn
__**b.** secretive   __**e.** outgoing
__**c.** animated

122c

a cu men (ə kyü′mən), *n.* sharpness and quickness in seeing and understanding; keen insight; discernment. [< Latin < *acuere* sharpen]

1. Which of the following is *least* similar to **acumen**?
   __**a.** discernment __**c.** discrimination
   __**b.** wisdom   __**d.** perseverance
2. **Acumen** correctly describes:
   __**a.** a quality of a good businessman
   __**b.** a characteristic of a good telescope
   __**c.** a characteristic of a fox

148a

en sconce (en skons′)

The body of each Pharaoh was **ensconced** in a sarcophagus, an elaborately carved stone coffin.

Write a definition or synonym:

279b

Such a **metamorphosis** has taken place that the tycoon once pictured in cartoons as a greedy tyrant is likely nowadays to be a respected leader in civic and charitable affairs.

Metamorphosis means:

___a. progression
___b. sudden event
___c. complete change
___d. resurrection

254b

Van Gogh's occasional **aberrations** may have disrupted his personal life, but they did not affect his paintings. Even the works he created while he was in a sanitarium have the beauty and clarity of the paintings of his normal periods.

Aberration means:

___a. leave of absence
___b. period of experimentation
___c. temporary mental disorder
___d. temporary change of residence

229c

c

pred·a·to·ry (pred'ə tôr'ē, pred'ə tōr'ē), *adj.* 1 living by preying upon other animals. Hawks and owls are predatory birds. 2 of or inclined to plundering or robbery: *Predatory pirates infested the seas.* [< Latin *praedā- torius* < *praedam* prey upon, plunder < *praeda* prey] —**pred'a·to'ri·ly,** *adv.*

1. Which of the following would you describe as **predatory**?

___a. a safecracker   ___d. a leopard
___b. a pickpocket   ___e. flies
___c. a robin

2. Which of the following would **predators** do?

___a. simulate
___b. raze
___c. pillage

204c

b

ver·nac·u·lar (vər nak'yə lər), *n.* 1 a native language; language used by the people of a certain country or place. 2 everyday lan- guage; informal speech. 3 language of a profession, trade, etc.: *the vernacular of lawyers.* 4 the common name of a plant or animal, as contrasted with its scientific name. —*adj.* 1 used by the people of a certain country or place; native: *English is our ver- nacular tongue.* 2 of or in the native lan- guage, rather than a literary or learned language. [< Latin *vernaculus* domestic, na- tive < *verna* home-born slave] —**ver·nac'u- lar·ly,** *adv.*

ANALOGY vernacular : literary ::

___a. casual : formal
___b. prehistoric : modern
___c. trivial : banal
___d. obscure : clear
___e. optimistic : pessimistic

180a

b, d

cul·mi·nate (kul' mə nāt)

In 1976 the Democratic Convention **culminated** in the nomination of Jimmy Carter.

Write a definition or synonym:

155a

a, c

em·bod·y (em bod' ē)

The writers of the Constitution contrived to **embody** all those principles of government which had been proved workable during the colonial period.

Write a definition or synonym:

22b

The manager asserted that the loyalty checks at Tektron could not be improved on and should not be questioned. Sally found this **dogmatic** attitude annoying. Obviously there was room for improvement since the plans had been stolen.

Dogmatic means:
___**a.** overbearing
___**b.** infallible
___**c.** hypocritical
___**d.** fervent

---

d

47c

e ques tri an (i kwes′trē ən), *adj.* 1 of horsemen or horsemanship; having to do with horseback riding, horses, or horseback riders: *equestrian skill.* 2 on horseback; mounted on a horse. An equestrian statue shows a person riding a horse. 3 having to do with or composed of knights. —*n.* rider or performer on horseback. [< Latin *equestris* of a horseman < *equus* horse]

ANALOGY equestrian : mount ::
___**a.** elongate : shorten
___**b.** stagnant : tributary
___**c.** eradicate : emboss
___**d.** steeple : church
___**e.** colleague : clientele

---

b

72c

am i ty (am′ə tē), *n., pl.* **-ties.** peace and friendship, especially between nations; friendly relations; friendliness: *a treaty of amity and commerce.* [< Middle French *amitié,* ultimately < Latin *amicus* friend. See AMICABLE.]

Amity is illustrated by which of the following expressions?
___**a.** "just one big happy family"
___**b.** "like cat and dog"
___**c.** "hand and glove"
___**d.** "at cross purposes"
___**e.** "like peas in a pod"
___**f.** "like pigs in the sunshine"

, d

98a

en treat (en trēt′)

After all the evidence had been presented, the counsel for the defense **entreated** the jury to decide that Mrs. Bast was innocent. Captain Salinger was still absent from the courtroom.

Write a definition or synonym:

. d
. a

123a

an i mos i ty (an′ ə mos′ ə tē)

For a while there was **animosity** between John Smith and some of the colonists.

Write a definition or synonym:

148b

The Egyptians believed that the body had to be preserved in a safe place to provide a home for the spirit. Thus the mummified bodies of the Pharaohs were **ensconced** in heavy stone coffins and tombs.

Ensconce means:
___**a.** imprison
___**b.** locate
___**c.** shelter
___**d.** consecrate

279a

d

met a mor pho sis (met'ə môr'fə sis)

Big Business has undergone a **metamorphosis** in the last few decades.

Write a definition or synonym:

254a

b

ab er ra tion (ab'ə rā'shən)

Vincent Van Gogh's **aberrations** are well known to students of art history.

Write a definition or synonym:

229b

Paula had never thought of herself as **predatory.** But she soon realized that humans must be **predatory** because they depend on other animals to supply them with food. The chimps were alarmed. If humans sometimes eat the flesh of sheep or cows, what would prevent them from eating the flesh of chimpanzees?

Predatory means:
- a. barbarous
- b. vagrant
- c. preying
- d. feline

204b

b

In the cartoons, Penny and the kids she terrorizes speak just the way young children actually speak. They use the same vocabulary and the same kinds of sentences that Tim's own children use. By writing in the **vernacular** this way, Tim made his cartoons much more lifelike.

Vernacular means:
- a. the first person
- b. everyday language
- c. extemporaneous speech
- d. flowery style of speaking or writing

179c

b

bu reau ra cy (byu rok'rə sē), n., pl. -cies. 1 system of government by groups of officials, each dealing with its own kind of business under the direction of its chief. 2 the officials running government bureaus. 3 concentration of power in administrative bureaus. 4 excessive insistence on rigid routine, resulting in delay in making decisions or in carrying out requests; red tape.

Where would you expect to find (a) **bureaucracy?**
- a. King Arthur's court
- b. Washington, D.C.
- c. a Boy Scout troop
- d. New York City government
- e. a tribe of nomads

154c

b

rel e vant (rel'ə vənt), adj.; bearing upon or connected with the matter in hand; to the point. See **pertinent** for synonym study. [< Latin *relevantem* relieving, refreshing < *re-* back + *levis* light?] —**rel'e vant ly,** adv.

Check the **relevant** sentence(s) in which **relevant** can be correctly used in the blank.
- a. The facts were not — to the case.
- b. John and Helen are — by marriage.
- c. The doctor asked the patient for information from his past which might be —.

a

22c

dog mat ic (dôg mat′ik, dog mat′ik), *adj.*
1 of dogma; doctrinal. 2 positive and emphatic in asserting opinions. 3 asserted in a positive and emphatic manner: *a dogmatic statement.* —**dog mat′i cal ly,** *adv.*

ANALOGY **dogmatic : uncertain :: fervent :**
__a. calm
__b. mistaken
__c. positive
__d. powerful
__e. excited

---

d

48a

zeal ous (zel′ əs)

At the third meeting, Linda's **zealous** efforts to secure land for a city park seemed to pay off.

Write a definition or synonym:

---

c, f

73a

lithe (līᴛʜ)

To joust successfully, a knight needed to be **lithe.**

Write a definition or synonym:

98b

The prosecution practically commanded the jury to convict Mrs. Bast. However, the defense counsel **entreated** the jury in eloquent terms not to convict. He pleaded with them to consider the evidence carefully, since a woman's life was at stake.

Entreat means:
__a. implore
__b. negotiate
__c. demand
__d. instruct

123b

Many of the settlers had expected to find gold in the New World. A great deal of **animosity** developed when John Smith criticized them harshly. He told them that they would go without food if they did not spend more time working in the fields and less time searching for gold.

Animosity means:
__a. annoyance
__b. activity
__c. hatred
__d. disappointment

---

c

148c

en sconce (en skons′), *v.t.,* -sconced, -sconc ing. 1 shelter safely; hide: *We were ensconced in the cellar during the tornado.* 2 settle comfortably and firmly: *The cat ensconced itself in the armchair.* [< en-¹ + sconce fortification, probably < Dutch schans]

In which of the following situations would a person be correctly described as **ensconced**?
__a. in a subway   __d. indoors during a storm
__b. in an easy chair __e. in a bomb shelter
__c. in a swimming pool

137

154b

Because time was precious, only items **relevant** to drafting the Constitution were considered. Speakers who digressed were quickly brought back to the matter at hand.

Relevant means:
__a. similar
__b. pertinent
__c. inherent
__d. assessable

179b

In a complex society in which the government is responsible for so many aspects of the people's lives, **bureaucracy** is inevitable. The many committees, agencies, bureaus, and offices become cumbersome and unwieldy.

The meaning of **bureaucracy** is:
__a. government by one family
__b. government by groups of officials
__c. pragmatic government
__d. government by divine right

204a

c, d
d, e

ver nac u lar (vər nak′ yə lər)

Tim was one of the first cartoonists to write in the **vernacular** of young children.

Write a definition or synonym:

229a

1. b
2. a

pred a to ry (pred′ ə tôr′ ē, pred′ ə tōr′ ē)

As soon as she heard Paula's news, the chief chimp became very thoughtful. "If what you say is true," she murmured, "then human animals must be **predatory** by nature."

Write a definition or synonym:

253c

b

syl van (sil′vən), *adj.* of, in, or having woods: *They lived in a sylvan retreat.* Also, **silvan**. [< Latin *sylvanus, silvanus < silva* forest]

ANALOGY sylvan : maritime ::
__a. vigilant : valiant
__b. forest : ocean
__c. urban : edifice
__d. arable : horticulture
__e. schooner : conveyance

278c

d

im pede (im pēd′), *v.t.,* **-ped ed, -ped ing.** stand in the way of; hinder; obstruct: *Our progress was impeded by the deep snow.* See **prevent** for synonym study. [< Latin *impedire < in-* on + *pedem* foot] **—im ped′er,** *n.*

ANALOGY impede : clear ::
__a. assist : help
__b. deny : claim
__c. wonder : amuse
__d. accelerate : retard
__e. prevent : predict

23a

a

au dac i ty (ô das′ ə tē)

Sally's next stop was the testing room at Tektron. If she had not been carrying her press card and her visitor's pass, she would not have had the **audacity** to enter.

Write a definition or synonym:

48b

a

Linda's eager excitement seemed to communicate itself to the others. Soon, the men were as **zealous** as Linda was. They began working to convince others that the park was a wonderful idea.

Zealous means:
__**a.** anxious
__**b.** fanatical
__**c.** crazed
__**d.** enthusiastic

73b

A man whose body was rigid and stiff might find it difficult to joust. To keep a seat on a horse while handling a lance required a **lithe** body and quick reflexes.

Lithe means:
__**a.** inflexible
__**b.** facile
__**c.** supple
__**d.** robust

98c

a

en treat (en trēt′), *v.t.* ask or keep asking earnestly; beg and pray: *The prisoners entreated their captors to let them go.* Also, **intreat**. [< Old French *entraitier* < *en-* in + *traitier* to treat] —**en treat′ing ly,** *adv.*

Check the sentence(s) in which a form of **entreat** is used correctly.
__**a.** He took them to the candy store for an entreat.
__**b.** She entreated the teacher a question.
__**c.** She entreated the governor to pardon her son.
__**d.** He saw an entreating mantis on the rose bush.

123c

c

an i mos i ty (an′ə mos′ə tē), *n., pl.* **-ties.** keen hostile feelings; active dislike or enmity; ill will.

ANALOGY **animosity : lethargy ::**
__**a.** reticence : shyness
__**b.** adamant : firm
__**c.** silhouette : shadow
__**d.** organism : automation
__**e.** boisterous : listless

149a

d, e

de i fy (dē′ ə fī)

Scholars were first able to decipher Egyptian hieroglyphics by means of the Rosetta Stone, which was discovered in 1799. This stone slab bore an inscription in three languages, describing how King Ptolemy had been **deified**.

Write a definition or synonym:

154a

rel e vant (rel' a vant)

All matters not **relevant** to the task were discarded.

Write a definition or synonym:

a, c

179a

bu reau c ra cy (byū rok' ra sē)

To some extent where there is democracy, there must be **bureaucracy.**

Write a definition or synonym:

c, d

a, d

203c

in de fat i ga ble (in'di fat'a ga bal), *adj.* never getting tired or giving up; tireless. [< Latin *indefatigabilis* < *in-* not + *defatigare* tire out < *de-* completely + *fatigare* to tire] —in'de fat'i ga ble ness, *n.* —in'de fat'i ga bly, *adv.*

1. Which of the following do you associate with the word **indefatigable**?
—a. snake   —c. beaver
—b. lion   —d. ant
2. Which of the following adjectives are *least* characteristic of an **indefatigable** worker?
—a. energetic   —d. indifferent
—b. determined   —e. nonchalant
—c. ambitious

b

228c

om niv o rous (om niv'ar as), *adj.* 1 eating every kind of food. 2 eating both animal and vegetable food: *Man is an omnivorous animal.* 3 taking in everything; fond of all kinds of books. [< Latin *omnivorus* < *omnis* all + *vorare* eat greedily] —om niv'or ous ly, *adv.* —om niv'or ous ness, *n.*

1. Which of the following persons can be described as **omnivorous**?
—a. a food faddist   —c. a vegetarian
—b. a "bookworm"
2. Check the correct synonym(s) for **omnivorous.**
—a. all-devouring   —c. gregarious
—b. universal

c

255b

Sometimes Van Gogh enhanced the beauty of a **sylvan** scene by showing the sunlight flickering through the leaves and branches. Sometimes he simplified the forest to show the essential shapes of the trees.

Sylvan pertains to:
—a. nature
—b. woods
—c. illumination
—d. color

278b

Some of the early labor leaders had such radical ideas that they actually **impeded** the growth of the unions. Many people who sympathized with the union movement were reluctant to ally themselves with such men, and progress was slower than it might have been.

Impede means:
—a. augment
—b. repel
—c. alter
—d. hinder

23b

Sally was not a timid or retiring person, but she was a bit frightened by the pairs of armed guards who stood at the doors to the locked rooms. How would anyone have the **audacity** to steal from Tektron and hope to escape?

Audacity means:
__a. modesty
__b. carelessness
__c. sincerity
__d. boldness

---

d

48c

zeal ous (zel′əs), *adj.* full of zeal; eager; earnest; enthusiastic: *The children made zealous efforts to clean up the house for the party.* —**zeal′ous ly,** *adv.* —**zeal′ous ness,** *n.*

Which of the following can be described as **zealous**?
__a. ditchdiggers __d. political campaigners
__b. missionaries __e. sunbathers
__c. invalids __f. fanatics

---

c

73c

lithe (līᴛʜ), *adj.* bending easily; supple: *lithe of body, a lithe willow.* [Old English *lithe* mild] —**lithe′ly,** *adv.* —**lithe′ness,** *n.*

Which of the following are **lithe**?
__a. a young tree __d. a ballet dancer
__b. a rubber hose __e. an elephant's trunk
__c. a snake __f. a telephone pole

---

c

99a

im passe (im pas′, im′ pas)

The jury had reached an **impasse** when Salinger walked into the courtroom with one arm in a sling. With him was a rough-looking man in handcuffs.

Write a definition or synonym:

---

e

124a

con cil i ate (kən sil′ ē āt)

Once Smith was able to **conciliate** the settlers, there was some hope that the colony of Jamestown would succeed.

Write a definition or synonym:

149b

The rulers of ancient Egypt exercised such enormous power that it was difficult to think of them as ordinary mortals. Perhaps that is why the rulers were **deified** and worshipped by the populace.

The meaning of **deify** is:
__a. make a god of
__b. pay homage to
__c. fear greatly
__d. make famous

153c

pro pound (prə pound′), *v.t.* put forward; propose: *propound a theory, propound a riddle.* [earlier *propone* < Latin *proponere* < *pro-* forth + *ponere* put] —**pro pound′-er,** *n.*

c

Check the sentence(s) in which **propounded** can be correctly substituted for the italicized word(s).

__**a.** She *put forward* a possible solution.
__**b.** He *proposed* to do his homework later.
__**c.** The professor *put forward* a hypothetical problem for the students.

178c

cred u lous (krej′ə ləs), *adj.* too ready to believe; easily deceived. —**cred′u lous ly,** *adv.* —**cred′u lous ness,** *n.* ➤ See **cred-ible** for usage note.

b

1. Which word(s) mean(s) about the same as **credulous**?
__**a.** confusing   __**c.** trusting
__**b.** faithful   __**d.** gullible
2. To be **credulous** one would need to be:
__**a.** naïve   __**c.** suspicious
__**b.** skeptical   __**d.** ignorant

203b

Tim spent many evenings at our house listening by the hour as I kept recalling more of the things Penny had done. Tim said I was **indefatigable** because I could go on and on without growing bored or weary.

Indefatigable means:
__**a.** brilliant
__**b.** tireless
__**c.** habitual
__**d.** vociferous

228b

Paula knew Paul's drowsiness was the result of the pineapple he had eaten. "Humans cannot stay awake on a diet of fruit or vegtables. They are **omnivorous**. They must also eat protein."
"You mean that humans eat every kind of food?" asked a chimp. "How disgusting!"

Omnivorous means:
__**a.** ravenous
__**b.** gluttonous
__**c.** eating all foods
__**d.** eating regularly

253a

b, c

syl van (sil′ vən)

Among Van Gogh's paintings there are many **sylvan** scenes.

Write a definition or synonym:

278a

a, b,
c
a

im pede (im pēd′)

At first, several factors **impeded** the development of labor organizations.

Write a definition or synonym:

23c

d

au dac i ty (ô das′ə tē), *n.* 1 reckless daring; boldness. 2 rude boldness; impudence; presumption. [< Latin *audacia* < *audax* bold < *audere* to dare]

Which person(s) would be likely to exhibit **audacity**?
__**a.** racing driver
__**b.** minister preaching a sermon
__**c.** surgeon performing an operation
__**d.** stunt man in the movies
__**e.** teacher grading examination papers

49a

d, f

in tel li gent si a (in tel′ ə jent′ sē ə, in tel′ ə gent′ sē ə)

However, one of the landowners nearly upset the plan when he refused to sell his land to the city unless provisions were made for the **intelligentsia**.

Write a definition or synonym:

74a

b, c, e

e lix ir (i lik′ sər)

Sorcerers of Arthur's day frequently claimed to have found an **elixir** of life.

Write a definition or synonym:

99b

After the man confessed to the crime, Salinger explained how he had solved the murder mystery with information provided by the note. With this evidence, the jury's **impasse** was ended and they were able to make a decision.

Another word for **impasse** is:
__**a.** dilemma
__**b.** mistrial
__**c.** paradox
__**d.** deadlock

124b

The profit from the great tobacco crops helped **conciliate** the disgruntled members of the colony. They began to find their new life more rewarding and bearable.

Conciliate means:
__**a.** reinforce
__**b.** coerce
__**c.** soothe
__**d.** confederate

149c

a

de i fy (dē′ə fī), *v.t.*, **-fied, -fy ing.** 1 make a god of. 2 worship or regard as a god: *deify wealth.* [< Old French *deifier* < Late Latin *deificare* < Latin *deus* god + *facere* make]

ANALOGY **deify : exalt :: sanctify :**
__**a.** spurn
__**b.** consecrate
__**c.** embezzle
__**d.** praise
__**e.** antagonize

153b

Whenever a member of the Constitutional Convention **propounded** a theory, it was subjected to intense criticism by other members. Their method was to listen to any and all ideas that were put forth and then consolidate their thinking.

Propound means:
__a. expose
__b. divulge
__c. propose
__d. resolve

178b

All through political history, there have been occasions when candidates for public office were dishonest and corrupt. There have always been **credulous** voters who were easily deluded into supporting such candidates.

Credulous means:
__a. ignorant
__b. gullible
__c. worthy of credit
__d. believable

203a

d

in de fat i ga ble (in′ di fat′ ə gə bəl)

When Tim first got the idea for the Penny Dreadful cartoons, he asked me to tell him all the stories I could remember about the real Penny. I was a good choice; I'm an **indefatigable** storyteller myself.

Write a definition or synonym:

228a

c, e

om niv or ous (om niv′ ə rəs)

"The problem is our captive humans," the chief chimp said. "They no longer work in the fields for us. All they do is eat their pineapples and sleep!" At once, Paula knew how to solve the chimps' problem. "You must remember that we human beasts are **omnivorous**," she explained.

Write a definition or synonym:

252c   **ver i ta ble** (ver′ə tə bəl), *adj.* true; real; actual. —**ver′i ta ble ness,** *n.* —**ver′i ta bly,** *adv.*

b

Veritable means:
__a. "worldly-wise"
__b. "sure-enough"
__c. "honest-to-goodness"
__d. "uppermost in one's thoughts"
__e. "like a bolt from the blue"

277c   **af fil i ate** (*v.* ə fil′ē āt; *n.* ə fil′ē it, ə fil′ē āt), *v.,* **-at ed, -at ing,** *n.* —*v.t.* join in close association; connect or associate: *The two clubs were affiliated with each other.* —*v.i.* connect or associate oneself *(with): affiliate with a political party.* —*n.* organization or group associated with another or larger organization or group. [< Medieval Latin *affiliatum* adopted < Latin *ad-* to + *filius* son] —**af fil′i a′tion,** *n.*

c

1. An **affiliate** can be:
   __a. a member   __c. an associate
   __b. a branch
2. Check the sentence(s) in which a form of **affiliate** is used correctly.
   __a. He is affiliated with a church.
   __b. He affiliates with his classmates after school.

24a

a, d

hi er o glyph ic (hī′ ər ə glif′ ik)

Sally studied the control panel and the computer printouts. But the signs and symbols she saw looked like **hieroglyphics**.

Write a definition or synonym:

49b

Quickly, Linda pointed out that a science center and a museum could be built in the park. Both projects would be educational. They would appeal to the **intelligentsia** as well as to the ordinary citizens.

Intelligentsia means:
—**a.** artists
—**b.** an exclusive set
—**c.** intellectuals
—**d.** nonconformists

74b

The people of the time had great faith that there were **elixirs** that would change metal to gold or prolong life if someone could only discover them.

An **elixir** is:
—**a.** an incantation
—**b.** a divine leader
—**c.** a sorcerer
—**d.** a magical substance

99c

d

im passe (im pas′, im′pas), *n.* 1 position from which there is no escape; deadlock. 2 road or way closed at one end. [< French]

Which of the following might be described as an **impasse**?
—**a.** dirt road   —**d.** standstill
—**b.** dead end   —**e.** roadblock
—**c.** strike   —**f.** detour

124c

c

con cil i ate (kən sil′ē āt), *v.t.,* **-at ed, -at ing.** 1 win over; soothe: *I conciliated the angry child with a candy bar.* 2 gain (good will, regard, favor, etc.) by friendly acts. 3 bring into harmony; reconcile. [< Latin *conciliatum* brought together, made friendly < *concilium.* See COUNCIL.] —**con cil′i-a′tor,** *n.*

You would be **conciliating** if you:
—**a.** invited a group of friends in for an evening of singing
—**b.** gave your friend a gift after having quarreled with him
—**c.** were elected most popular student in your class
—**d.** settled a dispute between two of your neighbors

150a

b

ap pa ri tion (ap′ ə rish′ ən)

One night as we inspected the most recent excavations in the Valley of the Kings, we thought we saw **apparitions** moving across the desert sands.

Write a definition or synonym:

153a

e

pro pound (prə pound′)

As each item of the Constitution was **propounded,** it was analyzed.

Write a definition or synonym:

178a

d, e

cred u lous (krej′ ə ləs)

Sometimes the voters are a **credulous** group.

Write a definition or synonym:

202c   **fig ment** (fig′mənt), *n.* something imagined; made-up story. [< Latin *figmentum* < *fingere* to form, fashion]

c

ANALOGY figment : imagination ::
__**a.** dwelling : barracks
__**b.** adversary : celebrity
__**c.** fact : fiction
__**d.** dream : subconscious
__**e.** pigment : color

227c   **leth ar gy** (leth′ər jē), *n., pl.* **-gies.** 1 drowsy dullness; lack of energy; sluggish inactivity. 2 (in medicine) a state of prolonged unconsciousness resembling deep sleep, from which the person can be roused but immediately loses consciousness again. [< Greek *lēthargia* < *lēthē* forgetfulness + *argos* lazy < *a-* not + *ergon* work]

a

How would you describe a person in a state of **lethargy**?
__**a.** effervescent   __**d.** exhilarated
__**b.** animated   __**e.** apathetic
__**c.** slothful   __**f.** stoic

252b

Van Gogh knew a number of successful artists who were truly skilled. However, Van Gogh's art shows more than skill; he was a **veritable** genius.

Veritable means:
__**a.** artistic
__**b.** genuine
__**c.** sincere
__**d.** probable

277b

All these organizations sought reforms for the workers. Unions found that they could operate more effectively if they **affiliated.** This made it possible to have spokesmen in common, and promotion directed toward their common goals.

To **affiliate** means to:
__**a.** assimilate
__**b.** concur
__**c.** connect closely
__**d.** become a subsidiary

24b

If Sally had known computer language, she might have been able to make some sense out of the intricate little diagrams. Without special training, they made no more sense to her than ancient picture writing found in Egyptian **hieroglyphics**.

Hieroglyphics means:
- __a. ancient artwork
- __b. ancient spoken language
- __c. ancient buildings
- __d. picture writing

---

c

49c

in tel li gent si a (in tel′ə jent′sē ə, in tel′ə-gent′sē ə), *n.pl.* persons representing, or claiming to represent, the superior intelligence or enlightened opinion of a country; the intellectuals. [< Russian *intelligentsiya* < Latin *intelligentia* < *intelligentem* intelligent]

Check the sentence(s) in which **intelligentsia** is used correctly.
- __a. Only the intelligentsia can make the football team.
- __b. Chess is an intelligentsia game.
- __c. The intelligentsia are a small but influential group.

---

d

74c

e lix ir (i lik′sər), *n.* **1** substance supposed to have the power of changing lead, iron, etc., into gold or of lengthening life indefinitely. The alchemists of the Middle Ages sought for it. **2** cure-all. **3** medicine made of drugs or herbs mixed with alcohol and syrup. [< Medieval Latin < Arabic *al-iksīr*]

Check the sentence(s) in which **elixir** is used correctly.
- __a. The pharmacist prepared an elixir.
- __b. The Fountain of Youth sought by Ponce de Leon was believed to contain an elixir of life.
- __c. There is no elixir for unhappiness.
- __d. The plumber poured an elixir into the clogged drain.

---

d, e

100a

ab solve (ab solv′, ab zolv′)

After a brief session, the jury returned and **absolved** Mrs. Bast.

Write a definition or synonym:

---

b, d

125a

dif fe ren ti ate (dif′ ər en′ shē āt)

In a society such as Jamestown, it was hard to **differentiate** among the various social classes.

Write a definition or synonym:

150b

These disturbing visions had been seen many times before. Always they would appear unexpectedly at night, like phantoms. The down-to-earth explanation was that the shapes were tomb-robbers. The supernatural explanation was that they were **apparitions**.

A synonym for **apparition** is:
- __a. plunderer
- __b. hallucination
- __c. ghost
- __d. illusion

147

277a

af·fil·i·ate (*v.* ə fĭl′ē āt; *n.* ə fĭl′ē ĭt, ə fĭl′ē ət)

Labor organizations sprang up and began to **affiliate.**

Write a definition or synonym:

b

252a

ver·i·ta·ble (vĕr′ ə tə bəl)

Only one of Van Gogh's paintings was sold during his lifetime. Today, his paintings are worth a **veritable** fortune.

Write a definition or synonym:

b, c

227b

When she heard the chimp's news, Paula was never more wide-awake and alert. But Paul's reaction was just the opposite. His **lethargy** was so great he seemed about to fall asleep on his feet.

Another word for lethargy is:

__a. stupor
__b. hypnosis
__c. anesthesia
__d. acquiescence

202b

Penny Dreadful was certainly not a **figment** of Tim's mind. She was based on a person who actually existed. Tim merely wrote down a few of the things that the real Penny did back when she, Tim, and I were in grade school together.

A **figment** is:

__a. a fallacy
__b. a consequence
__c. an invention
__d. a hallucination

177c

de·lude (dĭ lūd′), *v.t.,* -lud·ed, -lud·ing. mislead the mind or judgment of; trick or deceive. [< Latin *deludere* < *de-* + *ludere* to play] —de·lud′er, *n.*

ANALOGY **delude : deride ::**

__a. usurp : wean
__b. canvass : chide
__c. repudiate : sanctify
__d. embalm : embroil
__e. dismantle : disqualify

c

152c

pro·pi·tious (prə pĭsh′əs), *adj.* 1 holding well; favorable: *propitious weather for our trip.* 2 favorably inclined; gracious. [< Latin *propitius,* originally, falling forward < *pro-* forward + *petere* go toward] —pro·pi′tious·ly, *adv.* —pro·pi′tious·ness, *n.*

ANALOGY **propitious : promising ::**

__a. spinster : wife
__b. nucleus : cell
__c. brandish : flail
__d. premature : preoccupy
__e. deft : adept

a

d

24c

hi er o glyph ic (hi′ər ə glif′ik), *n.*
1 picture, character, or symbol standing for a
word, idea, or sound; hieroglyph. The ancient
Egyptians used hieroglyphics instead of an
alphabet like ours. 2 letter or word that is
hard to read. 3 **hieroglyphics,** *pl.* **a** system
of writing that uses hieroglyphics. **b** writing
that is hard to read. 4 a secret symbol. —*adj.*
1 of or written in hieroglyphics. 2 hard to
read. [< Late Latin *hieroglyphicus* < Greek
hieroglyphikos < *hieros* sacred + *glyphē* a
carving] —**hi′er o glyph′i cal ly,** *adv.*

Check the sentence(s) in which a form of
hieroglyphics is used correctly.
—**a.** My teacher jokingly said he couldn't read the
hieroglyphics I used for handwriting.
—**b.** The flag is a hieroglyphic of our country.
—**c.** The hieroglyphic of the secret society could be
interpreted only by members.

50a

c

pas tor al (pas′ tər əl)

On the day the land for the park was turned over to
the city, Linda was interviewed by a newspaper
reporter. "Exactly why do we need this huge
pastoral playground?" he demanded.

Write a definition or synonym:

75a

b, c

e ther e al (i thir′ ē əl)

Queen Guinevere was a woman of **ethereal** beauty.

Write a definition or synonym:

100b

The jury **absolved** Mrs. Bast by declaring her not
guilty. However, if Salinger had not tracked down
the actual murderer and captured him, Lucy Bast
would almost certainly have been convicted and
punished.

Absolve means:
—**a.** condemn
—**b.** acquit
—**c.** indict
—**d.** condone

125b

One could not use clothing as a means of
differentiating among the colonists. Rich and
poor alike wore simple, homespun garments.

Differentiate means:
—**a.** characterize
—**b.** distinguish
—**c.** segregate
—**d.** separate

150c

c

ap pa ri tion (ap′ə rish′ən), *n.* 1 a supernatural sight or thing; ghost or phantom.
2 the appearance of something strange,
remarkable, or unexpected. [< Late Latin
apparitionem]

Check the sentence(s) in which a form of
apparition is used correctly.
—**a.** The apparition at the window proved to be a
child in a Halloween costume.
—**b.** The pianist left on a tour of personal
apparitions.

152b

The excellence of its Constitution and the high caliber of its leaders were **propitious** signs for the new country. Americans had every reason to be optimistic about the future.

Propitious means:
___a. promising
___b. beneficial
___c. congenial
___d. potent

177b

An artful politician who distorts the truth can **delude** an uninformed voter. A citizen who is fully aware of the issues cannot be so easily swayed.

Delude means:
___a. coerce
___b. convince
___c. mislead
___d. outwit

202a

b

fig ment (fig′ mənt)

Some people mistakenly think the characters in the Penny Dreadful cartoons are **figments** of the author's imagination.

Write a definition or synonym:

227a

, d,

leth ar gy (leth′ ər jē)

"Who would have dreamed that our assistance would come from two giant hairless beasts with ugly faces!" the chief chimp exclaimed. Paul received this greeting with a curious **lethargy**.

Write a definition or synonym:

251c   **fir ma ment** (fėr′mə mənt), *n.* arch of the heavens; sky. [< Latin *firmamentum*, ultimately < *firmus* firm¹]

b

Which of the following mean the same as **firmament**?
___a. galaxy
___b. celestial space
___c. heavens
___d. four corners of the earth
___e. creation

276c   **no to ri e ty** (nō′tə rī′ə tē), *n., pl.* -ties. 1 a being famous for something bad; ill fame: *The scandal brought much notoriety to those involved in it.* 2 a being widely known. 3 a well-known person.

b

ANALOGY notoriety : ill fame ::
___a. aesthetic : caustic
___b. defunct : deceased
___c. admonish : reproach
___d. divulge : secrete
___e. astute : studious

25a

av o ca tion (av′ ə kā′ shən)

a, c

The people who worked in the lab were quite open and friendly when Sally interviewed them. The director remarked that he and the missing worker had become friendly because they shared an absorbing **avocation**.

Write a definition or synonym:

50b

"In the years to come," Linda said, "these will be the only trees and meadows for miles around. This will be the only place in our city where we can ride horses. It will be a **pastoral** oasis." The reporter thought Linda was crazy, but time has proved her to be right.

Pastoral means:
__a. agricultural
__b. uncivilized
__c. rustic
__d. provincial

75b

The queen's **ethereal** appearance made other women appear heavy, fleshy, and solid. Indeed, she did seem like a creature from another world.

Ethereal means:
__a. celestial
__b. fabulous
__c. imaginary
__d. magical

100c

b

ab solve (ab solv′, ab zolv′), *v.t.*, **-solved, -solv ing.** 1 pronounce or set (a person) free from sin, guilt, blame, or their penalties or consequences. 2 set free (*from a promise, obligation, or duty*); release. [< Latin *absolvere* < *ab*- from + *solvere* loosen] —**ab-solv′er,** *n.*

ANALOGY absolve : vindicate :: segregate :
__a. surveillance
__b. visualize
__c. separate
__d. recuperate
__e. infatuate

125c

b

dif fe ren ti ate (dif′ə ren′shē āt), *v.,* **-at ed, -at ing.** —*v.t.* 1 make different; cause to have differences: *Consideration for others differentiates good manners from mere politeness.* 2 tell the difference in or between; find or show to be different: *The botanist differentiated varieties of plants.* See **distinguish** for synonym study. 3 (in biology) make different in the process of growth or development; make unlike by modification. 4 (in mathematics) find the derivative of. —*v.i.* 1 become different. 2 tell the difference; find or show what is different. 3 (in biology) become differentiated or specialized: *The cells of an embryo differentiate into organs and parts as it grows.*

Check the sentence(s) in which a form of **differentiate** is used correctly.
__a. She differentiated that it had grown late.
__b. Her fair coloring differentiated her from her family.
__c. An insane person cannot differentiate right from wrong.
__d. She differentiated her costume by adding a ruffle at the neck.

LESSON 16 — The Wisdom of the Constitution

a

The Constitution of the United States of America is a remarkable document. Although it has been in existence since 1787, it has been amended only twenty-two times. Changing conditions in the political world have forced many other countries to modify their constitutions drastically or to discard them altogether. It is a tribute to our Constitution that it continues to serve its original purpose so effectively.

151

276b

Factory fires in New York City and elsewhere achieved **notoriety** when it was learned that the workers perished with no chance to escape. Demands for reform increased as a result of this unfavorable publicity.

Notoriety means:

__a. popularity
__b. ill fame
__c. coverage
__d. criticism

251b

The movements of the stars against a night sky is painted so dramatically and with such emotion that it shows the mystery and scope of the entire **firmament**.

The **firmament** is:

__a. the satellites
__b. the expanse of the heavens
__c. the mountains of the moon
__d. the visible planets

226c

junc ture (jungk'chər), *n.* 1 point or line where two things join; joint. 2 point of time. 3 state of affairs. 4 a critical state of affairs; crisis. 5 a joining. 6 a being joined. 7 the way in which sounds and sound sequences are joined: *There is a difference in juncture between "night rate (nīt' rāt')" and "nitrate (nī'trāt)."* 8 **at this juncture**, when affairs are in this state; at this moment. [< Latin *junctura* a joining < *jungere* to join. Doublet of JOINTURE.]

c

Which of the following are **junctures**?

__a. a knuckle
__b. convalescence
__c. line between sections of a bridge
__d. the putting together of sections
__e. critical point of an illness

201c

pseu do nym (süd'n im), *n.* a fictitious name used by an author instead of his real name; pen name. [< Greek *pseudōnymon* < *pseudés* false + *onyma* name]

b

Check the sentence(s) in which **pseudonym** is used correctly.

__a. "NASA" is a pseudonym for the National Aeronautics and Space Administration.
__b. To ensure privacy, the author used a pseudonym.
__c. "Loyalty" is a pseudonym for "devotion."
__d. "Ike" was the pseudonym of Dwight D. Eisenhower.

177a

de lude (di lüd')

An uninformed voter is easily **deluded**.

Write a definition or synonym:

, a

2, c

152a

pro pi tious (prə pish'əs)

The Constitution gave the United States **propitious** conditions for its start.

Write a definition or synonym:

, c

25b

Although the workers at Tektron were highly trained scientists whose duties on the job were extremely specialized, they enjoyed the same **avocations** that many office workers enjoy. The director and the missing worker had both become interested in growing rare tropical plants.

Avocation means:
—**a.** business
—**b.** mania
—**c.** hobby
—**d.** zeal for

50c

c

pas tor al (pas′tər əl), *adj.* 1 of shepherds or country life: *a pastoral occupation, a pastoral poem.* 2 simple or naturally beautiful like the country: *a pastoral scene.* See **rural** for synonym study. 3 of a pastor or his duties. —*n.* 1 a pastoral play, poem, or picture. 2 letter from a bishop to his clergy or to the people of his church district. —**pas′tor al ly,** *adv.*

Check the sentence(s) in which **pastoral** can be correctly used in the blank.
—**a.** The fashion model was elegantly attired in __ style.
—**b.** He drove out beyond the city limits to paint a __ scene.
—**c.** He led the cows back from the __.
—**d.** Everyone in the congregation received a copy of the __.

75c

a

e ther e al (i thir′ē əl), *adj.* 1 light; airy; delicate: *the ethereal beauty of a butterfly.* 2 not of the earth; heavenly. 3 of or having to do with the upper regions of space. Also, **aethereal.** —**e ther′e al ly,** *adv.* —**e ther′e al ness,** *n.*

ANALOGY **ethereal : celestial :: ultimate :**
—**a.** saturate
—**b.** reverie
—**c.** final
—**d.** foreign
—**e.** galaxy

LESSON 11 | Linda Superstar Learns How to Act

c

Although she had received two small parts in feature-length films, Linda Superstar felt her career was in trouble. None of the film critics had liked her performances, and no one was willing to give her a leading role in a movie. Everyone told Linda that the Stanton Acting Academy was the best place to master the acting skills that Linda felt she was missing. Linda felt she was a little too old to go back to school, but she was willing to give it a try.

126a

b, c

ho mo ge ne ous (hō′ mə jē′ nē əs, hō′ mə jē′ nyəs; hom′ ə jē′ nē əs, hom′ ə jē′ nyəs)

Although they were dressed alike, the backgrounds of the colonists were far from **homogeneous**.

Write a definition or synonym:

151a

pre ten tious (pri ten′ shəs)

The U.S. Constitution is not a **pretentious** document.

Write a definition or synonym:

151c

pre ten tious (pri ten/shəs), *adj.* 1 making claims to excellence or importance: *a pretentious person, a pretentious book, a pretentious speech.* 2 doing things for show or to make a fine appearance; showy; ostentatious: *a pretentious style of entertaining guests.* —**pre ten/tious ly,** *adv.* —**pre ten/tiousness,** *n.*

When you act in a **pretentious** manner you are:
__a. "hiding your light under a bushel"
__b. "putting on the dog"
__c. "putting on airs"
__d. "following the crowd"
__e. "singing a different tune"

176c

in val i date (in val/ə dāt), *v.t.,* -dat ed, -dat ing. make valueless; deprive of force or effect: *A contract is invalidated if only one party signs it.* —**in val/i da/tion,** *n.* —**in val/i da/tor,** *n.*

1. Which of the following can be **invalidated**?
__a. an agreement
__b. a blow
__c. a diamond
2. Which word is closest in meaning to **invalidate**?
__a. deteriorate
__b. injure
__c. annul

201b

There's nothing wrong with **pseudonyms**, of course. Samuel Langhorne Clemens wrote under the name "Mark Twain." William Sydney Porter used the name "O. Henry" to sign his stories.

A **pseudonym** is:
__a. a scion
__b. a pen name
__c. an alternate
__d. a relative

226b

Using a machine that made her language intelligible, the chief chimp explained how odd it was that Paul and Paula had arrived at this **juncture**. The chimps had been expecting a visitation from space at this point in time. The visitors were expected to assist the chimps in solving a great problem.

Juncture means:
__a. special method
__b. manner of speech
__c. significant moment
__d. important hour

251a

fir ma ment (fėr/ mə mənt)

Starry Night, a painting by Van Gogh, captures the dazzling power and beauty of the **firmament** as no other painting has done.

Write a definition or synonym:

276a

no to ri e ty (nō/ tə rī/ ə tē)

Several events gave **notoriety** to the poor conditions in factories.

Write a definition or synonym:

25c

c

av o ca tion (av′ə kā′shən), *n.* something
that a person does besides his regular business; minor occupation; hobby: *He is a law-*
yer by vocation, but writing stories is his
avocation. [< Latin *avocationem* < *avocare*
call away < *ab-* away + *vocare* to call] ➤ See
vocation for usage note.

Which of the following activities would be
considered **avocations**?

___**a.** stamp-collecting   ___**d.** flower-arranging
___**b.** going to the movies   ___**e.** sketching
___**c.** watching television   ___**f.** racing sports cars

Go back to page 1 and continue on frame 26a.

---

b, d

LESSON

The First Age of Exploration

When people began exploring the world systematically, the long period of
European history known as the Middle Ages came to an end. People demanded
a share in the wonders and riches that lay in the Middle East and Asia.
Explorers ventured forth in ever-increasing numbers to the New World,
around Africa, and then around the globe. It all started with the Crusades.

Go back to page 1 and continue on frame 51a.

76a

c

gos sa mer (gos′ ə mər)

Queen Guinevere wore gowns of **gossamer** fabrics.

Write a definition or synonym:

Go back to page 1 and continue on frame 76b.

101a

tu te lage (tü′ tl ij, tyü tl ij)

On the first day of school, Linda learned that she was
under the **tutelage** of the Stanton Acting Academy
from that day until her graduation.

Write a definition or synonym:

Go back to page 1 and continue on frame 101b.

126b

Many people came over to find gold, others to escape
religious persecution, and some simply for
adventure. The interests of the colonists were
certainly not **homogeneous**.

Homogeneous means:
___**a.** similar
___**b.** ordinary
___**c.** conventional
___**d.** amicable

Go back to page 1 and continue on frame 126c.

151b

Both its compact physical size and concise manner of
expression reveal that it is not a **pretentious**
document. Its aims are set forth simply, humbly, and
directly.

The meaning of **pretentious** is:
___**a.** nebulous
___**b.** profound
___**c.** showy
___**d.** redundant

Turn the book upside down and continue on frame 151c.

EDL WORD CLUES MASTERY TESTS*

Paul A. Fuchs
and
Mary Ellen Grassin
Rumson-Fair Haven (N.J.) Regional High School

When you finish each Word Clues lesson, how well do you remember the meanings of the words you have studied? The Word Clues Mastery Tests will help you answer this question.

There is one test for each lesson in the book. Each test has ten questions, one on each word taught in the lesson. These target words are set in **boldface** type.

Five kinds of questions are used in the tests. Here are the directions for each kind.

Definitions in Context: Choose the best meaning of the target word in each sentence.

Synonyms or Similar Meanings: Select the word or phrase that is closest in meaning to the target word.

Antonyms or Opposite Meanings: Select the word or phrase that is most nearly opposite in meaning to the target word.

Words in Context: Choose the word that best completes the sentence.

Analogies: Choose the word or phrase that best completes each analogy.

Answer all questions as directed by your instructor. Caution: Pay attention to the headings because the kinds of questions are not always in the same order.

---

*The authors of the Word Clues Mastery Tests for the various levels are as follows:

G	Carolyn A. Hill	**K**	Joseph J. Dignan
H	Marie H. Hughes	**L**	Paul A. Fuchs and
I	Margaret B. Holton		Mary Ellen Grassin
J	Elinor H. Kinney	**M**	William A. Speiser

NOTE: This edition of Word Clues L contains a final posttest. For this test, 25 words have been randomly chosen as representative of the total number of words taught. Students who score 80% or higher can move to the next higher book.

ANALOGIES

11. **magnanimous : highminded ::**
    a. gregarious : reflective   d. vacillate : bitter
    b. impetuous : rash   e. squalid : sacred
    c. interminable : unfair

12. **procrastinate : act swiftly ::**
    a. carnage : confuse
    b. vacillate : stand firm
    c. embroil : withdraw an offer
    d. askance : invent
    e. pungent : tremble in fear

SYNONYMS OR SIMILAR MEANINGS

13. **extemporaneous**
    a. offhand   d. expected
    b. rehearsed   e. unnecessary
    c. unusual

14. **gregarious**
    a. talkative   d. irate
    b. overdressed   e. isolated
    c. sociable

ANTONYMS OR OPPOSITE MEANINGS

15. **astute**
    a. unattractive   d. decisive
    b. idealistic   e. gullible
    c. irritating

16. **cantankerous**
    a. intelligent   d. confident
    b. moderate   e. friendly
    c. witty

WORDS IN CONTEXT

17. Secret Service agents must be ____ when talking about their work.
    a. plaintive   d. astute
    b. magnanimous   e. facetious
    c. discreet

18. It is difficult to ____ someone who has very little to say.
    a. procrastinate   d. characterize
    b. embroil   e. gregarious
    c. extemporaneous

DEFINITIONS IN CONTEXT

19. The guests were asked to leave the party before they became **embroiled** in an argument.
    a. excluded   d. enchanted
    b. denied   e. entangled
    c. debated

20. Jane could barely stay alert during the politician's **interminable** speech.
    a. endless   d. intellectual
    b. fascinating   e. evasive
    c. complex

DEFINITIONS IN CONTEXT

1. The answers to the second question of the history test were rather vague, and I found myself **vacillating** between the last two choices.
   a. brooding   d. marauding
   b. postponing   e. wavering
   c. exasperating

2. Tourists to the city avoided riding through the **squalid**, garbage-filled streets of the ghetto.
   a. unique   d. spicy
   b. dejected   e. wretched
   c. fragrant

SYNONYMS OR SIMILAR MEANINGS

3. **paraphernalia**
   a. excess baggage   d. sporting goods
   b. equipment   e. appearance
   c. luggage

4. **askance**
   a. anxiously   d. humorously
   b. disapprovingly   e. carefully
   c. strangely

5. **plaintive**
   a. excruciating   d. raucous
   b. shrill   e. joyous
   c. mournful

ANTONYMS OR OPPOSITE MEANINGS

6. **impetuous**
   a. impulsive   d. humorous
   b. bizarre   e. rash
   c. calm

7. **pungent**
   a. mild   d. violent
   b. irritating   e. sharp
   c. strange

WORDS IN CONTEXT

8. At the termination of the legal hearings, the lawyers involved found it a relief to be ____ rather than serious.
   a. dejected   d. squalid
   b. composed   e. facetious
   c. despondent

ANALOGIES

9. **askance : sideways :: carnage :**
   a. garage   d. plunder
   b. slaughter   e. trouble
   c. havoc

10. **deluge : cloudburst :: demeanor :**
    a. innocence   d. stiff
    b. hurricane   e. sedate
    c. conduct

WORD CLUES MASTERY TEST L-4

DEFINITIONS IN CONTEXT

31. Attempts by firemen to revive the victims of the hotel fire proved **ineffectual**.
    - a. useless
    - b. unique
    - c. brutal
    - d. isolated
    - e. worthy

32. The prisoners threatened that any effort to **harass** them would be met with severe retaliation.
    - a. accept
    - b. embrace
    - c. supply
    - d. annoy
    - e. befriend

SYNONYMS OR SIMILAR MEANINGS

33. **vulnerable**
    - a. susceptible
    - b. arrogant
    - c. weak-willed
    - d. proud
    - e. potent

34. **vociferous**
    - a. futile
    - b. frustrating
    - c. calm
    - d. shrewd
    - e. loud

ANTONYMS OR OPPOSITE MEANINGS

35. **unwitting**
    - a. moody
    - b. energetic
    - c. accidental
    - d. deliberate
    - e. sustained

36. **succumb**
    - a. survive
    - b. plague
    - c. praise
    - d. delete
    - e. contribute

WORDS IN CONTEXT

37. The police decided to maintain ____ on the three suspects until more information could be obtained.
    - a. unwitting
    - b. vociferous
    - c. harass
    - d. surveillance
    - e. vulnerable

38. The code of rules dated 1980 will ____ the rules in effect for the past ten years.
    - a. succumb
    - b. surreptitious
    - c. inalienable
    - d. supercede
    - e. harass

ANALOGIES

39. **surreptitious : obvious ::**
    - a. adroit : refined
    - b. vociferous : fragrant
    - c. plaintive : serious
    - d. squalid : immaculate
    - e. dogmatic : defeated

40. **inalienable : irrevocable ::**
    - a. latent : clumsy
    - b. adroit : skillful
    - c. impetuous : wicked
    - d. ineffectual : simple
    - e. facetious : dreary

WORD CLUES MASTERY TEST L-3

DEFINITIONS IN CONTEXT

21. The drama coach recognized the timid student's **latent** ability for acting.
    - a. hidden
    - b. sluggish
    - c. rampant
    - d. refreshing
    - e. burning

22. With little knowledge of **hieroglyphics**, I was unable to interpret the meaning of the pictures and symbols on the cave walls.
    - a. ancient art work
    - b. picture writing
    - c. ancient spoken language
    - d. ancient building
    - e. ancient architecture

SYNONYMS OR SIMILAR MEANINGS

23. **adroit**
    - a. appropriate
    - b. skillful
    - c. honest
    - d. awkward
    - e. inept

24. **affidavit**
    - a. typed paper
    - b. testimonial
    - c. summary
    - d. application
    - e. sworn statement

25. **avocation**
    - a. experience
    - b. business
    - c. zeal for
    - d. hobby
    - e. mania

ANTONYMS OR OPPOSITE MEANINGS

26. **dogmatic**
    - a. superior
    - b. infallible
    - c. assertive
    - d. meek
    - e. fervent

27. **audacity**
    - a. carelessness
    - b. shyness
    - c. wealth
    - d. demeanor
    - e. boldness

WORDS IN CONTEXT

28. The unwillingness of the class officer to allow his fellow classmates to offer suggestions marked him as a(n) ____ person.
    - a. astute
    - b. magnanimous
    - c. gregarious
    - d. discreet
    - e. bigoted

ANALOGIES

29. **connoisseur : expert :: interminable :**
    - a. unrewarding
    - b. hasty
    - c. complex
    - d. limitless
    - e. insoluble

30. **confidant : trust :: bigot :**
    - a. astuteness
    - b. intolerance
    - c. discretion
    - d. procrastination
    - e. adroitness

DEFINITIONS IN CONTEXT

51. The groups which supported the bond issue were composed of many **heterogeneous** elements.
    a. confusing
    b. varied
    c. annoying
    d. stale
    e. attractive

52. After he was ejected from the game, the quarterback made a number of **acrimonious** remarks to the referee.
    a. lengthy
    b. foolish
    c. bitter
    d. loud
    e. unfortunate

SYNONYMS OR SIMILAR MEANINGS

53. **consensus**
    a. bitterness
    b. foolishness
    c. beautification
    d. agreement
    e. theory

54. **incessant**
    a. vital
    b. cruel
    c. ornate
    d. continual
    e. smooth

ANTONYMS OR OPPOSITE MEANINGS

55. **coerce**
    a. welcome
    b. allow
    c. overlook
    d. deprive
    e. deny

56. **capitulate**
    a. facilitate
    b. follow
    c. persist
    d. reject
    e. wander

WORDS IN CONTEXT

57. The supervisor was ____ in her refusal to allow some workers to come in late.
    a. arduous
    b. acrimonious
    c. heterogeneous
    d. incessant
    e. adamant

58. The force of the blast was sufficient to ____ certain objects through the walls of the building.
    a. impel
    b. consensus
    c. coerce
    d. capitulate
    e. epoch

ANALOGIES

59. **arduous : effortless ::**
    a. herbivorous : hungry
    b. zealous : eager
    c. admonish : warn
    d. dogmatic : strict
    e. arid : verdant

60. **epoch : nuclear age ::**
    a. demeanor : habit
    b. avocation : term
    c. equestrian : lion tamer
    d. monument : Eiffel Tower
    e. bigot : carnage

SYNONYMS OR SIMILAR MEANINGS

41. **zealous**
    a. fanatical
    b. excitable
    c. anxious
    d. apathetic
    e. fervent

42. **herbivorous**
    a. living on flesh
    b. eating all kinds of food
    c. feeding on grass
    d. belonging to a group of animals
    e. types of herbs and spices

ANTONYMS OR OPPOSITE MEANINGS

43. **verdant**
    a. exotic
    b. vigorous
    c. barren
    d. luxuriant
    e. green

44. **pastoral**
    a. uncivilized
    b. audacious
    c. provincial
    d. urban
    e. agricultural

45. **languid**
    a. sad
    b. insensible
    c. bored
    d. impassive
    e. energetic

DEFINITIONS IN CONTEXT

46. The firemen had to **reiterate** their pleas for caution as curious onlookers gathered before the burning building.
    a. announce
    b. corroborate
    c. retract
    d. repeat
    e. warn

47. The organization called MENSA is limited to the **intelligentsia**.
    a. noncomformists
    b. intellectuals
    c. artists
    d. an exclusive set
    e. fanatics

WORDS IN CONTEXT

48. Sometimes the ordinarily shy person must display some ____ in order to secure a job.
    a. modesty
    b. audacity
    c. carelessness
    d. sincerity
    e. fanaticism

ANALOGIES

49. **equestrian : horsemanship :: architectural :**
    a. private home
    b. design of buildings
    c. new structure
    d. domed church
    e. engineer

50. **admonish : reprove :: procrastinate :**
    a. decide
    b. refuse
    c. defer
    d. vacillate
    e. terminate

WORD CLUES MASTERY TEST L-8

DEFINITIONS IN CONTEXT

71. The beauty queen wore a dress of **gossamer** fabric.
- **a.** delicate
- **b.** coarse
- **c.** stiff
- **d.** exotic
- **e.** shiny

72. To participate in gymnastics, the athlete must have a strong and **lithe** body.
- **a.** tall
- **b.** heavy
- **c.** durable
- **d.** hearty
- **e.** supple

SYNONYMS OR SIMILAR MEANINGS

73. elixir
- **a.** cleanser
- **b.** forgery
- **c.** medicine
- **d.** criminal
- **e.** lubricant

74. dub
- **a.** defend
- **b.** reject
- **c.** label
- **d.** dismiss
- **e.** infer

ANTONYMS OR OPPOSITE MEANINGS

75. amity
- **a.** tardiness
- **b.** deference
- **c.** hostility
- **d.** insolence
- **e.** discretion

76. piquant
- **a.** bland
- **b.** excessive
- **c.** skeptical
- **d.** arduous
- **e.** festive

WORDS IN CONTEXT

77. The school principal issued an _____ to the effect that all students will park their cars in the west lot.
- **a.** allegory
- **b.** edict
- **c.** amity
- **d.** elixir
- **e.** alarm

78. It is difficult to describe the _____ sounds which were heard last night at the concert of sacred music.
- **a.** gossamer
- **b.** piquant
- **c.** lithe
- **d.** usurp
- **e.** ethereal

ANALOGIES

79. usurp : overthrow ::
- **a.** sanctify : solve
- **b.** admonish : confess
- **c.** succumb : rejoice
- **d.** procrastinate : delay
- **e.** dissent : ignore

80. allegory : literature ::
- **a.** photography : avocation
- **b.** afternoon : epoch
- **c.** liar : connoisseur
- **d.** argument : consensus
- **e.** sailor : equestrian

WORD CLUES MASTERY TEST L-7

DEFINITIONS IN CONTEXT

61. The wedding of the two young people was **sanctified** by a church ceremony.
- **a.** sacrificed
- **b.** cited
- **c.** admonished
- **d.** rewarded
- **e.** consecrated

62. Because the soldiers were **adherents** to the cause of liberty, they were willing to sacrifice their lives for the cause.
- **a.** protectors
- **b.** lovers
- **c.** followers
- **d.** students
- **e.** agitators

SYNONYMS OR SIMILAR MEANINGS

63. repudiate
- **a.** deride
- **b.** disclaim
- **c.** reprove
- **d.** reiterate
- **e.** repulse

64. heretic
- **a.** insurrectionist
- **b.** heathen
- **c.** atheist
- **d.** dissenter
- **e.** adherent

ANTONYMS OR OPPOSITE MEANINGS

65. credible
- **a.** impractical
- **b.** impossible
- **c.** intolerant
- **d.** unsure
- **e.** unbelievable

66. ingenuous
- **a.** intolerant
- **b.** insane
- **c.** inalienable
- **d.** insincere
- **e.** intelligent

WORDS IN CONTEXT

67. Although her decision seemed correct at the time, in _____ she realized that she had made a mistake.
- **a.** embroilment
- **b.** retrospect
- **c.** procrastination
- **d.** facetiousness
- **e.** repudiation

68. The trapeze artist's delay in continuing his performance caused the crowd of onlookers to have a(n) _____ .
- **a.** adherence
- **b.** presentiment
- **c.** admonition
- **d.** heresy
- **e.** credibility

ANALOGIES

69. posthumous : happening after death ::
ineffectual :
- **a.** irrelevant
- **b.** tentative
- **c.** futile
- **d.** unwitting
- **e.** impractical

70. dissent : agree :: audacity :
- **a.** vulnerability
- **b.** zeal
- **c.** pungency
- **d.** timidity
- **e.** dogmatism

WORD CLUES MASTERY TEST L-10

ANALOGIES
91. ancestor : scion ::
   a. carnage : siege
   b. gratis : privation
   c. mansion : tenement
   d. avocation : hobby
   e. epoch : era

92. allege : innocence ::
   a. assert : truth
   b. impel : invader
   c. deride : contribution
   d. dub : actor
   e. sanctify : removal

SYNONYMS OR SIMILAR MEANINGS
93. caustic
   a. mellow
   b. friendly
   c. trustworthy
   d. burning
   e. enormous

94. reticence
   a. reluctance
   b. bitterness
   c. fatigue
   d. amusement
   e. rejection

ANTONYMS OR OPPOSITE MEANINGS
95. convene
   a. confer
   b. dismiss
   c. regard
   d. relieve
   e. discharge

96. vindicate
   a. rely on
   b. reinstate
   c. exhaust
   d. convict
   e. exterminate

DEFINITIONS IN CONTEXT
97. The anguished mother **entreated** the kidnappers not to injure her child.
   a. rejected
   b. implored
   c. demanded
   d. baited
   e. encouraged

98. Mr. Jones showed that he was a **vindictive** person when he refused to allow a neighbor's child to compensate him for the damaged window.
   a. bright
   b. hysterical
   c. sincere
   d. casual
   e. spiteful

WORDS IN CONTEXT
99. I cannot ____ you of all responsibility in the matter, since you did stand by and watch the affair.
   a. absolve
   b. entreat
   c. convene
   d. vindicate
   e. allege

100. Negotiations reached the point of ____ when the union representatives stood up and left the meeting room.
   a. reticence
   b. caustic
   c. vindictive
   d. scion
   e. impasse

WORD CLUES MASTERY TEST L-9

DEFINITIONS IN CONTEXT
81. Many derelicts would starve without food they receive **gratis** from city agencies.
   a. grateful
   b. free
   c. rewarding
   d. regular
   e. profuse

82. The young tennis **prodigy** was quickly accepted into the world of adults.
   a. individualist
   b. spectacle
   c. radical
   d. idealist
   e. wonder

SYNONYMS OR SIMILAR MEANINGS
83. privation
   a. destitution
   b. procrastination
   c. dispossession
   d. seclusion
   e. bereavement

84. voluble
   a. vigorous
   b. fluent
   c. voluntary
   d. plaintive
   e. overbearing

ANTONYMS OR OPPOSITE MEANINGS
85. staid
   a. frivolous
   b. sedate
   c. discreet
   d. extemporaneous
   e. plaintive

86. innate
   a. natural
   b. ordinary
   c. acquired
   d. internal
   e. inborn

WORDS IN CONTEXT
87. Rather than accept money from his family, John chose to live on a(n) ____ while attending college.
   a. privation
   b. pittance
   c. surveillance
   d. abstraction
   e. derision

88. The child's ____ behavior in front of guests brought him a severe scolding from his parents.
   a. plaintive
   b. pastoral
   c. prodigious
   d. languid
   e. flippant

ANALOGIES
89. abstract : real :: ethereal :
   a. zealous
   b. allegorical
   c. latent
   d. retrospective
   e. substantial

90. derisive : scornful :: lithe :
   a. facetious
   b. unwilling
   c. supple
   d. piquant
   e. languid

WORD CLUES MASTERY TEST L-12

ANALOGIES

111. limbo : forgotten ::
- **a.** carnage : party
- **b.** reality : tangible
- **c.** heretic : believer
- **d.** privation : satisfaction
- **e.** avocation : talent

112. infectious : contagious ::
- **a.** prodigy : slow learner
- **b.** ineffectual : efficient
- **c.** credible : believable
- **d.** edifice : hut
- **e.** latent : liberal

SYNONYMS OR SIMILAR MEANINGS

113. raiment
- **a.** garb
- **b.** distortion
- **c.** equipment
- **d.** illusion
- **e.** wisdom

114. fetid
- **a.** remote
- **b.** reeking
- **c.** unrealistic
- **d.** vague
- **e.** unreliable

ANTONYMS OR OPPOSITE MEANINGS

115. ignoble
- **a.** magnanimous
- **b.** ignorant
- **c.** huge
- **d.** deceitful
- **e.** remarkable

116. garish
- **a.** rejected
- **b.** isolated
- **c.** colorless
- **d.** unpolitical
- **e.** defaced

DEFINITIONS IN CONTEXT

117. Some turtles and other reptiles are known for their **longevity.**
- **a.** overweight
- **b.** bad temper
- **c.** color
- **d.** habitat
- **e.** long life

118. A small child was **abducted** last week when his mother left him unattended.
- **a.** injured
- **b.** kidnapped
- **c.** beaten
- **d.** scolded
- **e.** ridiculed

WORDS IN CONTEXT

119. One of the players who quit the team had the ____ to ask the coach for a recommendation to college.
- **a.** longevity
- **b.** abduct
- **c.** raiment
- **d.** effrontery
- **e.** limbo

120. The guests began to leave the party after one person started telling ____ stories.
- **a.** ignoble
- **b.** fetid
- **c.** infectious
- **d.** garish
- **e.** ribald

WORD CLUES MASTERY TEST L-11

ANALOGIES

101. stature : height ::
- **a.** reticent : withdrawal
- **b.** entreat : compromise
- **c.** amity : peace and friendship
- **d.** impasse : solution
- **e.** absolve : indict

102. solicitous : concerned ::
- **a.** credible : unbelievable
- **b.** ingenuous : insincere
- **c.** flippant : polite
- **d.** vindicated : cleared
- **e.** stature : station

SYNONYMS OR SIMILAR MEANINGS

103. gauche
- **a.** inane
- **b.** ponderous
- **c.** familiar
- **d.** cumbersome
- **e.** awkward

104. deference
- **a.** concurrence
- **b.** yielding
- **c.** fidelity
- **d.** futility
- **e.** availability

ANTONYMS OR OPPOSITE MEANINGS

105. banal
- **a.** droll
- **b.** standard
- **c.** free
- **d.** significant
- **e.** merry

106. pseudo
- **a.** obscure
- **b.** pretended
- **c.** authentic
- **d.** meaningless
- **e.** false

WORDS IN CONTEXT

107. The upperclassmen of the school frequently ____ the incoming class with offensive remarks.
- **a.** inspire
- **b.** stimulate
- **c.** implore
- **d.** corroborate
- **e.** upbraid

108. The teacher's ____ remarks to the boisterous youngster were intended as a lesson to the other students.
- **a.** disinterested
- **b.** inaccurate
- **c.** scathing
- **d.** magnanimous
- **e.** latent

DEFINITIONS IN CONTEXT

109. George is under the **tutelage** of a military academy that is very much concerned with the academic success of its students.
- **a.** franchise
- **b.** privilege
- **c.** surveillance
- **d.** guardianship
- **e.** usurpation

110. Since Lillian's school is **secular,** her religious training is fulfilled at a nearby house of worship.
- **a.** atheistic
- **b.** neutral
- **c.** worldly
- **d.** specialized
- **e.** diplomatic

Name _____ Date _____

WORD CLUES MASTERY TEST **L-14**

DEFINITIONS IN CONTEXT

131. In his attempts to **ingratiate** himself with the boss, Peter succeeded only in making his position more uncertain.
- **a.** bring himself into favor
- **b.** demonstrate friendliness
- **c.** create stability
- **d.** generate sympathy
- **e.** demand special treatment

132. Many of the troubled areas of the world suffer from a shortage of **arable** land.
- **a.** oil-bearing
- **b.** fit for farming
- **c.** heavy with timber
- **d.** near mountains
- **e.** close to a river or seaport

WORDS IN CONTEXT

133. Many oil tankers are registered in foreign countries that have rather lax _____ regulations.
- **a.** arable
- **b.** pallid
- **c.** maritime
- **d.** overt
- **e.** tortuous

134. Carol tried to use her sore finger as a(n) _____ for not having to take the test.
- **a.** pallid
- **b.** tortuous
- **c.** pretext
- **d.** moot
- **e.** overt

ANALOGIES

135. tortuous : twisting ::
- **a.** adroit : careless
- **b.** lithe : complex
- **c.** gratis : costly
- **d.** adamant : unyielding
- **e.** caustic : delightful

136. somnolent : alert ::
- **a.** nebulous : clear
- **b.** ribald : anxious
- **c.** garish : established
- **d.** flippant : secular
- **e.** cantankerous : unusual

SYNONYMS OR SIMILAR MEANINGS

137. pallid
- **a.** rapid
- **b.** sensible
- **c.** colorless
- **d.** brown
- **e.** listless

138. insatiable
- **a.** uncertain
- **b.** unbelievable
- **c.** unknown
- **d.** unsatisfiable
- **e.** unforgiving

ANTONYMS OR OPPOSITE MEANINGS

139. overt
- **a.** hidden
- **b.** allowable
- **c.** concise
- **d.** sensitive
- **e.** stern

140. moot
- **a.** talkative
- **b.** inadmissible
- **c.** adroit
- **d.** credible
- **e.** indisputable

Name _____ Date _____

WORD CLUES MASTERY TEST **L-13**

ANALOGIES

121. homogeneous : heterogeneous ::
- **a.** adroit : honest
- **b.** usurp : conquer
- **c.** repudiate : reject
- **d.** edict : decree
- **e.** adamant : yielding

122. acclimate : become accustomed to ::
- **a.** happiness : depression
- **b.** audacity : modesty
- **c.** elixir : nutritive value
- **d.** entreat : beg
- **e.** lithe : inflexible

SYNONYMS OR SIMILAR MEANINGS

123. conciliate
- **a.** become acquainted with
- **b.** reinforce
- **c.** coerce
- **d.** believe
- **e.** gain by friendly acts

124. acumen
- **a.** enthusiasm
- **b.** efficiency
- **c.** jurisdiction
- **d.** insight
- **e.** reticence

ANTONYMS OR OPPOSITE MEANINGS

125. nebulous
- **a.** revenge
- **b.** supple
- **c.** indistinct
- **d.** published after death
- **e.** vivid

126. animosity
- **a.** revenge
- **b.** love
- **c.** disappointment
- **d.** enmity
- **e.** activity

WORDS IN CONTEXT

127. The success of our football team's first game provided the _____ to face the most challenging team in the state.
- **a.** longevity
- **b.** homogeneity
- **c.** limbo
- **d.** impetus
- **e.** acumen

128. The _____ attitude of our early forefathers enabled them to endure the hardships with which they were confronted.
- **a.** ignoble
- **b.** languid
- **c.** cantankerous
- **d.** stoic
- **e.** conversant

DEFINITIONS IN CONTEXT

129. It is sometimes difficult for a child to **differentiate** right from wrong.
- **a.** characterize
- **b.** segregate
- **c.** reinforce
- **d.** distinguish
- **e.** clear

130. Fred's frequent trips to Montreal had left him **conversant** with a number of Canadian traditions.
- **a.** familiar
- **b.** congenial
- **c.** agreeable
- **d.** learned
- **e.** naïve

WORD CLUES MASTERY TEST **L-16**

DEFINITIONS IN CONTEXT

151. The title of Miss America **embodies** the ideals of beauty, talent, and personality.
- **a.** devises
- **b.** expresses
- **c.** refrains
- **d.** describes
- **e.** foretells

152. A secondary benefit of drug research is the development of **derivative** compounds which are quite useful.
- **a.** substitute
- **b.** overt
- **c.** unnecessary
- **d.** elixir
- **e.** by-product

SYNONYMS OR SIMILAR MEANINGS

153. propitious
- **a.** haphazard
- **b.** deceitful
- **c.** powerful
- **d.** promising
- **e.** desperate

154. relevant
- **a.** related
- **b.** immaterial
- **c.** improbable
- **d.** obvious
- **e.** worthy

ANTONYMS OR OPPOSITE MEANINGS

155. pretentious
- **a.** flippant
- **b.** available
- **c.** unaffected
- **d.** ambitious
- **e.** caustic

156. harangue
- **a.** discredit
- **b.** overpower
- **c.** reject
- **d.** disappear
- **e.** whisper

WORDS IN CONTEXT

157. The American Cancer Society has conducted research which ____ smoking with lung cancer.
- **a.** entreats
- **b.** embodies
- **c.** embroils
- **d.** correlates
- **e.** convenes

158. In classical mythology Helen of Troy was regarded as the ____ of beauty.
- **a.** elixir
- **b.** paragon
- **c.** consensus
- **d.** impetus
- **e.** apparition

ANALOGIES

159. propound : doctrine ::
- **a.** dub : concession
- **b.** repudiate : belief
- **c.** upbraid : violation
- **d.** embody : edifice
- **e.** admonish : partner

160. pragmatic : practical ::
- **a.** moot : precise
- **b.** ineffectual : efficient
- **c.** staid : nervous
- **d.** ingenuous : natural
- **e.** infectious : interesting

WORD CLUES MASTERY TEST **L-15**

ANALOGIES

141. defunct : extinct ::
- **a.** ignoble : degraded
- **b.** banal : novel
- **c.** homogeneous : heterogeneous
- **d.** languid : energetic
- **e.** lithe : inflexible

142. orifice : entrance ::
- **a.** longevity : moderation
- **b.** limbo : confinement
- **c.** raiment : habitat
- **d.** effrontery : investigation
- **e.** abduction : threat

SYNONYMS OR SIMILAR MEANINGS

143. ensconce
- **a.** imprison
- **b.** locate
- **c.** surrender
- **d.** consecrate
- **e.** hide

144. apparition
- **a.** plunderer
- **b.** example
- **c.** dissenter
- **d.** phantom
- **e.** heretic

ANTONYMS OR OPPOSITE MEANINGS

145. comely
- **a.** witty
- **b.** shrewd
- **c.** pallid
- **d.** homely
- **e.** pretty

146. aesthetic
- **a.** abstract
- **b.** pastoral
- **c.** ethereal
- **d.** unaware
- **e.** utilitarian

WORDS IN CONTEXT

147. On the playing field, the referee's ruling is ____ .
- **a.** aesthetic
- **b.** definitive
- **c.** staid
- **d.** secular
- **e.** dissenting

148. In one of the early religions, people ____ the sun.
- **a.** ensconced
- **b.** upbraided
- **c.** deified
- **d.** coerced
- **e.** admonished

DEFINITIONS IN CONTEXT

149. To help **defray** the expenses of our leader's trip, we each agreed to contribute five dollars.
- **a.** determine
- **b.** pay
- **c.** liquidate
- **d.** repay
- **e.** disperse

150. The couple living in the apartment above us sold most of their ____ before moving to another state.
- **a.** companions
- **b.** bonds
- **c.** movable possessions
- **d.** necessities of life
- **e.** comforts

WORD CLUES MASTERY TEST **L-18**

ANALOGIES

171. caucus : planning ::
- **a.** elixir : healing
- **b.** scion : spying
- **c.** raiment : protecting
- **d.** avocation : disturbing
- **e.** edict : rejecting

172. electorate : voters ::
- **a.** stature : weight
- **b.** epoch : legend
- **c.** abstraction : idea
- **d.** pretext : purpose
- **e.** allegory : puzzle

SYNONYMS OR SIMILAR MEANINGS

173. hackneyed
- **a.** reversed
- **b.** restricted
- **c.** worn out
- **d.** lively
- **e.** overdressed

174. delude
- **a.** invoke
- **b.** avoid
- **c.** withdraw
- **d.** deceive
- **e.** scold

ANTONYMS OR OPPOSITE MEANINGS

175. credulous
- **a.** trusting
- **b.** friendly
- **c.** awkward
- **d.** suspicious
- **e.** uncertain

176. culminate
- **a.** defend
- **b.** continue
- **c.** disperse
- **d.** eject
- **e.** demonstrate

WORDS IN CONTEXT

177. The high officials met in _____ to elect a successor to their late leader.
- **a.** conclave
- **b.** bureaucracy
- **c.** credulous
- **d.** electorate
- **e.** culminate

178. Mr. Johnson's countless applications to have his license restored always seem to become snarled in the _____ .
- **a.** caucus
- **b.** bureaucracy
- **c.** invalidate
- **d.** harangue
- **e.** conclave

DEFINITIONS IN CONTEXT

179. Judge Ann Jones is known for the **colloquial** tone of her speech.
- **a.** learned
- **b.** rapid
- **c.** cautious
- **d.** philosophical
- **e.** informal

180. Because of a number of questions about several crucial ballots, the election results had to be **invalidated**.
- **a.** reviewed
- **b.** restored
- **c.** annulled
- **d.** deteriorated
- **e.** injured

WORD CLUES MASTERY TEST **L-17**

DEFINITIONS IN CONTEXT

161. Many professionals show an **affinity** for their particular field during their childhood years.
- **a.** inclination
- **b.** indifference
- **c.** disgust
- **d.** consensus
- **e.** admonition

162. The rumor of the impending invasion **emanated** from the state department.
- **a.** evoked
- **b.** absolved
- **c.** succumbed
- **d.** infused
- **e.** came forth

SYNONYMS OR SIMILAR MEANINGS

163. charlatan
- **a.** blunderer
- **b.** drone
- **c.** criminal
- **d.** imposter
- **e.** zealot

164. poignant
- **a.** affecting
- **b.** veritable
- **c.** painless
- **d.** incredulous
- **e.** manifest

165. pathology
- **a.** study of medicine
- **b.** study of germs
- **c.** study of cells
- **d.** study of life
- **e.** study of diseases

ANTONYMS OR OPPOSITE MEANINGS

166. extol
- **a.** remain
- **b.** reiterate
- **c.** reproach
- **d.** praise
- **e.** supercede

167. haggard
- **a.** gaunt
- **b.** impassive
- **c.** languid
- **d.** mean
- **e.** vigorous

WORDS IN CONTEXT

168. Sue was _____ at not receiving an invitation to the wedding.
- **a.** admonished
- **b.** conciliated
- **c.** piqued
- **d.** dogmatic
- **e.** succumbed

ANALOGIES

169. decry : extol ::
- **a.** deride : reiterate
- **b.** entreat : beseech
- **c.** procrastinate : delay
- **d.** allege : claim
- **e.** repudiate : accept

170. exorbitant : immoderate ::
- **a.** haggard : robust
- **b.** relevant : pertinent
- **c.** interminable : limited
- **d.** discreet : infallible
- **e.** astute : gullible

WORD CLUES MASTERY TEST L-20

DEFINITIONS IN CONTEXT

191. The junior high school's production of *Hamlet* was a **fiasco**.
    - **a.** success
    - **b.** suspension
    - **c.** failure
    - **d.** strike
    - **e.** skirmish

192. The new manager is better respected than his ill-mannered **predecessor**.
    - **a.** servant
    - **b.** follower
    - **c.** one who comes after
    - **d.** one who went before
    - **e.** one who belongs to the same family

WORDS IN CONTEXT

193. The government withdrew its ____ troops from the disputed territory so as not to embroil itself in a total war.
    - **a.** fiasco
    - **b.** austerity
    - **c.** mercenary
    - **d.** languish
    - **e.** bourgeois

194. A person with inadequate job skills can expect to ____ in low-paying jobs throughout his or her lifetime.
    - **a.** sojourn
    - **b.** austerity
    - **c.** fiasco
    - **d.** languish
    - **e.** anarchy

ANALOGIES

195. **despot : tyrant ::**
    - **a.** anarchy : fiasco
    - **b.** avocation : allegory
    - **c.** affidavit : edict
    - **d.** charlatan : friend
    - **e.** impasse : solution

196. **bourgeois : middle class ::**
    - **a.** proletariat : high class
    - **b.** paragon : low class
    - **c.** tutelage : helper
    - **d.** stature : political party
    - **e.** patrician : nobility

SYNONYMS OR SIMILAR MEANINGS

197. **anarchy**
    - **a.** refinement
    - **b.** energy
    - **c.** serenity
    - **d.** sorrow
    - **e.** chaos

198. **austerity**
    - **a.** amusement
    - **b.** disappointment
    - **c.** fatigue
    - **d.** severity
    - **e.** imagination

ANTONYMS OR OPPOSITE MEANINGS

199. **proletariat**
    - **a.** patrician
    - **b.** militarist
    - **c.** revolutionary
    - **d.** bibliography
    - **e.** withdrawal

200. **autocracy**
    - **a.** dictatorship
    - **b.** democracy
    - **c.** police state
    - **d.** anarchy
    - **e.** martial law

WORD CLUES MASTERY TEST L-19

ANALOGIES

181. **patrician : plebeian ::**
    - **a.** garish : gaudy
    - **b.** verdant : green
    - **c.** harass : restrict
    - **d.** credible : believable
    - **e.** ecclesiastical : secular

182. **sojourn : stay ::**
    - **a.** emanate : come forth
    - **b.** succumb : adhere
    - **c.** cantankerous : good-natured
    - **d.** supersede : strengthen
    - **e.** vacillate : brood

SYNONYMS OR SIMILAR MEANINGS

183. **macabre**
    - **a.** decaying
    - **b.** gruesome
    - **c.** intimidating
    - **d.** ominous
    - **e.** exotic

184. **itinerary**
    - **a.** condition of finances
    - **b.** place of origin
    - **c.** route of travel
    - **d.** location of a church
    - **e.** taste of individual

ANTONYMS OR OPPOSITE MEANINGS

185. **raze**
    - **a.** consecrate
    - **b.** plow
    - **c.** destroy
    - **d.** deify
    - **e.** construct

186. **decadence**
    - **a.** improvement
    - **b.** delusion
    - **c.** impetus
    - **d.** depression
    - **e.** extravagance

187. **sumptuous**
    - **a.** patrician
    - **b.** extravagant
    - **c.** magnificent
    - **d.** celestial
    - **e.** inexpensive

WORDS IN CONTEXT

188. From an airplane, a passenger may note that the ____ of Minnesota, ranging from hills and mountains to streams and rivers, varies greatly.
    - **a.** climate
    - **b.** carnage
    - **c.** biology
    - **d.** topography
    - **e.** paraphernalia

DEFINITIONS IN CONTEXT

189. The leaders of the church never tired in their discussion of **ecclesiastical** matters.
    - **a.** provincial
    - **b.** pretentious
    - **c.** meticulous
    - **d.** clerical
    - **e.** fraudulent

190. The temple stands on **hallowed** ground.
    - **a.** memorable
    - **b.** composed
    - **c.** dedicated
    - **d.** idealized
    - **e.** consecrated

WORD CLUES MASTERY TEST L-22

ANALOGIES

211. prosaic : banal ::
- **a.** lithe : zealous
- **b.** caustic : scathing
- **c.** insatiable : relevant
- **d.** ostentatious : arduous
- **e.** innate : adroit

212. dissuade : persuade ::
- **a.** conclave : confine
- **b.** emanate : retire
- **c.** ingratiate : praise
- **d.** overt : tragic
- **e.** dismiss : convene

SYNONYMS OR SIMILAR MEANINGS

213. affluent
- **a.** rich
- **b.** exciting
- **c.** ornate
- **d.** complex
- **e.** intelligent

214. ostentatious
- **a.** plain
- **b.** spectacular
- **c.** sorrowful
- **d.** devoted
- **e.** uninformed

ANTONYMS OR OPPOSITE MEANINGS

215. conjecture
- **a.** estimation
- **b.** suspicion
- **c.** inkling
- **d.** certainty
- **e.** confusion

216. meticulous
- **a.** polite
- **b.** embarrassed
- **c.** belated
- **d.** convenient
- **e.** careless

WORDS IN CONTEXT

217. The old dam stood in _____ danger of collapse.
- **a.** meticulous
- **b.** omnibus
- **c.** ostentatious
- **d.** imminent
- **e.** prosaic

218. The senate committee has developed a(n) _____ energy package to cover many of the gaps in current policy.
- **a.** ostentatious
- **b.** omnibus
- **c.** affluent
- **d.** prosaic
- **e.** imminent

DEFINITIONS IN CONTEXT

219. Houses in **proximity** to the new shopping mall are much desired.
- **a.** nearness
- **b.** family
- **c.** social club
- **d.** identity
- **e.** charm

220. The government agency decided to **allocate** emergency resources on the basis of income level.
- **a.** recall
- **b.** earmark
- **c.** refer
- **d.** suspend
- **e.** restore

WORD CLUES MASTERY TEST L-21

SYNONYMS OR SIMILAR MEANINGS

201. vicarious
- **a.** on a small scale
- **b.** having common characteristics
- **c.** serving to gain vengeance
- **d.** felt by sharing others' experience
- **e.** having a pragmatic philosophy

202. guile
- **a.** trickery
- **b.** intelligence
- **c.** honesty
- **d.** secrecy
- **e.** effrontery

203. impotent
- **a.** entangled
- **b.** helpless
- **c.** snared
- **d.** inclined
- **e.** enraged

ANTONYMS OR OPPOSITE MEANINGS

204. figment
- **a.** fantasy
- **b.** fallacy
- **c.** actuality
- **d.** illusion
- **e.** creation

205. intrepid
- **a.** impassive
- **b.** fearless
- **c.** staid
- **d.** overt
- **e.** cowardly

DEFINITIONS IN CONTEXT

206. Uncle Dennis, an **indefatigable** storyteller, held the attention of his little niece with countless tales.
- **a.** habitual
- **b.** fatigued
- **c.** tireless
- **d.** vociferous
- **e.** deceiving

207. The first aid squad had a difficult time trying to **extricate** the driver from the wrecked car.
- **a.** escape
- **b.** disentangle
- **c.** excavate
- **d.** sever
- **e.** plunder

WORDS IN CONTEXT

208. Some authors enjoy the anonymity provided by use of a(n) _____ .
- **a.** antonym
- **b.** synonym
- **c.** presentiment
- **d.** pseudonym
- **e.** colloquialism

ANALOGIES

209. vernacular : language ::
- **a.** allegory : meaningless
- **b.** credibility : reality
- **c.** paraphernalia : gear
- **d.** convene : disband
- **e.** patrician : plebeian

210. slave : subservient ::
- **a.** abstraction : concrete
- **b.** reticent : outgoing
- **c.** hermit : gregarious
- **d.** flippant : courteous
- **e.** missionary : zealous

WORD CLUES MASTERY TEST L-24

ANALOGIES
231. **pirouette : dancer ::**
   - a. embroil : acid
   - b. raze : statue
   - c. imbue : landscape
   - d. foray : sea
   - e. delude : charlatan

232. **protégé : patron ::**
   - a. edict : editor
   - b. beginner : expert
   - c. harangue : politician
   - d. privation : pirate
   - e. scion : farmer

SYNONYMS OR SIMILAR MEANINGS
233. **diffident**
   - a. interested
   - b. provincial
   - c. different
   - d. shy
   - e. vain

234. **taciturn**
   - a. sardonic
   - b. silent
   - c. overweight
   - d. cruel
   - e. nervous

ANTONYMS OR OPPOSITE MEANINGS
235. **apathy**
   - a. boredom
   - b. curiosity
   - c. anesthesia
   - d. refusal
   - e. zeal

236. **precocious**
   - a. trusting
   - b. energetic
   - c. slow-witted
   - d. complicated
   - e. hateful

WORDS IN CONTEXT
237. Some contemporary writers use ____ to create a humorous effect.
   - a. apathy
   - b. parody
   - c. prowess
   - d. transcend
   - e. diffident

238. The beauty of Mount Everest ____ one's ability to describe it.
   - a. imbues
   - b. prevails
   - c. pirouettes
   - d. transcends
   - e. underlies

DEFINITIONS IN CONTEXT
239. Napoleon's troops were noted for their **prowess** in combat.
   - a. pride
   - b. enthusiasm
   - c. concern
   - d. disinterest
   - e. bravery

240. The sight of the old war veteran standing at attention **imbued** the crowd with a sense of pride.
   - a. compelled
   - b. inspired
   - c. frustrated
   - d. displayed
   - e. rejected

WORD CLUES MASTERY TEST L-23

DEFINITIONS IN CONTEXT
221. Barbara's **sardonic** glance told me that it would be a long time before we became friends.
   - a. unpleasant
   - b. satirical
   - c. inane
   - d. derisive
   - e. complimentary

222. After my long flight, I was so overcome by **lethargy** that I quickly fell asleep.
   - a. stupor
   - b. hypnosis
   - c. acquiescence
   - d. anesthesia
   - e. procrastination

SYNONYMS OR SIMILAR MEANINGS
223. **succulent**
   - a. savory
   - b. rare
   - c. juicy
   - d. luxurious
   - e. palatable

224. **juncture**
   - a. special method
   - b. speech mannerism
   - c. important hour
   - d. significant moment
   - e. casual meeting

225. **omnivorous**
   - a. eating all foods
   - b. ravenous
   - c. gluttonous
   - d. eating regularly
   - e. habitual

ANTONYMS OR OPPOSITE MEANINGS
226. **ponderous**
   - a. dull
   - b. sarcastic
   - c. astounding
   - d. weighty
   - e. trivial

227. **ludicrous**
   - a. gregarious
   - b. sorrowful
   - c. grotesque
   - d. whimsical
   - e. contented

WORDS IN CONTEXT
228. Certain species of birds may become unknown to future generations unless they begin to ____ quickly.
   - a. propagate
   - b. vindicate
   - c. succumb
   - d. vacillate
   - e. extricate

ANALOGIES
229. **pandemonium : uproar ::**
   - a. epoch : growth
   - b. unwitting : deliberate
   - c. astute : gullible
   - d. proximity : closeness
   - e. flippant : mannerly

230. **predators : pillage ::**
   - a. instructors : learn
   - b. admonishers : neglect
   - c. propagators : breed
   - d. repudiators : accept
   - e. deluders : coerce.

WORD CLUES MASTERY TEST **L-26**

WORDS IN CONTEXT

251. When dealing with the bureaucracy, one is often caught in a _____ tangle of confusion.
  - **a.** voluptuous
  - **b.** sylvan
  - **c.** fiscal
  - **d.** staid
  - **e.** veritable

252. Since she was generally very mild tempered, the teacher's sudden outburst was considered a momentary _____.
  - **a.** festoon
  - **b.** remiss
  - **c.** firmament
  - **d.** aberration
  - **e.** sylvan

SYNONYMS OR SIMILAR MEANINGS

253. firmament
  - **a.** dungeon
  - **b.** cement
  - **c.** earth
  - **d.** area
  - **e.** heavens

254. festoon
  - **a.** discolor
  - **b.** decorate
  - **c.** silhouette
  - **d.** rejoice
  - **e.** mask

ANTONYMS OR OPPOSITE MEANINGS

255. voluptuous
  - **a.** exhausting
  - **b.** extensive
  - **c.** restrained
  - **d.** academic
  - **e.** ornate

256. remiss
  - **a.** missing
  - **b.** wholesome
  - **c.** derelict
  - **d.** conscientious
  - **e.** uneventful

DEFINITIONS IN CONTEXT

257. If the government continues its present **fiscal** policy, the rate of inflation can be expected to persist.
  - **a.** athletic
  - **b.** welfare
  - **c.** foreign
  - **d.** urban
  - **e.** financial

258. The painting depicts a **sylvan** scene on the bank of a lake.
  - **a.** industrial
  - **b.** polar
  - **c.** ocean
  - **d.** forest
  - **e.** desert

ANALOGIES

259. documents : archives ::
  - **a.** forms : bureaucracy
  - **b.** visions : despot
  - **c.** weather : magnate
  - **d.** garden : orifice
  - **e.** complaint : stature

260. light : suffuse ::
  - **a.** confusion : conciliate
  - **b.** funds : allocate
  - **c.** souvenir : relegate
  - **d.** issue : emanate
  - **e.** livelihood : ingratiate

WORD CLUES MASTERY TEST **L-25**

DEFINITIONS IN CONTEXT

241. It is generally known by students of mythology that Neptune was **omnipotent** in his realm, the sea.
  - **a.** having unlimited power
  - **b.** never wrong
  - **c.** respected and influential
  - **d.** having little power
  - **e.** having much power

242. Considerable interest will **accrue** to you from that investment.
  - **a.** come unexpectedly
  - **b.** come as a result
  - **c.** be donated
  - **d.** be handed down
  - **e.** come without surprise

WORDS IN CONTEXT

243. Lack of proper sanitary precautions may lead to _____ of epidemic proportions.
  - **a.** ignobleness
  - **b.** allegation
  - **c.** admonition
  - **d.** pestilence
  - **e.** vindictiveness

SYNONYMS OR SIMILAR MEANINGS

244. indiscretion
  - **a.** imprudence
  - **b.** exhibition
  - **c.** satire
  - **d.** impoliteness
  - **e.** inhibition

245. volatile
  - **a.** vociferous
  - **b.** devious
  - **c.** temperamental
  - **d.** taciturn
  - **e.** powerless

246. relegate
  - **a.** retire
  - **b.** admit
  - **c.** entice
  - **d.** banish
  - **e.** heed

ANTONYMS OR OPPOSITE MEANINGS

247. obesity
  - **a.** lightness on feet
  - **b.** stature
  - **c.** obedience
  - **d.** senselessness
  - **e.** leanness

248. abstinence
  - **a.** gluttony
  - **b.** religion
  - **c.** refraining
  - **d.** franchise
  - **e.** sanctification

ANALOGIES

249. opulent : affluent ::
  - **a.** volatile : taciturn
  - **b.** supercilious : diffident
  - **c.** inexplicable : credible
  - **d.** succulent : juicy
  - **e.** exorbitant : negligible

250. obviate : avert ::
  - **a.** languish : wither
  - **b.** hallowed : dedicated
  - **c.** transcend : depreciate
  - **d.** allocate : segregate
  - **e.** innate : congenial

WORD CLUES MASTERY TEST L-28

ANALOGIES
271. **intrinsic : innate ::**
- a. languid : astute
- b. opulent : gauche
- c. piquant : poignant
- d. flippant : insatiable
- e. defunct : pragmatic

272. **undergo : metamorphosis ::**
- a. employ : fiasco
- b. discover : impasse
- c. devise : edict
- d. respect : apathy
- e. swear : affidavit

SYNONYMS OR SIMILAR MEANINGS
273. **candor**
- a. carelessness
- b. affection
- c. sincerity
- d. confusion
- e. contempt

274. **censure**
- a. censor
- b. abuse
- c. interrogate
- d. flatter
- e. reprove

ANTONYMS OR OPPOSITE MEANINGS
275. **notoriety**
- a. oblivion
- b. laziness
- c. revulsion
- d. alteration
- e. intensity

276. **impede**
- a. define
- b. pertain
- c. promote
- d. assess
- e. withstand

WORDS IN CONTEXT
277. Next month many industrial ____ will meet to discuss the rising costs of labor.
- a. magnates
- b. censures
- c. notorieties
- d. subsidiaries
- e. candors

278. At the last meeting of the board, the chairman proposed opening a number of ____ outlets in Los Angeles.
- a. candor
- b. subsidiary
- c. magnate
- d. avid
- e. intrinsic

DEFINITIONS IN CONTEXT
279. Mr. Brownlee is an **avid** reader of mystery stories.
- a. bold
- b. frequent
- c. amateur
- d. deliberate
- e. eager

280. Several splinter groups in the reform movement anticipated more success after they became **affiliated**.
- a. redesigned
- b. expanded
- c. disbanded
- d. associated
- e. funded

WORD CLUES MASTERY TEST L-27

ANALOGIES
261. **idiosyncratic : eating whipped cream for breakfast ::**
- a. nonentity : as big as life
- b. incognito : wearing dark glasses
- c. voluptuous : of world-wide renown
- d. commending : repudiating
- e. diffident : shy

262. **modulated : adjusted ::**
- a. remiss : justifiable
- b. precocious : unusually muscular
- c. fiscal : financial
- d. allocate : segregate
- e. emanate : imitate

DEFINITIONS IN CONTEXT
263. At first hesitant, Julie soon found herself **amenable** to the rules of the summer camp.
- a. compelling
- b. affable
- c. responsive
- d. fearful
- e. hospitable

264. Although Anne was a **nonentity** among the members of the cast, she was treated as if she were a celebrity.
- a. stupid person
- b. giant
- c. notorious person
- d. nobody
- e. bore

SYNONYMS OR SIMILAR MEANINGS
265. **lucrative**
- a. remunerative
- b. praiseworthy
- c. stimulating
- d. pleasant
- e. aesthetic

266. **paraphrase**
- a. make a rough draft
- b. make a copy
- c. spell correctly
- d. recite
- e. translate

267. **plaudit**
- a. listen
- b. comment
- c. praise
- d. ridicule
- e. publicize

ANTONYMS OR OPPOSITE MEANINGS
268. **supercilious**
- a. typical
- b. diffident
- c. haughty
- d. acrid
- e. brusque

269. **impeccable**
- a. exotic
- b. conscientious
- c. inimitable
- d. imperfect
- e. free from guilt

WORDS IN CONTEXT
270. To escape identification, spies often travel ____ .
- a. incognito
- b. gratis
- c. zealously
- d. pretentiously
- e. nebulously

WORD CLUES MASTERY TEST L-30

ANALOGIES

291. indolent : loafer ::
    a. impotent : military force
    b. credulous : alibi
    c. arable : cultivated
    d. pastoral : environment
    e. haggard : beggar

292. abject : squalid ::
    a. supercilious : intrinsic
    b. cantankerous : overt
    c. hackneyed : banal
    d. tortuous : exorbitant
    e. moot : dogmatic

DEFINITIONS IN CONTEXT

293. Among some primitive tribes, members afflicted with serious disease are **ostracized**.
    a. killed
    b. respected
    c. banished
    d. nursed
    e. bewitched

294. Fred is usually regarded by his classmates as the **quintessence** of artistic skill.
    a. best example
    b. poorest performer
    c. most enthusiastic participant
    d. least likely to succeed
    e. best impersonation

SYNONYMS OR SIMILAR MEANINGS

295. ignominious
    a. incendiary
    b. terminal
    c. belligerent
    d. humiliating
    e. potent

296. supplant
    a. nourish
    b. reinforce
    c. replace
    d. surpass
    e. convict

ANTONYMS OR OPPOSITE MEANINGS

297. comprise
    a. denote
    b. refer
    c. understand
    d. cultivate
    e. exclude

298. inundate
    a. specify
    b. drain
    c. reject
    d. welcome
    e. extract

WORDS IN CONTEXT

299. For some ____ reason the student group decided not to take a class trip this year.
    a. ignominious
    b. affluent
    c. secular
    d. inexplicable
    e. abject

300. If the military does not see an increase in the number of enlistments, it will have to resort to ____ to fill its manpower needs.
    a. quintessence
    b. conscription
    c. supplant
    d. ignominious
    e. abject

WORD CLUES MASTERY TEST L-29

DEFINITIONS IN CONTEXT

281. Because he had no commitments, John was free to go to Europe for an **indeterminate** time.
    a. dubious
    b. ultimate
    c. primeval
    d. indefinite
    e. lengthy

282. The monumental rocks at Stonehenge are **vestiges** of an ancient civilization.
    a. symbols
    b. artifacts
    c. traces
    d. hypotheses
    e. models

SYNONYMS OR SIMILAR MEANINGS

283. agrarian
    a. agricultural
    b. peaceful
    c. legislative
    d. financial
    e. exotic

284. effigy
    a. vestige
    b. mummy
    c. memento
    d. portrait
    e. statue

285. wreak
    a. desire
    b. return
    c. seek
    d. twist
    e. inflict

ANTONYMS OR OPPOSITE MEANINGS

286. venerate
    a. scorn
    b. praise
    c. revere
    d. fear
    e. personify

287. erode
    a. obliterate
    b. build up gradually
    c. change in nature
    d. suffuse
    e. wear away

WORDS IN CONTEXT

288. In need of food, the stray dogs made a successful ____ on our garbage.
    a. juncture
    b. exploration
    c. foray
    d. sojourn
    e. edict

ANALOGIES

289. caste : social class ::
    a. raiment : clothing
    b. charlatan : blunderer
    c. transcend : depreciate
    d. affluence : poverty
    e. meticulous : civil

290. expound : set forth ::
    a. imbue : impel
    b. decry : forbid
    c. modulate : simulate
    d. dissuade : surrender
    e. allocate : assign

1 *Reticence* does not usually win juries. A witness who speaks freely impresses them much more favorably than one who does not.

A synonym for *reticence* is:
  a. emotion
  b. ingenuousness
  c. reserve
  d. simplicity

2 Since she had not yet been found guilty, the newspaper reporters could only *allege* that she had committed the crime.

Allege means:
  a. surmise   c. infer
  b. claim   d. hope

3 I *dissuaded* my friend from his choice of first class travel over tourist, because traveling tourist was less expensive.

To *dissuade* is to:
  a. effect a compromise
  b. render an opinion
  c. divert by persuasion
  d. give advice

4 A man lacking John Smith's *acumen* would not have been able to see the problems of the early settlers as clearly or to make such sound decisions concerning them.

Acumen means:
  a. skill   c. strength
  b. repute   d. insight

5 Life in Greenwich Village could not be characterized as dignified and conventional. This Bohemian life could be unsettling for a *staid* person.

Staid means:
  a. sedate   c. pompous
  b. dull   d. inhibited

6 When they realized that their attempts were *ineffectual*, the British began to pass sterner acts, which they hoped would succeed.

Ineffectual means:
  a. irrelevant
  b. useless
  c. tentative
  d. impractical

7 If a President is rash or reckless, either in speech or action, he can jeopardize the country's position. He must be *discreet* at all times.

A synonym for *discreet* is:
  a. decisive   c. infallible
  b. cautious   d. critical

8 The spirit and liveliness of the people who surrounded King Arthur, and the aura of mystery about the King himself, have made stories about him universal favorites. People everywhere find them *piquant*.

Piquant means:
  a. stimulating
  b. popular
  c. famous
  d. in print

9 The prime minister's efforts to *usurp* the throne threatened not only the king's supremacy, but also the stability of the entire kingdom.

Usurp means:
  a. to use illegally
  b. to regain
  c. to seize without right
  d. to conquer

10 For some reason, I assumed that almost all zoo animals would be carnivorous. It appeared that many of them are *herbivorous*, however.

Herbivorous means:
  a. living on flesh
  b. eating herbs and spices
  c. feeding on grass and plants
  d. belonging to a group of animals

11 The work of a beginning artist rarely brings in any money. He would probably starve if he did not receive some food *gratis* from kind restaurateurs and friends.

Gratis means:
  a. gratefully
  b. free of charge
  c. as a tip
  d. at regular intervals

12 The prosecutor's sneer matched his *caustic* remarks. Both angered the defense attorney.

Caustic means:
  a. sarcastic
  b. erroneous
  c. deceitful
  d. aggressive

13 The queen's *ethereal* appearance made other women seem heavy, fleshy, and stolid. Indeed, she did seem like a creature from another world.

Ethereal means:
  a. celestial
  b. fabulous
  c. imaginary
  d. magical

14 It is still possible for a stock clerk to become a *magnate* by using his wits and ability.

A *magnate* is:
a. a benevolent ruler
b. a person prominent in industry
c. an autocratic officer
d. an educational leader

15 She must be completely *vindicated* by the jury, or she would never be able to live in this town again.

Another word for *vindicate* is:
a. corroborate   c. avenge
b. prove   d. clear

16 The Crusaders pledged their lives to regaining the Holy Land. However, the Moslems were *adamant* in their determination to stay there. Thus, battle ensued and lasted for almost two centuries.

A synonym for *adamant* is:
a. unyielding   c. dauntless
b. remitting   d. devious

17 If one tried to *characterize* Warren Harding, one would have to mention how handsome and friendly he was.

A synonym for *characterize* is:
a. describe
b. impersonate
c. evaluate
d. visualize

18 While it is true that many residents of the Bowery are basically *ignoble,* there are others who are worthy people, reduced by circumstance.

Ignoble means:
a. unknown
b. vulgar
c. dishonorable
d. ignorant

19 The ship Vasa was not *vulnerable* to attack since it was protected by the cannon of the powerful Swedish fort.

A synonym for *vulnerable* is:
a. strong   c. important
b. susceptible   d. vacillating

20 Many great people attain only *posthumous* fame. Society is often too late in recognizing and rewarding greatness.

Posthumous means:
a. short-lived
b. belated
c. after proof
d. after death

21 King Charles *repudiated* Joan of Arc after he saw that she was more interested in France than in his personal interests. He left her to the mercy of the English invaders.

Repudiate means:
a. repulse
b. reject
c. reprove
d. deride

22 A less suspicious, more understanding person might have enjoyed our teen-age exuberance. Our waiter, however, looked *askance* at our table and breathed a sigh of relief when we left the restaurant.

Askance means:
a. furiously
b. uncertainly
c. anxiously
d. disapprovingly

23 Artists tend to have strong opinions and to be *voluble.* For these reasons there is always much animated conversation at their gatherings.

Voluble means:
a. vigorous
b. voluntary
c. loud
d. talkative

24 The discoveries of Columbus and later explorers began a new *epoch,* which was characterized by a renewed interest in science and a flourishing of the arts.

A synonym for *epoch* is:
a. learning
b. era
c. knowledge
d. growth

25 We *allocated* part of our money for travel expenses and hotel accommodations. We planned to use the rest for food and entertainment.

A synonym for *allocate* is:
a. determine
b. compile
c. segregate
d. assign

Check your answers with the key in the front of this book. If you have 20 or more correct answers, proceed to the next level.